RANDOM HOUSE
LARGE PRINT

PRAISE FOR
THE WAY OF INTEGRITY

"This is a book I will read over and over again. The journey within is a pilgrimage that can help to heal the soul and make a world whole."

—Bishop Michael Curry

"The perfect guide for anyone who wants greater happiness and clarity of purpose. As always, Martha Beck's writing is beautiful and perceptive, and the insights and exercises . . . will certainly lead you to a better place."

—Marci Shimoff, #1 **New York Times** bestselling author of **Happy for No Reason**

"[A] masterpiece, initiating a new path forward, one of integrity, showing us how to embrace our authentic self for unlimited freedom."

—Shannon Kaiser, international bestselling author of **The Self-Love Experiment**

"**The Way of Integrity** is about the redemptive power of discovering, speaking, and living the truth about who you are. . . . It brims with humor, spirituality, fascinating science, and even Dante's **Divine Comedy.**"

—Elizabeth Gilbert, #1 **New York Times** bestselling author of **Eat, Pray, Love**

"Martha Beck's genius is that her writing is equal parts comforting and challenging."

—Glennon Doyle, #1 **New York Times** bestselling author of **Untamed** and founder of Together Rising

"Beck identifies the ways culture works against integrity and touches on Dante's **Inferno,** includes quizzes, and rethinks suffering."

—Good Morning America

"Martha Beck at her finest: one hundred percent pure distilled wisdom, truth, and illumination, delivered always with humor. There's no one I'd trust more to get me out of the dark woods."

—Susan Casey, **New York Times** bestselling author of **Voices in the Ocean**

"Profound, funny, and beautifully crafted."

—Elizabeth Lesser, cofounder of Omega Institute and **New York Times** bestselling author of **Broken Open**

"Beck's holistic interpretation of integrity is refreshing. It doesn't feel stiff and constricting. It feels like truth."

—**Houston Chronicle**

"Many will be moved by Beck's sincerity and lucid techniques."

—**Booklist**

BEYOND ANXIETY

BEYOND ANXIETY

Curiosity, Creativity, and Finding Your Life's Purpose

Martha Beck

RANDOM HOUSE
LARGE PRINT

Original cover design: Lynn Buckley
Design adapted for Large Print
Cover art: **Rare Moments of Beauty—Free,** Pawel Nolbert

The Library of Congress has established a
Cataloging-in-Publication record for this title.

ISBN: 978-0-593-94908-5

https://www.penguinrandomhouse.com/

FIRST LARGE PRINT EDITION

Printed in the United States of America

1st Printing

Dear Reader,

Years ago, these words attributed to Rumi found a place in my heart:

> *Out beyond ideas of*
> *wrongdoing and rightdoing,*
> *there is a field. I'll meet you there.*

Ever since, I've cultivated an image of what I call "the Open Field"—a place out beyond fear and shame, beyond judgment, loneliness, and expectation. A place that hosts the reunion of all creation. It's the hope of my soul to find my way there—and whenever I hear an insight or a practice that helps me on the path, I love nothing more than to share it with others.

That's why I've created The Open Field. My hope is to publish books that honor the most unifying truth in human life: We are all seeking the same things. We're all seeking dignity. We're all seeking joy. We're all seeking love and acceptance, seeking to be seen, to be safe. And there is no competition for these things we seek—because they are not material goods; they are spiritual gifts!

We can all give each other these gifts if we share what we know—what has lifted us up and moved us forward. That is our duty to one another—to help each other toward acceptance, toward peace, toward happiness—and my promise to you is that the books published under this imprint will be maps to the Open Field, written by guides who know the path and want to share it.

Each title will offer insights, inspiration, and guidance for moving beyond the fears, the judgments, and the masks we all wear. And when we take off the masks, guess what? We will see that we are the opposite of what we thought— we are each other.

We are all on our way to the Open Field. We are all helping one another along the path. I'll meet you there.

Love, *Maria S*

For my wild, creative global family.
If I knew every word of every language,
there still wouldn't be enough to say how
much I love you.

CONTENTS

Part Two
THE CREATIVE

Part Three
THE CREATION

INTRODUCTION

As the year 2020 began, Bo Burnham finally felt ready for his return to the stage. Burnham had been an up-and-coming comedian until 2016, when he began experiencing panic attacks onstage and had to step back from his career. Three long years later, he was ready to start performing again.

Then someone in China came down with a dry cough.

Bo Burnham's plans changed, along with yours, mine, and everyone's. But instead of giving up on his dream of being a performer, Burnham began creating—with a vengeance. Locked down in his home, he single-handedly wrote, performed, filmed, and edited a comedy and music routine he called **Inside.** The show was digitally released in June of 2021 to rave reviews.

Inside captures the experience of living in the twenty-first century with unnerving accuracy. "There it is again, that funny feeling," Burnham sings at one point, sitting alone in his apartment, cameras rolling.

> **A gift shop at the gun range, a mass**
> **shooting at the mall . . .**
> **The quiet comprehending of the ending of**
> **it all.**

Burnham calls our reaction to the perils of our time—rising temperatures, violence in the news and in video games, avalanches of data, disassociation— "that funny feeling." But of course, the feeling is anything but amusing. Burnham's work conjures the strange, slow terror of belonging to the most tech- nologically advanced, well-informed population in history . . . and watching human activity destroy the conditions we need for our own survival.

As we doomscroll our way through horrible news, swap jokes about environmental collapse, shake our heads in disbelief at political chaos, and watch news stories about the multiple ways our species may be flirting with apocalyptic catastrophes, most of us feel at least a dark shadow of "that funny feeling." Another name for it, as Bo Burnham knew all too well, is anxiety.

THE AGE OF UNBELIEVABLE ANXIETY

In 1948, W. H. Auden won the Pulitzer Prize for his long poem **The Age of Anxiety.** With all due respect, Mr. Auden, if you thought your age was anxious, you should give ours a try. In 2022, **The New York Times** labeled anxiety among adolescents "the inner pandemic." The phrase is based on not only the prevalence of anxiety but also the rapidity with which it's zooming upward.

Back in 2017, **Forbes Health** reported that over 284 million people worldwide had been diagnosed with some kind of anxiety disorder—and unreported cases almost certainly outnumber the recorded ones. When the **Journal of Psychiatric Research** set out to document rates of anxiety in the United States, it concluded that the condition was rising rapidly due to "direct and indirect . . . exposure to anxiety-provoking world events."

When was that study published? you may ask.

In the year of our Lord two thousand and eighteen. Hahahahaha!

Remember the olden days, back in 2018? Remember how we all thought we'd been exposed to "anxiety-provoking world events" back **then**?

In the first year of the COVID-19 pandemic, global prevalence of anxiety disorders skyrocketed by a full 25 percent. According to **Forbes Health,** the number of people affected by anxiety disorders grew from about 298 million to 374 million. By 2020, nearly half (47 percent) of human beings surveyed said they experienced regular bouts of this life-draining, health-destroying, torturous condition. By 2023, even with fears about the pandemic easing off for some people, a full 50 percent of young adults aged eighteen to twenty-four reported symptoms of anxiety. All of this gives anxiety disorder the dubious distinction of being the most common mental illness in the world.

They say that statistics are people with the tears washed off. Well, I, for one, can feel the pain of those afflicted by high anxiety. I'm one of them.

MY OWN FUNNY FEELING

I've been studying anxiety all my life, because I have it. Have had it. Have had it in white-hot volcanic eruptions and foul, sky-darkening billows. Have had it for years on end, for richer and for poorer, in sickness and in health. I remember being knotted up with anxiety on the eve of one birthday, worried sick because time was passing so fast and I had yet to accomplish anything significant. I was turning four.

Things only got worse once I started school. The first time I was assigned to write a poem, my fear of inadequacy kept me awake for five consecutive hallucinatory days and nights, until my pediatrician— my pediatrician!—put me on a short, blessed course of Valium. In high school, when I joined the debate team and stood up to speak in front of a judge, I passed out cold.

The only reason I even tried public speaking was that sometime around puberty, I realized I had a choice: I could do things that caused me horrific anxiety, or I could live in a box under my bed. Luckily, inactivity made me just as anxious as everything else. So I charged forward into life, not so much bravely as frenetically, like someone running from a swarm of bees.

Filled with dread, I applied to college, then graduate school, then various jobs. In stark terror, I married, traveled, and had some children, then set about raising them. I went places and did things—more than some people, fewer than others. But wherever I went and whatever I did, I was always, always, always anxious.

God, that sucked.

All this anxiety was one of the reasons I gravitated toward the social sciences. If I could understand the mind, my own mind, then—maybe? someday?— I could free myself from constant unease. At first, this yielded a lot of discouraging information. For several years, from many books, I learned that every human brain is fully formed by the age of five. Fixed and finished. Done and dusted. I remember staring glumly at page after page, devastated that my horribly anxious brain would always remain horribly anxious.

Luckily, I kept reading.

As the years went by, new technologies allowed neurologists to examine the brain with more accuracy. It turns out that the idea of an unchanging brain is pure fiction. Our gray matter is a wonder of self-revision. It can and does constantly reshape itself, depending on how we use it, throughout our lives.

This discovery made my heart soar like the Goodyear Blimp. I began devouring everything I could find on **neuroplasticity,** a term that describes the malleability of our brains. Each new study I read gave me more hope, especially a study where neurologists peered into the brains of Tibetan monks who had spent years in meditation. These men, it was found, had unusually dense tissue in the brain regions associated with happiness, compassion, and calm.

In one specific monk, this effect was so pronounced that the scientists measuring his brain activity thought their equipment must be malfunctioning. This guy was a veritable superhero of tranquility. But he hadn't always been so relaxed. In fact, he had spent his whole childhood battling crippling anxiety and panic attacks.

YES!

I mean, not YES! A CHILD HAD PANIC ATTACKS! but YES! HE GOT OVER IT!

By the time I learned about the amazing plasticity of our brains, I'd finished graduate school, taught college for a while, and left academia to write books and work as a life coach. In the end, my career was based less on my intellectual training than on my near-pathological conviction that every one of us can fulfill our deepest longing and make the world a better place. After I read the Tibetan monk study, this conviction grew roots so deep nothing could shake it. I was convinced I could fix my brain, maybe without even moving to the Himalayas or training as a monk. I believed that the way to peace was already inside me. I just had to find it.

DISCOVERING THE ART OF CALM

In 2021, as Bo Burnham put the finishing touches on his darkly brilliant **Inside,** several things converged to make me more obsessed with overcoming anxiety than I'd ever been before. They included these factors:

- Many of my clients (now consulting me on Zoom) were climbing the walls with anxiety—and who could blame them? They worried about the pandemic, their financial futures, political upheaval, the steadily weirding weather, and myriad other problems. In order to help them,

I began researching anxiety more intensely than ever before.

• During lockdown, I spent several months developing and teaching an online course about creativity. The goal was to help people come up with innovative ways to navigate a world that had become overwhelmingly uncertain. As part of my preparation, I learned everything I could about the way creativity works in the brain.

• I began having regular conversations with different scientists and psychologists, including Jill Bolte Taylor, a neuroanatomist whose time at Harvard had overlapped with mine. Jill once had a massive stroke that shut down much of her brain's left hemisphere. Her experience, as both a scientist and a stroke survivor, contains powerful lessons about how our brains produce anxiety, and how we might let it go.

These experiences gave me new ideas for dealing with my own unquiet mind. I became fascinated with the neurological dynamics of anxiety—how it works in our brains and also in our behaviors and social interactions. I was particularly intrigued by the evidence that shows a kind of toggle effect between anxiety and creativity: when one is up and running, the other seems to go silent. I began to play with something I called "the art of calm," because it was all about using creativity to calm my anxiety.

The results of this experimentation astonished me. At a time of worldwide crisis, when I fully expected to be feeling extremely uneasy, my anxiety dropped to near zero. Events that once would have triggered anxiety attacks—physical pain and disability, financial uncertainty, potential critical illness and loss of loved ones—no longer caused me to panic. As I developed and practiced this "art of calm," I found myself caring more than ever about other people and the world but simultaneously experiencing far less anxiety.

Since the lockdown had moved pretty much every social interaction besides diapering babies onto the internet, I also found myself doing a lot of group coaching, including free online meetings that drew hundreds of participants. My sociology-nerd mind thrilled at the opportunity to test my new anxiety-calming methods. I walked thousands of people through these strategies, and thanks to the wonders of technology, those people could give me real-time feedback about how the techniques worked for them. The overwhelming majority of every group reported that the methods I'd developed helped lower their anxiety immediately and consistently. That's when I decided to write this book.

THE BASICS OF GOING BEYOND ANXIETY

Stacked on the desk where I'm writing these words are many wonderful books on how to reduce the chronic worries of the reading public. They all contain terrific advice. I've read them carefully and repeatedly. I've used their advice in my own quest to feel less anxious. I've taught many of the methods I've learned from them (always with attribution!) when working with clients. A lot of the information I've gleaned from them has really helped.

But until recently, this felt like shoveling out the Augean stable. After years of diligent mental hygiene and thousands of hours of meditation, something many of those books advise, I'd learned how to drill down through my anxiety and connect with a state of inner peace. For a while. On most days. But then something worrying would come up—a work deadline, an alarming news report, a weird pain in my belly—and my brain would start producing anxiety like all of King Augeas's cows and horses on Ex-Lax. I could stabilize myself enough to smile during the day and sleep at night, but it took constant effort.

Then, researching away from a number of different disciplines, I realized Three Important Things that would change my life. They helped me see how anxiety was always scratching its way into my mind, and how to turn it from something vicious into something downright gentle. As I experimented with new calming strategies, my anxiety dropped to nearly nonexistent and stayed there almost all the time. Here are the Three Important Things, which I hope will form the foundation for your own path beyond anxiety.

IMPORTANT THING NO. 1: We're all taught to unconsciously activate an "anxiety spiral" in our brains. We keep this spiral spinning and accelerating without any awareness that we're doing so.

From early childhood, you have been constantly rewarded for thinking in a certain way: verbally, analytically, in organized lines of logic. You're doing this right now as you decode symbols on a page, turn them into language, follow my reasoning. This kind of focus has built up (is building up) a certain part of your brain, the way weight lifting might build your muscles. The part of your brain that you're strengthening is located largely in your left hemisphere, though your entire brain is active almost all the time. While there are huge advantages to focusing on this kind of thought, at least one major **dis**advantage exists: inside everyone's buffed-up left hemisphere is a neurological mechanism I call the "anxiety spiral."

The anxiety spiral works like one of those tire rippers you may have driven over while leaving a parking lot: it allows the brain to go forward into higher anxiety but not to drop back into relaxation. All animals have fear responses when they're in danger. But because of our fancy powers of speech and imagination, we humans can keep that fear response elevated indefinitely, whether we're in danger or not. In fact, the more left-brain dominant our society becomes, the more we as individuals receive messages to keep our angst spiraling up and up and up and **up** into ever-higher levels of anxiety.

IMPORTANT THING NO. 2: As society makes us more anxious, we make it more anxious.

Anxiety is contagious. Even if we learn techniques that bring down our personal anxiety, engaging with a culture that's full of anxiety can put us right back into the dread zone. Our brains and emotions are shaped by the cultural influences we experience every day: the pressure to perform in schools that rank students against each other; the need to secure some form of income; the constant barrage of alarming news from all over the globe; encounters with family members, friends, and strangers who may be flailing around in their own difficult life situations. Staying calm in a society of uneasy people is like walking down the up escalator.

As society makes us anxious, we make it anxious.

Our uneasy feelings, thoughts, and actions bleed into the world around us, making others more anxious still. Then those people increase the social pressure that makes **us** even more anxious, and we pump that increased anxiety back to other people . . . You see where this is going. The anxiety spiral inside our heads—the one that keeps our anxiety climbing— replicates itself in a bigger circle, then whirls between individual minds and society.

The social influences pushing us toward anxiety are infinite, subtle, and powerful. The mirror cells in our brains shift to automatically reflect whatever the people around us are feeling. Images of danger and horror are being communicated more rapidly and universally, so we constantly hear and see reports of terrible things happening all over the world. The structures of our work lives often push us to stay nervous and make us continually fear that we'll lose our competitive edge or our way of making a living.

To counteract all this, we need more than a few relaxation techniques. We need a culture-wide transformation in the way we approach our lives.

IMPORTANT THING NO. 3:
Anxiety can't just be ended.
It must be **replaced**.

Nature abhors a vacuum, so even if we can relax our highly developed anxiety circuits, they collide with many forces (inside and outside our brains) that rev them right back up—unless we fill the space where the anxiety used to be.

To live with joy and optimism instead of constant worry, we don't just need to subtract our troubles; we need to use our brains differently. We need practices that guide our thinking into new habitual pathways, new modes of perceiving and relating to the world. Though some psychologists and neurologists are beginning to articulate this idea, modern Western culture doesn't teach us any major skills for rerouting anxious energy into more peaceful ways of thinking. But other cultures (think Tibetan monastic orders) do teach such skills.

Here's what the people who developed early antianxiety practices knew: The human mind is endlessly, unstoppably generative. It's always making something. Always. The part of our brains that we've been taught to use is constantly creating concepts, stories, theories, competitive strategies, a sense of lack—and, of course, anxiety.

To stop doing this, we can shift our neural activity to a different set of brain structures and functions—the ones that generate curiosity, wonder, connection, compassion, and awe. Learning to use our brains in this way relies on science, but as I've said, it's ultimately an art. The strategies I'll teach you in this book won't merely make you a less anxious person; they'll turn you into an artist of calm, a creative genius.

This doesn't mean you'll start painting portraits or composing symphonies (though you may). It means you'll begin bringing the full power of your infinitely resourceful human mind to bear on anything you make or do. We all have favorite forms of creative expression: cooking, poetry, engineering, animal husbandry, whatever. But no matter where our individual interests lie, we all share one form of creative expression: the shaping of our life experiences. Anything you happen to do can become a creative medium, and as you leave anxiety behind and free up your innate creativity, your magnum opus will be the most thrilling, fulfilling life you can imagine.

This way of living beyond anxiety is radically liberating. It sets us free in more ways than we can count: Free to sustain an ongoing inner state of peace and self-compassion. Free to interact with others with confidence and wisdom rather than insecurity and tension. Free to engage with the pressures of society as powerful navigators and pathbuilders rather than as hapless wanderers. Free to create our own futures and approach them not as random avalanches of frightening events but as unfolding beneficent miracles. The capacity for all this freedom is your birthright; it's been in you since the day you were born. As you leave anxiety behind, you'll see that for yourself.

WHERE WE'RE HEADED: THE CREATURE, THE CREATIVE, AND THE CREATION

Like any other art, living beyond anxiety takes practice. I like to approach it in three phases, so this book has three parts. In part 1, you'll learn about how to handle your biological and psychological tendency to get anxious. I call this process "calming the creature."

In part 2, you'll begin utilizing parts of your brain that pull you out of anxiety and into curiosity, fascination, and inventiveness. Since this process makes you your most creative self, I call it activating the "creative" or "creator" self. Again, this side of yourself may be interested in what society calls "art" (music, painting, poetry, etc.), but its biggest role will be discovering or inventing creative problem-solving approaches to **any aspect of your life.** Your creative self sees "problems" not as anxiety-driving terrors but as opportunities to design original responses to any situation whatsoever.

In part 3, you will move so far away from anxiety and into creativity that you may begin experiencing something I call "commingling with creation." This phrase sounds odd to the typical Western ear, since our culture doesn't teach us much about it. In fact, "commingling with creation" may sound silly or nonsensical to you, especially since words can't really describe it. The closest I can come here is to tell you that this union with creation is a state of effortless flow in which you completely forget your anxiety—and even the part of yourself that felt anxious. In fact, your whole sense of self may dissolve. But this kind of dissolution—the dissolving of all anxiety—unleashes your full potential for joy, just as the dissolution of dragonfly larvae ultimately gives earthbound creatures the ability to fly.

This progression beyond anxiety and into your inborn creative genius is a continuing process. As long as you have a normal human brain, you'll also have the capacity to slip back into anxiety. But as you learn the concepts and skills laid out in this book, it will get easier and easier to calm the frightened creature in your brain and liberate your creative side. Every time you do this, you'll move into greater heights of inventiveness, adventure, and exhilaration.

All of this may generate a brand-new "funny feeling" that you will carry with you everywhere. Even when confronting a world of chaos, destruction, anger, and threat, you'll feel a bloom of calm that ripples outward into creativity, connection, and joy. You'll learn to work with your own mind and heart the way a sculptor works with clay, the way a musician composes songs. Everything you do will contribute to your most important artistic creation: your own life. And as you construct your own best life, you may just change the world.

BEFORE WE BEGIN

As you learn to use the ideas and processes suggested in this book, swapping your anxiety for joyful creativity, you may start to seem peculiar to the (anxious) folks around you. These people may watch you with furrowed brows, blank stares, and the occasional critical comment. Learning to live beyond anxiety is one of the best things you'll ever do for yourself, your loved ones, and the world, but it may not be the easiest.

Here are some questions I'd like you to consider right now. If the answer to any of them is a flat no, it's okay. Read through the book—or maybe just lie down for a while—and see if the answers change as your anxiety goes up. When you're really, truly sick of feeling anxious, you may decide that the challenge is worth taking.

- Are you prepared to question the conventional wisdom of our culture so deeply that you physically shift the gray matter in your head—in other words, develop a brain that doesn't quite fit in with society?

- Can you accept that abandoning anxiety may cause you to think and act in ways that are compassionate and creative but unusual, ways that the people around you might find incomprehensible?

- Do you have the will and courage to shape all your actions according to what emerges from your inherent originality rather than from anything you've ever been taught?

Think carefully about these questions. Living beyond anxiety is a gentle art—in fact, it will teach you the paradoxical truth that gentleness is extraordinarily powerful. But in this world, being gentle can require a lot of grit. I don't want to scare you—you've spent enough time being scared. I just want you to know that living beyond anxiety, like any radical art, is countercultural. It will definitely take you out beyond the conventional wisdom of our society. No one can predict what you may do then. I can't promise you that it will look "normal"; I can only tell you that it will take you to the unimaginable joy of your best destiny.

Still in?

Let's do this.

Part One

THE CREATURE

1

The Nuts and Bolts of Why You Go Nuts and Want to Bolt

I'm writing this under the thatched roof of a cottage in one of my very favorite places: a South African game reserve called Londolozi. A few minutes ago, as I sat here typing away, a sharp, guttural noise shattered the evening stillness. I recognized the sound as a leopard calling; I've heard it many times before. But I've never heard it when I happened to be alone, in pajamas, at night, six feet away from the source of the sound.

For a moment, I genuinely thought the leopard was in the room with me—specifically, **below** me, because I'd instantly levitated, straight up into the mosquito netting over my bed, like a rocket fueled by pure adrenaline.

But only in my mind.

What actually happened was much less dramatic.

I glanced over just in time to see the animal's half-lit form gliding past a screen door. Before I'd even thought the word **leopard,** I realized I was completely safe. My visitor stalked off into the tall grass, proclaiming his presence with a sound like a revving chain saw while I sat here beaming, feeling as if my blood had been replaced by fine champagne.

This is an example of something violence-prevention expert Gavin de Becker calls "the gift of fear." What I felt just now, when I heard the leopard, wasn't calm. But it wasn't anxiety, either. Before we talk more about what anxiety is, we need to be clear about what it isn't.

Three words: anxiety isn't fear.

That leopard's call flipped on my fight-or-flight response, a resource most animals possess. It created a surge of true fear, which is meant to hit hard, get us moving, and then disappear. Most of the time, these "true fear" reactions hang around like off-duty firefighters, scrolling through social media, dozing lightly, examining their moles. If—and only if—our senses detect clear and present danger, true fear snaps into action, giving us the mental clarity and physical energy required to deal with the threat. As soon as safety is reestablished (the fire is out, the leopard is walking away), it relaxes again.

It's astonishing how quickly this can happen. Just now, in less than a second, I went from peaceful contentment to five-alarm fear, then all the way back to peace. I didn't experience any crippling negative emotion, only sudden, sharp mental focus and a jolt of physical energy. Real fear tells us what to do while giving us the speed and strength we need to do it. It's like being shot from a cannon.

Anxiety, on the other hand, is more like being haunted. It pulls our attention inward to worrisome thoughts and fantasies, away from our actual physical situation in the present. Its vague sense of doom presses down on us without suggesting any constructive action. And unlike healthy fear, anxiety never relents. It may not only persist but also **increase** in situations where we're completely safe. This constant dread worsens our health, our relationships, our ability to fulfill our hopes and dreams.

So how does fear—a priceless gift without which we'd all be dead by Tuesday—become the grinding torture of anxiety? Excellent question! I'm so glad I asked.

In this chapter, I'll tell you how your healthy fear can end up stuck in the "on" position, turning a quick, reflexive impulse into an endless, rising spiral of anxiety. I'll show you how both your biology and your culture pull you toward anxiety like a riptide, often sweeping you up before you're even aware of it, and how you can begin to free yourself. The chapter at hand has some rudimentary science in it, drawn from the treasure trove of exciting discoveries that are emerging as technology teaches us more and more about ourselves, our thoughts, and our behavior. This branch of science is not only fascinating but profoundly liberating. Understanding the nuts and bolts of anxiety is key to escaping it.

HOW FEAR BECOMES ANXIETY

When you encounter anything unfamiliar, from a strange-looking bug to a newfangled hairstyle, it grabs the attention of an ancient structure at the center of your brain, one that's been passed down from creature to creature for hundreds of millions of years. The word for it is **amygdala,** Greek for "almond," because—textbooks never fail to mention this—it's about the size and shape of an almond. Every creature with a spine has one, or a close homologue.

Actually, saying that you have "an amygdala" isn't quite accurate. You really have two—one on the left side of your brain, another on the right—and we'll talk more about what this means later on. For now, just picture your two-part inner almond picking up on any threatening or unfamiliar sense impression: the sight of an object flying toward you, the sound of a leopard chuffing, a whiff of your mother-in-law's hair spray. Immediately, your brain's inner almond sends out a pulse of alarm, like a little silent shriek: **Yawp!**

In a flash, this yawp of alarm reaches other structures: the emotion-generating brain layers we share with other mammals and the logical, verbal parts that are unique to humans. During moments of high danger, this fear response can make us almost super-human. Without even thinking, we leap away from the rattlesnake, launch the lifeboats, lift the car off our trapped lover. (Not, one hopes, all at once.)

For most creatures, the experience of fear ends when the immediate danger is gone. That's what happened in my brain as my leopard visitor skulked away. I've seen many other animals relax after escaping danger—and I mean **right** after. I once watched a lion who had just eaten most of a wildebeest decide to attack an entirely different wildebeest. The antelope took off like a shot. After a hundred yards or so, the overfed cat gave up and simply stood there, panting. Instantly, with its would-be murderer still in plain sight, the wildebeest relaxed and went back to grazing.

Humans would react the same way if we weren't so damn smart (as opposed to your average wildebeest, which would lose a battle of wits with a spoon). Our brains, unlike those of any other animal, can hold information as a verbal story and elaborate on it with imagination. We like to believe that we are the "rational" species, as coolly logical as Sherlock Holmes. But, in fact, our thoughts and decisions are driven largely by what's happening at the emotional levels of our brains.

This means that your brilliant human mind often reacts more to the yawp of the inner almond and the emotional flash of fear than to your actual situation. We can be startled by almost anything—footfalls behind us, a boss's frown, a news story. This is what happens when we see that a threat is real and present. The whole brain springs into action to deal with the danger. But even if the threat isn't real, even if we see that the person behind us is a loved one, that the boss is grimacing because of gout rather than anger, and that the news story requires long-term wisdom rather than an immediate freak-out, the left side of the brain tends to react to every threat alarm by doing two things: (1) it comes up with **explanations** that justify our feeling of fear, and (2) it figures out ways we might **take control** of the situation.

EXPLANATIONS AND CONTROL: HOW ANXIETY TAKES ROOT

The scary stories our brains create to justify any feeling of fear tend to sound completely rational to the person experiencing them. So do the control tactics we use to make ourselves feel in command. As a coach, I've seen people spend astonishing amounts of time and energy trying to control all sorts of life situations. Some people track their spouses through phone apps every moment of every day on the theory that constant surveillance is the way to keep love alive. I've seen parents practically move into their children's schools, believing that if they can control every aspect of the curriculum, their darlings will be guaranteed a happy future. I've seen bosses destroy their companies by controlling every aspect of their employees' work lives until those employees broke free and ran for the hills.

The impulse to control is so deep and powerful that we may believe we're acting logically even when our control strategies become downright bizarre. For instance, a couple of years ago, my friend Jennifer was staying in the very same Londolozi cottage where I'm writing this. In the middle of her first night here, she woke to see—you guessed it—a leopard, right outside the screen door. It may have been the very same animal that just strolled past me. But when it visited Jennifer, it brought a snack. My friend was stirred from slumber by the stimulating sound of fangs scronching through bone and cartilage. The huge cat was just a few feet away, eye deep in the bloody carcass of an impala.

Of course, Jennifer's amygdala let out an almighty yawp. But her jet-lagged neocortex went further than mine. It instantly formed a theory ("This is why you **should** be scared!") and a control strategy ("This is what you **must** do to stay safe!"). Jennifer's theory was that since she was wearing fuzzy leopard-print pajamas, the animal would perceive her as a territorial rival. Her control strategy, which she swiftly and decisively enacted, was to sit bolt upright, wrap herself in a beige blanket, and pose as a termite mound.

When she told this story the next day at breakfast, Jennifer laughed so hard she could barely breathe. Her nervous system, just like mine, had reset itself to "safe" after her leopard visitation ended. But in many situations, a jittery human brain doesn't relax after danger has passed. Instead, it keeps conjuring more scenarios about what could go wrong. And here's a key point: the thoughts remembered and imagined by the neocortex feed back to the left amygdala as if they are **actually happening.**

THE ENDLESS FEEDBACK LOOP OF THE ANXIETY SPIRAL

Right now, listening to the symphony of animal calls in the African night around me, I could put myself into a welter of anxiety. My brain might generate thoughts and stories that would keep me awake all night. It could start silently shouting things like:

- **This place is** filthy **with leopards. They're everywhere!**

- **That animal is just waiting for me to fall asleep. Then it'll smash through the screen door and attack.**

- **I've heard they kill you by biting your neck until you suffocate. What would** that **feel like?**

- **Or . . . wait . . . do they claw out your intestines first? That could be even worse— I could** linger!

THE NUTS AND BOLTS

- **Maybe it would just pin me down and start eating me alive. Oh no! Where would it start?**

As these fear stories played out, my left amygdala would react to each new thought as if that terrifying scenario were actually happening. Every thought would get a bigger yawp. And each time, my left hemisphere would respond to the new yawp by thinking, **Oh my God, this is even worse than I thought!** Then it would spin out even **scarier** stories to justify the new, imagination-fortified level of fear, which would make my left amygdala yawp ever more loudly, causing my neocortex to create **even worse** horror stories, and so on.

And on. And on.

This is what engineers call an "unregulated feedback cycle"—something that feeds on its own energy so that it only goes up, never down. When this happens in the fear-generating part of our brains, I call it the "anxiety spiral."

THE ANXIETY SPIRAL, INSIDE AND OUTSIDE

If you're a worrier, you know how it feels to lie awake, safe and sound, getting more and more terrified—not by actual events but by **possible** ones. (As an unknown author once said, "I am an old man and have known many troubles, but most of them never happened.") You probably also know what it's like to calm yourself down through heroic amounts of self-discipline, rising after a sleepless night filled with determination to make this a better day—only to find yourself spinning into anxiety all over again after getting stuck in traffic, or staring at an unexpected bill, or catching hell from a stressed-out coworker.

There's a nauseating circularity to the anxiety spiral, like a merry-go-round that keeps speeding up and creating more centrifugal force. For me, there have been many times when the process is just a blur: jolts of intense alarm followed by terrifying thoughts about potential disaster followed immediately by even more intense jolts of alarm. You may not be able to slow down your own anxiety at first, but if you set an intention to **observe** your anxiety without trying to change it, you'll start to recognize the sharp kick of a fear impulse and notice how it increases the momentum of your frightening thoughts.

For example, a client I'll call Kayla once walked into a room where her husband was typing on his cell phone. He immediately swiped the screen clear and turned to her with a little too much enthusiasm. "I felt this horrible jolt," Kayla told me. "I thought, **He's lying. What's he into? Gambling? Porn? Is he having an affair?**" With each thought, the jolt of dread repeated, growing worse as the stories multiplied. "I felt so betrayed I started an argument," Kayla said. "By the time he admitted he'd been planning my birthday party, I was half-convinced my marriage was over."

Simon had a similar pattern at work, where he held a management position leading a team of three older men. A tech whiz, Simon genuinely had more skills than his subordinates. But he felt intensely anxious about being seen as immature, so he tried to act "more authoritative" by showing off his superior knowledge. This made him come across as critical and arrogant. Simon's colleagues soon felt as anxious around him as he did around them.

Jared and Sophie got caught in an anxiety spiral when their daughter Ruby was born. Every cough or sneeze from little Ruby triggered a bolt of fear that sent her parents to the internet on a mission to learn (and control) every possible thing that could go wrong with their baby's health. As their story-telling minds grasped labels like "respiratory syncytial virus" and "gastroesophageal reflux disease," Sophie and Jared would get so tense that Ruby would sense the mood and begin to wail, accelerating her parents' anxiety spirals, sending the whole family out for multiple unnecessary medical appointments.

Kayla and her husband, Simon and his coworkers, and Ruby's little family are far from unusual. Anxiety spirals start in individuals but spread to groups in almost any social situation. Remember, anxiety is contagious. Every time we interact with other people, we run a high risk of getting caught up in their anxiety spirals, which will accentuate our own. And we humans have built a macro version of our brains' anxiety mechanism into the society we've created. Modern culture is like a massive anxiety spiral in which countless clever brains busily spin out terrifying stories and control strategies 24/7. Our ability to instantly communicate with huge numbers of people allows us to spread the misery faster and farther than ever before.

Here's one example of a very large collective anxiety spiral. A few days ago, when I boarded my plane to South Africa, my luggage contained—I confess it—an eyelash curler. The security screeners at the airport scowled at this little gadget, pronounced it dangerous, and confiscated it. I knew better than to ask how they thought I was going to use it as a weapon. (Curl my eyelashes until they became distractingly prominent, causing the crew to lose focus and open the doors while in flight? Curl the pilot's eyelashes until he became unrecognizable to himself and had an existential collapse? Lethally shame other passengers whose lashes were disgracefully straight?)

If my joking about this offends you, I apologize. And I understand. The terrorist attacks of 2001 were very real and utterly horrifying. Air travel makes a lot of people feel uneasy at the best of times, and since 9/11, that uneasiness has twisted far, far up our collective anxiety spiral. Just seeing a passenger jet can trigger a huge yawp as our minds replay the images from that ghastly day. In response to those memories, and other cases of attempted terrorism, our society has generated many control strategies—some logical, some not. For instance: **If all travelers pack their liquids in tiny bottles, we will be safe. If everyone takes off their shoes before boarding, we will be safe. If we confiscate all eyelash curlers, we will be safe. If we attack anything or anyone we're not used to, we will be safe.** And above all: **If we always stay worried about this, we will be safe.**

This is the self-defeating logic of anxiety; it makes us truly believe that the only way to feel safe is to never feel safe. Because of the unregulated feedback systems inside us, it's easy to get caught in this kind of circular reasoning that pervades the society around us.

Collective anxiety fantasies shape the way we interact with our families, our institutions, our religions—in short, all our social structures and activities. Operating from anxiety, family members try to micromanage their loved ones' lives; conspiracy theorists post dark conjectures online, goading one another into higher and higher levels of paranoia; people on either side of political issues frantically try to control one another, becoming louder, more insulting, and more extreme as their anxiety mounts.

Sometimes, frightening rumors or imagined dangers can whip up a collective anxiety spiral that has the size and suction power of a tornado. It's as if someone just yelled "FIRE!" in a theater packed with a billion people. Whole nations can fall into shared fantasies of threat, with people growing so suspicious that they can barely see one another through the roaring horror stories in their minds. Collective anxiety spirals have created untold violence, injustice, discrimination, slaughter, suffering, and war.

This is **legitimately scary**! We really have to **get control** of it! Right?

See how that works?

The bad news is that however frightened we become, and however hard we try to control other people and situations, anxiety-based actions tend to breed more anxiety, leading to upward spirals of terror and violence. The good news is that we have another option.

ONE BRAIN, TWO VIEWPOINTS

This whole time we've been talking about what happens in the **left hemisphere** of your brain when you perceive something threatening. Now let's consider your right hemisphere. That's as far as you have to go to begin freeing yourself from anxiety. It's also the best position from which to solve the real, valid difficulties we face as individuals and as a species.

Throughout this book, I'll talk a lot about the differences between the left and right brain hemispheres. I realize this is a simplification; at any given moment, both your brain hemispheres are up and running, trading information, shaping your behavior in complex, multipart harmony. Scientists hate it when nonscientists generalize about being a "left-brained" or "right-brained" person. But as Oxford psychiatrist Iain McGilchrist says, "It would be just as foolish to believe that therefore there are no important hemisphere differences. There are massively important ones, which lie at the core of what it means to be a human being."

Neurologists have long known that the left hemisphere is responsible for analytical, logical, and verbal thinking, while the right hemisphere is more attuned to sense perceptions, emotions, and intuition. This becomes obvious when people lose function in specific parts of their brains through illness or accident. Their impairments show neuroscientists what was going on in the various parts of their brains before tragedy struck.

My friend Jill Bolte Taylor understands this about as well as anyone ever could. For one thing, she's a highly trained neuroanatomist. For another, while working as a brain scientist at Harvard, Jill suffered a massive stroke that temporarily disabled much of her left hemisphere. She is the person who first told me—both in her written work and in conversation—that talking about "the amygdala" or "the neocortex" as a singular structure is misleading. Having studied and lived the difference between the two hemispheres, Jill is exquisitely aware that the two halves of the brain perform very different functions, in very different ways.

The View from the Right

One morning, as Jill prepared for another busy day at Harvard, a vein ruptured inside her head. Blood pulsed into Jill's left hemisphere with each beat of her heart. Gradually, parts of her brain became flooded, then sputtered, flickered, and finally shut down. Within hours, Jill had lost her ability to use language, follow sequential reasoning, and track linear time.

She'd also lost every trace of anxiety.

With her left hemisphere inactive, Jill experienced herself as a field of energy the size of the entire universe. In this right-hemisphere consciousness there was no time, just an infinite present moment. Jill couldn't remember the names of common objects, let alone of people, but she was extraordinarily attuned to her fellow humans' physical and emotional energy. She later wrote that her consciousness felt "like a great whale gliding through a sea of silent euphoria." She was intensely aware, filled with inexpressible compassion and gratitude.

Fortunately, Jill also happened to be surrounded by other brain scientists. They had faith she could recover, because they knew that our brains are malleable—we can change their structures from the inside just by thinking differently. It took Jill over eight years to perform the near-miraculous task of rebuilding her brain's left hemisphere. She regained her ability to use language, logic, and time. But she deliberately chose to remain less left-hemisphere dominant than she'd once been. She now knew how to, as she put it, "step into the consciousness of my right hemisphere."

At first, I was confused by Jill's description of a blissful right hemisphere, because it clashed with something she herself called "a mountain of neuro-science research that supports the idea that our left brain is the source of our happiness." But, she wrote in her book **Whole Brain Living,** "happiness is not the same as joy. Although both happiness and joy are positive emotions, they are very different psychologi-cally and neuroanatomically." The happiness of the left hemisphere comes from positive external con-ditions, while the right hemisphere feels a joy born from within.

This difference shows up in many books on how to be happy. For example, here's some advice from psychologist John B. Arden:

> Let's say that you've been sad recently and have been pulling back from your friends. Maybe you've said to yourself, "I don't want to put on a happy face." You should force yourself to call a friend and go out to lunch when you don't feel like it.

This advice is based on Arden's conviction that the left hemisphere, if given total control, can lock down what he sees as the glumness or moodiness of the right brain. Arden states that people are depressed after a left-hemisphere stroke but not after a stroke that affects the right hemisphere—exactly the opposite of what Jill Bolte Taylor experienced.

When I asked Jill about this, she told me that doctors who want verbal reports of happiness usually can't get them from people whose left hemispheres are offline, because those patients can't use language. As for being depressed after her stroke, she said, "People thought I must be depressed, because I wept a lot. But I wasn't depressed. I was in awe." As a social scientist, I've been trained to take the word of observers as important but to give primary credence to the reports of people who have actually lived through an experience. For this reason, among others, I favor Jill's perspective.

WHY OUR BRAINS TEND TO TURN LEFT

You'd think that since we all have access to the state of awe and bliss Jill found in her right hemisphere, we'd go into this state as often as we could and stay for as long as possible. But evolution has given us the opposite tendency—we tend to focus on whatever makes us feel **worse,** or at least more uneasy. Two of the mechanisms responsible for this are the brain's "negativity bias" and something I call the "hall of mirrors." Recognizing and understanding these neurological quirks can help us step away from their influence.

The Negativity Bias

One holiday, my family received a life-size cardboard cutout of Lin-Manuel Miranda, the genius who brought the musical **Hamilton** to the world. The cutout looks just like the real guy: same height, same silhouette, same adorably dimpled smile. After we unwrapped the cutout, we all toasted Lin-Manuel's health, put our arms around his shoulder, and took some selfies.

The problem was that our cockapoo, Bilbo Baggins of Bag End, Pennsylvania, did not perceive this as a hilarious sight gag. He only knew that our home had been invaded by a weirdly motionless two-dimensional human that exuded all the wrong smells. Now, Bilbo isn't easily shaken, but when he is, the drama can get positively Shakespearean. **WHAT HO!** he screamed, catching sight of the cutout. Then he courageously attacked it, shouting **BEGONE, YE NIGHTMARE FIEND! RETURN TO THINE ODIOUS LAIR AND TORMENT US NO MORE!**

For almost an hour, we tried to help Bilbo stop saving us from Lin-Manuel Miranda. Nothing worked. He nobly sustained the fight until we gave up and stashed the cutout in a closet. Which is when things got really intense.

Now, everyone in my family knows what's in that closet. We've all seen it many times. Nevertheless, we are frequently treated to an event that gives us all a bracing frisson of terror. First, there's the squeak of hinges as someone opens that particular door. Next comes the bloodcurdling scream, then the thunder of feet in flight, then finally the shaky laughter of the unfortunate person who has once again surprised Lin-Manuel Miranda lurking in the darkness, just waiting for Bilbo to drop his guard.

The reason this piece of cardboard has the power to terrify my family over and over again is that we—and all humans—share Bilbo's tendency to perceive any possible danger in every situation. The second we notice something odd, our fight-or-flight responses flash into action. If you want to see how strongly and quickly this happens, google "invisible danger prank" and watch a few videos. (Trigger alert: This prank involves someone faking fear, which causes an immediate fight-or-flight reaction in someone else. I would **never** play this prank on anyone. Nor do I want anyone to play it on me. But damn is it ever a vivid illustration of how quick we are to panic, even with no evidence of danger.)

The negativity bias is our hair-trigger tendency to see danger everywhere. It's a big evolutionary plus, because fearing everything motivates us to avoid the few things that really are dangerous. If you come across a snake, for example, you might not know whether it's a harmless species or a venomous one. Assuming that the snake is dangerous when it isn't could rob you of a beautiful relationship with a friendly serpent. But assuming that it's harmless if it's not could get you lethally chomped. It's best to err on the side of caution, so that's what our brains do.

The negativity bias makes us worry about social and emotional risks, as well as physical ones. If someone gives you three compliments and one bit of harsh criticism, your brain will focus on the insult. If your Instagram post gets a thousand Likes and one comment that simply says "BAD!" your brain will spotlight the troll. In the midst of almost universal approval, you may feel devastated by a single stranger's complaint that your mention of "hearty soups" brought up her fear of choking and should have come with a trigger warning.

When the negativity bias spurs our anxiety spirals into action, our thinking can quickly become delusional. In a state of anxiety, we actually stop noticing any information that tells us there's no need to fear. We think our anxious worldview is complete and perfect, because **the left hemisphere cannot believe that anything beyond its own perceptions is real.** As a result, we often get stuck in a neurological hall of mirrors.

The Hall of Mirrors

I was about five years old when I first entered a hall of mirrors at an amusement park. I was not amused. To my eyes, the "hall" (actually just a small room) looked like a horrifying alien universe. The walls, ceiling, and floor were all covered with mirrors that were warped to create grotesque reflections. Since every mirror reflected the other mirrors, the room also appeared endless. Terrified by all the monstrous images, I got so disoriented that I couldn't find the exit.

Fortunately, a friend pulled me out of that awful little room. But later, on many occasions, I got trapped in a metaphorical hall of mirrors that materialized from the anxious reflections of my brain's left hemisphere. You may have experienced the same thing, because the anxiety spiral, just like a carnivalesque hall of mirrors, is structured in a way that makes it hard for us to find the exit. The anxiety-producing part of the brain magnifies its own distorted thinking while denying that anything else exists.

It's amazing to see how literal this can be. For example, one day the famous neurologist and writer Oliver Sacks, then a psychiatric intern, showed up at the hospital to find one of his patients behaving strangely. This young man had woken up from a nap and started screaming that someone had put a **severed leg** into bed with him. He kept pointing at his own left leg, accusing the nurses of putting it there as a horrible sick joke.

Sacks listened to the patient rant about the alien leg. Then he asked, "If this—this thing—is **not** your left leg, then where **is** your own left leg?"

The patient looked around, gaped in horror, and said, "I have no idea. It's disappeared. It's gone." Then he grabbed his left leg—that ghoulish, repulsive object—and threw it to the floor. The rest of him went with it. The patient lay there in growing dread as he realized that the alien leg was somehow **attached to him.**

This bizarre condition, called "hemispatial neglect," only happens to people with right hemisphere damage (the opposite of the area where Jill's stroke occurred). Such patients may shave or put makeup on only the right sides of their faces, ignore anyone standing to their left, and draw pictures that are simply blank on one side. There's nothing wrong with these people's eyesight. But they've lost the ability to pay attention to anything that isn't perceived and controlled by their left hemispheres, including half of their own bodies.

This weird attention blindness also applies to the way the left hemisphere **thinks.** Once we've generated an anxiety-based story, our brains latch on to it as The Only Reality, becoming resistant to any other way of thinking. Take a group of anxious people—folks with extreme political beliefs, say, or cultists who are convinced that their leader, a former carpet salesman named Ralph, is a powerful wizard. Show these people irrefutable evidence that something they believe is factually incorrect. What happens? Research shows that **their belief in the disproven idea actually grows stronger.**

Confronted by new information, the left side of the brain doesn't open up. It sees the evidence not as valuable information but as a threat to its status quo, its truth—no, **The Truth!** Logical evidence that it's incorrect just puts the anxiety spiral on rocket fuel. The left hemisphere generates even more fear, magnifying its terrifying stories.

Once we're inside the left hemisphere's hall of mirrors—that is, our anxiety—anything and everything may seem monstrous. Simple kindness may look like a manipulative lie. Rest and relaxation appear weak. Optimism is stupid. Everything is out to get us, except for the things we want, which seem to be in terribly short supply. There is never enough good stuff in the world as seen from this mental perspective: never enough money, status, power, love, golden toilets, breakfast cereal, anything. This perspective makes the world look grim and joyless, but by God, **it feels real.**

Because the negativity bias and the hall of mirrors affect the way we identify what's true, anxiety can blind us to inconsistencies or errors in our own thinking. So how do we find the way out? By recognizing the sensation of suffering. Seeing the world from inside the anxiety spiral feels horrible. We can use that horrible feeling as a signal: "HELLO! YOU ARE BEING SPUN BY YOUR OWN NEGATIVITY BIAS! YOU ARE LOST IN THE HALL OF MIRRORS!" Once we realize this, we can step into a better mindset.

USING YOUR BEAUTIFUL MIND TO STEP OFF THE ANXIETY SPIRAL

In the movie **A Beautiful Mind,** based on a true story, mathematician John Nash fights through schizophrenia by using his prodigious rational brain to disprove his psychotic delusions. He notices that several important people in his life **never age,** even though they've been hanging out with him for decades. The real Nash described his own mental process: "Gradually I began to intellectually reject some of the delusionally influenced lines of thinking."

Rarely are people so scrupulously rational that they use logic to see the illogic in their own beliefs. But if we're going to live in peace, we need to learn this skill. Anxiety—feeling terrified and endangered all the time, even in situations where we're safe—isn't John Nash–level psychosis, but it is delusional. It's an imbalanced way of thinking that overemphasizes the perceptions of our left brains. Once we see that, we can reestablish a more balanced worldview by activating our right hemispheres. In fact, you can do that right now. Try the exercise below.

New Skill

STEP OUT OF YOUR ANXIETY SPIRAL

---

1. First, think about something that makes you mildly anxious—not anything truly horrifying but a situation that makes you just a bit nervous, like remembering to buy a gift for a relative or file your taxes on time. Notice how this mild anxiety feels in your body and emotions. Describe it here:

   _____

   _____

2. Now let that thought go for just a minute. Instead, think about three things you love to taste. Imagine tasting them. List them here:

   _____

   _____

   _____

3. Now list three things you love to hear. Imagine hearing them:

_____

_____

_____

4. Now list three things you love to see. Picture them as you write them here:

_____

_____

_____

5. Now list three things you love to smell. Remember the scents:

_____

_____

_____

6. Now list three things you love to feel against your skin. Imagine touching them:

_____

_____

_____

7. Next, see if you can remember or imagine a scenario in which all or most of the

items above were/are present. Because each person's brain is unique, some people find it easier to remember an experience, whereas others can easily conjure sensations through imagination. If neither imagination nor memory works for you, think of a place where you can assemble some things you love with each of your senses. Then spend time in that place, focused on sensing each object.

_____

_____

_____

_____

Right now (or whenever you can bring these sense perceptions into your mind), write a brief description of the scenario that combines some of your favorite sense perceptions. As you do this, use present-tense language. Include at least one image from each of your five senses. For example: **I'm sitting in my favorite easy chair, sipping champagne and munching on Belgian chocolate. My cat is purring on my lap while I stroke her fur. Outside, I can see a beautiful forest, and my children playing. I can hear their laughter, wind in the trees, and birds singing. A cool breeze drifts through the open**

window, carrying the scent of pine trees and the ocean. Also, I am receiving the best foot massage of my life.

8. Briefly describe the physical and emotional sensations that arose as you composed this fantasy situation:

_____

_____

_____

9. Notice what happened to your anxiety during the time you were composing, experiencing, and writing about this scene.

NOTICE WHAT JUST HAPPENED

If you actually did the exercise above—that is, if you really spent some time imagining, remembering, or experiencing all those lovely sense impressions—I hope you enjoyed your brief vacation from anxiety!

That said, it's more likely you read the instructions and thought, **Okay, right, got it. I see where this is going.** In fact, that's what you've been trained to do. Our culture is dominated by the verbal, abstract thinking most prominent in the left hemisphere, so your socialization pulls hard toward the assumption that reading about an experience, or thinking about it in words, is the same thing as actually living it. In fact, you've been trained to believe that thinking is **superior** to experiencing.

So maybe you dismissed the whole exercise above as being stupid, basic, or unimportant. Perhaps you filled in the blanks, felt your anxiety diminish for a few seconds, and then mentally invalidated the whole experience: **Well, sure, that's nice, but that scene is just something I dreamed up in my imagination. It isn't real.**

It's quite true that you created your calming scene by selectively focusing on certain memories, perceptions, and fantasies. **But that's exactly the same thing you're doing when you see the world as frightening and unsafe.**

When the left hemisphere whips us into miserably embracing the negativity bias and the hall of mirrors, we're primed to believe that our perceptions are factually correct. By contrast, when we use our right hemispheres to assemble an internal experience, we know this is a choice. If we step far enough away from the anxiety spiral, we can see that our fears, just like our positive fantasies, are constructed from selected bits of information. And this recognition can take us into a whole new way of living and thinking.

LIFE IN A BALANCED BRAIN

I first met Jill Bolte Taylor when she emailed me to schedule a Zoom call. As Jill's image popped onto my computer screen, I saw that she wasn't in a house. Behind her grew a lush forest, filled with rising mist. Jill was in her summer home: a boat on a lake somewhere in midwestern America. Living there, she told me, helped her abide in the kind of wonder and peace she first experienced when her left hemisphere went offline.

Jill told me that she'd structured her whole life to access the best aspects of her entire brain. (She'd just published **Whole Brain Living,** a wonderful book that I highly recommend.) In addition to engaging her left hemisphere through her scientific research and writing, Jill had shaped her life to light up the right side of her brain. When she wasn't communing with nature, she would jet-ski to land to buy necessities like groceries, boat parts, and art supplies. Yes, art supplies. Though still very much a scientist, Jill is also an artist who makes all sorts of beautiful things: paintings, stained-glass windows, limestone sculptures. She is a living example of the way a balanced brain creates. And creates. And creates.

THE CREATIVITY SPIRAL

When we step away from our anxiety and begin using both sides of our brains to shape our thoughts and perceptions, we encounter something I call the "creativity spiral." Just like the left hemisphere, the right hemisphere can form its own spiraling feedback system, from the inner almond to the upper layers of the brain and back. This pattern is the mirror image of the anxiety spiral. But in the right hemisphere, the effects of the spiral are about as far away as you can get from anxiety. Where the brain's left-side spiral sparks fear and makes us want to control things, its right-side spiral sparks **curiosity** and makes us want to **create** things.

When you see something unfamiliar, your right amygdala yawps along with its anxious twin on the left. But because the right hemisphere doesn't track time, it perceives only what's there in the moment. If the leopard is walking away or the snake is a rope, the right hemisphere drops fear and picks up curiosity. At this point, Jill writes, the deep layers of our right hemispheres are like fascinated children, eager to explore, feel, and experience, unconcerned about the past or the future.

The upper layers of your right brain, unlike their left-side counterparts, don't analyze, predict, or worry about control. Instead, they form connections between ideas, actions, and people. Where the left side analyzes (the word **analyze** means "to cut things apart"), the right side **synthesizes,** or puts things together. Working with the raw material of whatever we perceive in the present moment, the right brain harmonizes, blends, relates, and assembles things, often in highly original ways.

The anxiety spiral blocks out information coming from the right hemisphere. By contrast, the creativity spiral welcomes everything we perceive, including data flowing in through the left hemisphere. It can use the left hemisphere's insights to create items that are useful (like a labor-saving machine), satisfying (like the solution to a mystery), exciting (like meeting a new friend), or expressive (like singing a love song). These experiences often create positive feedback— a sense of fascination and "flow." We feel heightened curiosity and a desire for more experience, leading to more investigation, which leads to more inventive connection, and so on.

Research on creativity indicates that these two ways of thinking seem to toggle—that is, when one goes on, the other goes off. Anxiety shuts down creativity so completely that even the slight stress of being told we'll get paid for solving a puzzle makes us less able to think creatively. But by the same token, deliberately entering and moving further into the creativity spiral can pull us out of the anxiety spiral.

You just did this if you used the exercise above

to focus on your physical senses and to imagine, re-member, or construct a scene in which some of your favorite sights, smells, tastes, sounds, and tactile sensations came together. Now, to practice, let's do another exercise.

First, find a time when you can actually be in a place that feels like a sanctuary, even if it's just the corner of a room. We live in a world of sensations much more stimulating than anything our bodies and brains evolved to handle, so bright lights, loud noises, large groups of people, busy environments, and other aspects of your "normal" life may actually be quite stressful. If you know that's true for you—or even if you don't know it—take some quiet time in a naturally lit space without too much commotion.

Once you're in a sanctuary space, we're going to use your whole beautiful mind and a single physical object to anchor your nervous system in the here and now. By focusing all your senses on something you can hold and move around with your left hand, you activate something called "proprioception," or the sense that tells you how your body is positioned and how it's moving, and bring your whole brain to the task of perceiving something in the here and now. A full physical experience of something you appreciate in the present moment can stop the anxiety spiral in its miserable tracks.

New Skill

OBJECT APPRECIATION

1. Find a moment where you're not in immediate danger and where you won't have to interact with anyone for a few minutes.

2. Close your eyes. Imagine or remember looking at a vast, beautiful landscape. See if you can feel your eyes relax, as if they're taking in a broad vista. Allow your breathing to deepen, and notice whether your eyes can feel even more relaxed. If not, that's fine.

3. Now, while still breathing deeply, open your eyes and look around you for any smallish object that has positive associations—something that ignites a spark of pleasure. For example, you might notice a favorite coffee cup, a book, or your most lived-in T-shirt. Anything portable and positive will do.

4. Pick up the object. Heft it, feeling its weight, texture, and temperature. Examine

it with your eyes. Hold it up to your ears and scratch it to make a noise. Sniff the object. If tasting it feels interesting and sanitary, go right ahead and do that, too.

5. Now start to think about everything that had to happen to create the object and bring it into your life. Imagine how it was made—by nature, by humans, by both. Contemplate the ways this object has helped you in the past, and how it continues to add pleasure or ease to your life.

6. If you feel yourself sliding into anxiety, slow your breathing and let yourself come back to appreciative thoughts about the object. Replay some positive memories. For example:

- **I've sipped coffee from this cup on so many mornings. It's always here for me and never complains. I love to hold it on cold days and feel the coffee waking me up. This right here is a** fantastic **coffee mug!**

- **I remember buying this book off the remainder table. Best three dollars I ever spent. This book has comforted me so often, taught me things I really needed to know, and buoyed me up**

when I thought all was lost. Who would have thought that Plumbing for Dummies **could change my life so much?**

• **This T-shirt has survived being washed a thousand times. It's soft and faded and so, so comfortable. I love the word on the front: BREATHE. I love the fact that when I wear a jacket over it, you can only see the middle letters: EAT. Such good advice!**

7. If you feel like it, write down five positive thoughts about your object here:

_____

_____

_____

_____

_____

8. Notice that while you were actively appreciating the object, your anxiety backed off a step or two.

9. Anytime you feel a bit anxious, find an object to appreciate: a stop sign that keeps you safer, a cloud that brings needed rain, a pebble that feels good in your hand. Notice how many objects are present

to help you, without ever judging you or demanding anything.

10. If your friends think this is weird, know that you are making significant progress.

MOVING ON TO A CALMER PLACE

As long as we have typical brains, we'll always have a hair-trigger danger alarm, a negativity bias, and a tendency to get caught in the left hemisphere's hall of mirrors. As long as we're living with other people, especially in modern society, we'll continue to encounter scary information and worried people who are firmly ensconced in their own halls of mirrors. We can trust that our ancient biology will fire up its emergency alert system whenever we see a leopard by the screen door, a flat cardboard man in the closet, or someone acting jumpy nearby. But we can also learn to stop and deploy our **whole** brains so that healthy fear never runs off track and into an escalating spiral of anxiety.

Imagine how different your childhood might have been if every day, at school and at home, you'd been taught to slow down, breathe deeply, and let go of worry. What if you'd been taught by people like Jill, who deliberately access their whole brains and know how to find a place beyond anxiety? What if all the adults around you had agreed that stepping away from anxious perceptions, accessing your creativity, feeling safe in the present moment, and connecting with everything you love were the skills you most needed to live a successful life? You might have done almost anything. You might have been a completely different person.

But that's not what happened, is it?

Through no fault of anyone's, almost all of us ignore the countless moments when we're quite safe. Instead, we spend years stewing in anxiety, mentally screaming and running from the various versions of Lin-Manuel Miranda that fill the closets in our minds. We're taught that this constant anxiety is logical and prudent. We see that our society as a whole is heading up the anxiety spiral, taking us with it and rewiring our brains to be ever more anxious.

In the next chapter, we'll take a closer look at the constant social pressure that's trying to accelerate our anxiety spirals. Once we understand how this works, we can begin to separate our senses of reality from the stories that have been socialized into our heads. Then we can begin rewiring our brains to move toward wonder and delight.

As psychologist James Hollis wrote, anxiety "has crowded you into a diminished corridor of [the] vast mansion of possibilities." If you can trace the anxiety spiral in your own mind and life, if you can step away from it for even just a second or two, you're already leaving that shrunken, contorted world behind. It's time to explore the mansion.

2

Anxious Creatures in an
Anxious Culture

Nicky shows up promptly for her appointment on my laptop screen, which is where I do most of my coaching these days. From what I can see, Nicky is in three things: (1) a tastefully furnished Manhattan apartment, (2) a Versace suit, and (3) a state of astronomical anxiety.

Knowing that Nicky is a rising star at a prestigious law firm, I'm surprised by how wretched she looks. After greeting me, she bends forward like Atlas shouldering the world, clenching both hands to her chest, trying and failing to hold back tears.

I wait for a minute, then gently ask her what's wrong.

"Oh, nothing," Nicky says. "Or—I don't know—maybe everything." She rubs her temple with the tips of her perfectly manicured fingers. "I'm just not doing well. I'm nervous all the time. I can't sleep. I'm getting close to the end of my rope. I'm **so** anxious!"

"Okay," I say. "What makes you most anxious?"

"Everything." Nicky emits a mirthless laugh. "I'm anxious about failing. I'm afraid my career will fall apart. I'm scared that I'll disappoint people—my boss, my team, my parents. I'm afraid I'll never have a family of my own, because if I ever take the time to date, my career will collapse."

Nicky tells me a bit about her personal history: Born in Puerto Rico, she moved with her parents to New York City when she was ten, hoping for a better life. Nicky is the first in her family to graduate from college, let alone from law school, and her achievements are the pride of her whole extended clan. At school and work, she's always been the can-do prodigy, taking on the most grueling tasks with a cheerful smile. No one at her firm knows how tired she is, or how hard she has to fight every day to cope with the cutthroat, racist, sexist atmosphere that permeates her workplace.

A few months ago, Nicky went to her doctor hoping to get some sleeping pills. He sent her to a psychiatrist, who diagnosed her with anxiety disorder and prescribed medication and therapy. They helped. A little. For a while. But Nicky's anxiety kept slowly rising. Now, she says, she feels worse than ever.

At this point, let's put a pin in Nicky (not literally) and see if her story feels familiar to you. Maybe you, too, have worked insanely hard and achieved much, only to find yourself so anxious that you can't enjoy the fruits of your labor. Maybe after devoting yourself to hearth, home, and child-rearing, you feel overwhelmed by the low-prestige, high-demand grind of parenting. Maybe you decided to stick it to the man and become an artist, musician, actor, or writer, just to wind up anxiously scraping for money as your creativity goes weirdly dry. Or perhaps you're so daunted by the demands you face every day that you're too anxious to really commit to anything.

Well, at least you're not alone.

There's a common factor behind all these scenarios, but most of us have been trained not to see it. The people Nicky has consulted—family members, friends, doctors, her therapist—have focused on her anxiety as a problem, like a flat tire or a flu. None of them has suggested that Nicky's anxiety is a perfectly healthy, normal response to her lifestyle, which is extremely **abnormal.**

"What?" Nicky says when I tell her this. She stops crying and stares at me as though I've grown an extra ear. "My life is totally normal! No, **better** than normal. I mean, I'm living the American dream!"

"Mm," I say. "Well, it seems to be affecting you a lot like a nightmare."

As our session continues, Nicky and I discuss the three things I want you to learn from this chapter.

First: We're living in a culture that's heavily biased toward a very specific kind of thinking and behaving—the way preferred by the left hemisphere.

This bias is so strong that one expert, the psychiatrist and Oxford scholar Iain McGilchrist, says we all act like "people with right hemisphere brain damage." Because the left hemisphere is also the part of the brain that gets stuck in anxiety spirals, this makes us sitting ducks for anxiety.

Second: The way our culture goes about trying to reduce anxiety also tends to be very left-brain dominated. We subject ourselves to psychological analysis (remember, to analyze means to cut things up). We attack anxiety, fighting it like warriors on a search-and-destroy mission. This, as we'll see, ends up making us more anxious, not less.

Third: There's a better way to deal with anxiety, one that moves us away from our left hemisphere–dominated cultural models and allows our inherent wisdom to guide us into a more brain-balanced way of being. This approach helps us calm not only ourselves but also the people around us—even in extremely difficult or dangerous situations. By the end of this chapter, you should have the knowledge and the skills to do it.

THE UNNATURAL WAYS OF OUR SOCIETY

If Nicky had been born a few thousand years ago— an eyeblink, in evolutionary terms—her life would have been shaped by the rhythms and cycles of nature. For the vast majority of human history, people went to bed when it got dark, sleeping several more hours per night than most of us do these days and waking to the sounds of wind, water, birds, animals, and one another's voices. They lived in natural settings that contained few straight lines or right angles, doing daily tasks like hunting, foraging, gardening, fishing, pot-making, weaving, and cooking. These activities certainly require effort, but the fact that many modern humans still do them as hobbies, **for fun,** is a strong hint that we evolved to enjoy them.

Nicky's body, like yours and mine, knows that it evolved to live this way. Take Nicky to a forest and in just a few hours, there'd be a measurable drop in her stress hormones, muscle tension, and blood pressure. Her resistance to infection would increase, along with the number of her cancer-killing cells. She'd also raise her problem-solving abilities, lower her risk of depression, and sleep better. Scientists can measure these responses in people who visit natural environments even briefly—and we evolved to live there all the time.

By contrast, Nicky spends her life in environments full of straight lines, rigid angles, and artificial everything, from snack foods to fabrics to light. Our left brains heartily approve of this. As McGilchrist writes, "The left hemisphere likes things that are man-made . . . because we put them together. They are not, like living things, constantly changing and moving, beyond our grasp." They're also easier to handle with the left hemisphere's preferred tools: force, logic, and control.

To function in the artificial worlds we've made, we force our bodies to run on clock time rather than in accordance with the seasons, our states of health, or physical sensations like hunger, thirst, and fatigue. We sort our children into same-size groups and make them sit for hours, paying sharp attention to things they'd never find in nature—even though scientists have shown that children learn best when they're outside, moving, using a wide-open attention focus and all their senses to solve problems that are immediately useful to them.

But, of course, our school system wasn't designed to teach kids just any damn thing they like. It was designed not long after the industrial revolution to prepare them for jobs where they'd sit at assembly lines or desks under fluorescent lights, doing mechanical tasks or processing information, pretending to like it.

Those who land really coveted, high-prestige jobs like Nicky's may spend most of their lives fully focused on things that only the left hemisphere can understand: calendar deadlines, written text, spreadsheets, PowerPoint presentations so dull viewers can actively feel their minds turning to oatmeal. Most of these jobs—most jobs, period—will require them to leave their families and other loved ones so that they can spend most of their waking hours with strangers who've been assigned to perform similar work.

This profoundly imbalanced culture, says Princeton psychologist Les Fehmi, is "born of the left hemisphere." It's been moving further and further toward left-hemisphere thinking for the last few centuries, rewarding people who value its definition of productivity over things like empathy and meaning. It focuses overwhelmingly on one single goal: maximizing material wealth. Or, as McGilchrist puts it, "grabbing stuff." To the left hemisphere, this seems like the only task worth doing. "Its purpose is utility," McGilchrist says, "and its evolutionary adaptation lies in the service of grasping and amassing 'things.'"

This is the way of life that has crowded us into artificial environments, destroyed countless natural ecosystems, helped people slaughter each other by the hundreds of millions, and changed the planet's weather in potentially apocalyptic effect. It's driven many of us, including Nicky, to exhaustion, depression, and intense anxiety.

HOW THINGS GOT SO WEIRD

All of this has made us radically depart from the way our bodies and minds are designed to function. And our brains are struggling to keep up. In the year 2000, biological anthropologist Joseph Henrich coined the acronym WEIRD to describe countries that are Western, Educated, Industrialized, Rich, and Democratic. Henrich believes that we citizens of the WEIRD world have dramatically different psyches from our ancestors: more object obsessed, more driven, and—you guessed it—more anxious.

The template for WEIRD thinking arose a few hundred years ago in Western Europe. Rejecting the rule of religion, the thought leaders of this time set out to understand the world from a strictly material-ist perspective, by measuring, analyzing, calculating, and labeling things. In other words, they got all up in their left brains, and stayed there.

Don't forget, the left hemisphere's hall-of-mirrors effect makes it absolutely certain that its percep-tions are fundamentally correct, that no other way of thinking is, by God, **right.** This attitude inspired those European Enlightenment thinkers to spread their new mindset all over the globe.

By the left hemisphere's standards, this effort was a rousing success. When European explorers encoun-tered people with different values and lifestyles, they got right to work enslaving, exploiting, or simply kill-ing as many of these people as possible, grabbing all of their stuff, including their bodies and their children. Anyone from the conquered cultures who survived had to adopt Western values to navigate their new world. To the left hemisphere, this just made sense. It was all Progress! Divine Right! Manifest Destiny!

And it's still going on.

HOW OUR ECONOMY BECAME A FEAR FACTORY

As this left-hemisphere culture pushes us away from nature's rhythms, our neuroplastic brains have adapted themselves to the conditions we face. In other words, each of us is socialized to become more and more left-hemisphere dominated. That means we're also operating preferentially from the parts of our brains that create anxiety spirals. No wonder people like Nicky, who are sitting in various box-shaped offices, focused on information processing and competing with coworkers they barely know, tend to be anxious.

In fact, in our culture, anxiety is **encouraged** as a means of boosting productivity ever higher. Despite piles of evidence showing that we are most creative and ingenious when we're calm, we often tell ourselves (and one another) that fear is the great motivator, a necessary component of high achievement. To stay productive, we believe, we **should** stay anxious.

This is why Amazon's founder, Jeff Bezos, one of the wealthiest human beings in history, wrote to his stockholders, "I constantly remind our employees to be afraid, to wake up every morning terrified." Living in fear, he asserts, is the way to stay ahead. This philosophy has certainly helped Bezos acquire his staggeringly huge fortune. But is it really "normal" for over a million Amazon employees to be terrified from the moment they wake up every day so that some of the richest people in the world can get even richer?

Absolutely! the left hemisphere shouts.

Our culture's conventional wisdom tells us that our best chance at a good life is to **be** a Jeff Bezos, someone perched on the very tip-top of a social and financial pyramid. Because this is the way we've been taught to hope and dream, we help create and co-operate with systems in which the continuous oppression of many ordinary people, who are just scraping by financially, supports extreme wealth for a tiny minority. And to sustain this situation—to make it even more extreme, with greater wealth at the top of the pyramid—everyone lives in a state of perpetual dread that makes the enjoyment of life nearly impossible. Even more ironically, the people at the top of the pyramid usually also live in a state of anxiety. As Shakespeare put it, "Uneasy lies the head that wears a crown."

Most people I know accept this pyramid of anxiety as The Way Things Work, succumbing to the same resignation with which they tolerate the realities of gravity or weather. But producing extreme wealth for a few people by terrifying almost everyone else isn't natural law. It's something we've **made,** following our left hemisphere's most materialistic, frightened, and controlling tendencies.

And so we return to Nicky, curled up and weeping

in her beautiful apartment. She's spent her life complying impressively with WEIRD culture. And no one who's tried to help reduce her anxiety seems to have noticed that this effort has disconnected her from everything that sustained humans for tens of thousands of years: her own body, her loved ones, plants and animals, natural environments, her sense of spirit.

Remember Jill Bolte Taylor, living on a forest lake, studying science, and making art? Many people might see her lifestyle as odd, even eccentric. But biologically and psychologically, Jill's daily life is far more normal than Nicky's. After experiencing the "silent euphoria" of life with a disabled left hemisphere, Jill deliberately chose to live in a way that balanced the functions of her two hemispheres. She chose not to go back to the prestigious lifestyle she calls "climbing the Harvard ladder." Instead, she created a life where she can truly thrive—body, mind, and soul.

So how do we disengage from our "normal" way of thinking, the mindset that rules our culture and sends us spinning through anxiety cycles? Most of my clients assume that the best strategy is to fight back. They're ready to make war on anxiety with all their might and main. This is brave and admirable. And it doesn't work.

HOW WE MAKE OUR ANXIETY WORSE BY FIGHTING TO MAKE IT BETTER

The left hemisphere loves to fight. It thrives on competition and conquest. Among our left hemisphere–based cultural traits is our reverence for the way of the warrior. While most of us don't spend a lot of time physically attacking other people, we do urge ourselves and one another to fight for anything worth having. Fight to stay healthy! Fight to win your true love! Fight for self-esteem! Fight for peace, because that's not self-contradictory at all! Fight, fight, fight!

Even many styles of psychotherapy explicitly set out to "fight" mental illness. The first psychotherapists started out under the label "analysts," those who dissect the psyche. Ever since Freud, mental health experts have tried to isolate and examine every little bit of a disturbed mind, like pathologists slicing up tumor tissue or watchmakers disassembling a timepiece to see why it no longer ticks.

Nicky's therapist, for example, is devoted to detailed analysis. In every session, Nicky articulates more and more clearly all the early traumas that may have contributed to her anxiety disorder. After a year of this, Nicky says, "I understand my anxiety so much better. Why isn't it going away?" The reason why she and her therapist haven't found the loose cog in the machine of Nicky's mind is that her mind is not a machine. Anxious human beings aren't broken mechanisms. We're frightened creatures.

When you feel anxious, the primal creature at the core of your brain is working exactly as nature intended. It's trying to find your natural environment and ways of behaving, and when it can't, it gets worried. Subjecting it to analysis or attack doesn't help this situation. I often hear people say things like:

- "I'm trying so hard to beat this stupid anxiety thing!"
- "I need to get a grip and **end** my anxiety."
- "I'm totally committed to overcoming my anxiety."
- "I'm fighting my anxiety as hard as I can, but it always wins."

These are the valiant words of a warrior, and they sound perfectly normal to almost everyone in our culture. Now consider some things I've **never** heard a client say:

- "I plan to give my anxiety lots of space to do whatever it wants."
- "I'd love to help my anxiety thrive."
- "I'd really like to have a closer connection with my anxiety."
- "I value my anxiety so very much."

These statements may strike you as bizarre, because they contradict the way our culture teaches us to think. But consider how you yourself naturally respond to these different approaches. Say you've signed on for a change-your-life coaching session with me. I march in, look you in the eye, and rattle off the "normal" things people say about anxiety. I tell you:

- "I'm going to try so, so hard to beat you."

- "I want to get a grip on you and **end** you."

- "I'm totally committed to overcoming you."

- "I'm going to fight you as hard as I can until I win."

How does that make you feel? Relaxed and cooperative? Impressed and excited? Or very, **very** uneasy? Are you more interested in following my instructions or feeling around for your pepper spray?

Well, the part of you that feels anxiety responds the same way anytime you set out to "beat," "overcome," "end," or even "analyze" it. Faced with such antagonism, it gets more afraid than ever—how could it not? So it bulks up, digs in, and braces itself to survive your most warlike onslaughts. Your net anxiety increases.

Next, let's imagine that when you come to me for coaching, I start with my list of the "bizarre" statements no one makes about their anxiety:

- "I plan to give you lots of space to do whatever you want."

- "I'd love to help you thrive."

- "I'd really like to have a close connection with you."

- "I value you so very much."

You might raise a dubious eyebrow—I mean, we hardly know each other, and this is definitely third-date material—but I doubt it would make you flee the room. It might even make you feel curious about what I'd do next.

This isn't rocket science–level psychology, folks. We all know that no part of us—no creature that ever lived—wants to be attacked, controlled, or chopped up. We know that we're more likely to relax when we feel respected and understood. So for the rest of this chapter—maybe the rest of your life—I'd like to help you picture another approach to anxiety, one that begins with respecting the way we evolved to think and behave.

BECOMING AN ANXIETY WHISPERER

Relaxing our anxiety is a bit like learning how to "whisper" to horses, as opposed to following the

time-honored tradition of "breaking" them. For centuries, people have broken horses using the way of the
warrior: attack, overwhelm, injure, dominate. Some
horse trainers still do this. Popular methods include
hobbling a horse so that it can't run, then beating it,
kicking it, whipping it, and otherwise causing fear
and pain until it "breaks" and stops fighting back.

Happily, modern trainers are beginning to use
techniques popularly known as "horse whispering."
Experts in this method start by observing how horses
interact with one another. Then they mimic equine
"language," which is mainly composed of movement,
gesture, and energy. (For example, ambling along a
winding path while keeping your eyes in soft focus is
horse language for "I'm not here to hunt you or hurt
you; I just want to be part of your herd.")

I once watched horse whisperers work with some
wild mustangs that had just been relocated off public land. These animals were as wild as deer. They'd
rarely seen humans and had never been touched, only
herded—terrified, no doubt—into transport trucks.
Before the whisperers entered the pasture with them,
each donned a helmet and signed a waiver acknowledging that the horses might kill them. I went along
to watch, expecting some high drama.

It was actually kind of boring.

Over a period of about four days, the humans
spent hours standing near the mustangs. Sometimes,
someone would saunter toward a horse, then slowly
move away. The whisperers used tactics like shifting

their weight or relaxing their eyes to communicate safety to the horses in their own "language." A lot of it was so subtle that I didn't even notice it. But within a few days—in contrast to the weeks it might take to "break" a horse—those mustangs were happily allowing their new human friends to pet and brush them. The whole process was the extreme opposite of violent combat.

Horses and humans have very similar amygdalae—so, in fact, do most creatures. That's why calming yourself (and other people) using gentle, subtle skills works best like those used in horse whispering. This is true even in situations that seem to call for warlike action, situations where being gentle and subtle strikes most of us as just plain stupid.

Anxiety Whispering When the Stakes Are High

In the summer of 2000, a twenty-four-year-old American named Jeffrey Schilling was kidnapped by rebels in the Philippines. The rebel leader was an infamous terrorist named Abu Sabaya. He demanded a $10 million ransom from Schilling's parents, who checked their wallets thoroughly, then asked the US government for help. The FBI sent in a team of agents led by the bureau's best hostage negotiator, Chris Voss.

I think it goes without saying that hostage crises are high-anxiety affairs—everyone is hostile, armed, and ready to pull literal triggers. But when Voss got to the Philippines, he made no threats, tossed no hand grenades, kicked no one in the face. He was working with a Filipino colleague named Benjie, a decorated soldier who'd been communicating with Sabaya by phone in his native Tagalog. Here are some of the methods Voss asked Benjie to use in subsequent conversations with the kidnapper:

- a soft, low, gentle voice

- thoughtful silence

- curious questions

- attentive listening

- summarizing Sabaya's position out loud

- showing empathy

Benjie did not like this **at all.** He hated Sabaya with a white-hot passion. The man had killed one of his men, raped and murdered innocent people without the slightest remorse. So when Voss suggested listening attentively to Sabaya, even **empathizing** with him, Benjie went ballistic. And how did Voss react as Benjie yelled and cursed? He offered:

- a soft, low, gentle voice

- thoughtful silence

- curious questions

- attentive listening

- summarizing Benjie's position out loud

- showing empathy

Encountering this weirdly calm reaction, Benjie ranted for a while, then gradually ran out of steam. He soon began cooperating with Voss, practicing the negotiator's counterintuitive techniques as days of tension stretched into weeks. Gradually, Benjie became a skilled negotiator himself, right there in the field.

After many conversations, Sabaya seemed to grow bored with Benjie's thoughtful, muted tone. He also seemed bored with his hostage, because he dropped his guard, giving Schilling an opportunity to escape into the jungle, where he was rescued by a team of commandos.

Sabaya called Benjie one last time, to tell him he should have been promoted.

"I was going to hurt Jeffrey," he said. "I don't know what you did to keep me from doing that, but whatever it was, it worked."

This would make a terrible movie. You just can't eat popcorn while watching rugged men empathize with each other in slow, soft voices. Nevertheless, the story of Benjie and Sabaya thrilled me more than all the **Rambo** movies put together, because it showed me a radically simple truth: in any anxious situation, from a household spat to a hostage crisis, we're dealing with one basic thing—the triggered human amygdala.

All amygdalae, in every creature, respond to similar conditions; they sound the alarm whenever something dangerous or unfamiliar appears, and they calm down when given quiet, stillness, and space to relax. This means we can employ the same strategies with ourselves and one another that horse whisperers use to calm mustangs. The skills Voss taught Benjie can replace our habit of turning every disagreement into a war. Learning these skills starts with calming our own inner anxiety creatures. Once we do that, we will find that the people around us become calmer, too. Even in scary situations, we can pull ourselves—and often one another—out of the anxiety spirals that our culture virtually guarantees.

The Basic Skills

The approach Voss "taught" Benjie was actually already present in Benjie's instincts. We naturally access similar tactics when we're dealing with frightened creatures. You might have used amygdala-quieting techniques if you've ever cared for a human baby, a puppy, a kitten, or any other vulnerable being. You automatically knew that it would help to move gently, breathe deeply, make soft sounds, and avoid scaring the creature by attempting to totally immobilize and control it.

Because Benjie used this approach instead of threats of force or analytical argument, he was able to calm Sabaya **without the kidnapper even knowing what was happening.** Benjie's methods seemed to pull the antagonistic energy out of the conflict like magic. (As Iain McGilchrist says, "Magic is the way that the left hemisphere sees powers over which it has no control.")

The anxiety and stress in your own mind and body can be similarly dispelled if you're willing to direct some amygdala-whispering skills toward yourself. The exercise below will get you started. Approaching your anxiety this way may feel odd or counterintuitive at first (remember, it took Benjie a while before he agreed to try Voss's methods). But as you repeat the process and feel how it affects you, you'll get better and better at being a whisperer to your own anxious brain.

To start, take a few minutes when you won't be interacting with other people. Notice any sense of tightness or anxiety anywhere in your body. Focus on this uneasy feeling. Picture it as a young animal: a piglet, a lamb, a duckling. This is your "anxiety creature." In the box below, write down what your creature is and what you're going to name it. Scribble a small picture of it if you like.

My Anxiety Creature

Now close your eyes and imagine watching this anxiety creature curled up inside you, wary, wobbly, and worried. If you can't picture it, **feel** for it. See if you can find the tenuous, skittish part at your core that tenses when you feel anxious. Promise this creature that you have every intention of keeping it safe. Observe it. Notice that it can't **force** itself to relax, even when it wants to. Then gently apply the following amygdala-whispering techniques.

AMYGDALA-WHISPERING SKILL NO. 1: SIGH.

Every time you breathe out, your heartbeat slows a little. Exhaling taps the brakes on your fight-or-flight response so that your heart rate can't get dangerously high. That's why—across hundreds of human cultures and even other species—a long, slow outbreath is a universal way to begin reducing any stress reaction.

Right now, take in a deep breath and let it out in a long sigh. Try pursing your lips and pushing air out through a small opening, working your diaphragm a bit more than usual and making the outbreath last longer. Do this as many times as you like. (Take some normal breaths in between sighs if you start to feel lightheaded.) Notice that as you do this, your body feels slightly more relaxed.

AMYGDALA-WHISPERING SKILL NO. 2: SOFTEN THE FOCUS OF YOUR EYES.

As a child, you were probably subjected to a litany of orders like "Focus!" "Listen!" "Look at me!" "Pay attention!" These instructions really meant that you should concentrate laser-like left-hemisphere attention on whatever the speaker deemed important. This sharp attention focus, considered so productive in our culture, is actually part of the fight-or-flight response that may disturb or paralyze you when you want to do something constructive.

Softening the focus of our attention, especially the focus of our eyes, sends a powerful message to our anxiety creatures that it's okay to relax. Try this right now: If you're reading this book on a page or a screen, stop for a moment and look at **the space between** you and your reading surface. If you're listening to an audiobook, press pause, then listen to the silence that exists around and under any sounds you hear.

I sometimes invite people to do this when I'm on a Zoom call with dozens or hundreds of participants. First, I ask them to rate their anxiety from one to ten and type the number into the chat field. Most of the anxiety scores are over five. Then I ask everyone to gaze at the empty space between their eyes and their computers while listening to the silence under any sound they can hear. After a few seconds of this, I ask them to rate their anxiety again. Virtually everyone reports a dramatic drop, with most people typing in a big fat zero.

Give this a try. Then move on. And I do mean "move."

AMYGDALA-WHISPERING SKILL NO. 3: LET YOUR ANXIETY CREATURE MOVE.

When we're dealing with frightened children, we often try to confine them, hug them, get them to be still. To an anxiety creature, this can feel like forceful captivity. Voss didn't try to stop Benjie from ranting and stomping; he just waited for the soldier to work out his adrenaline. Later, Benjie used the same strategy on Sabaya.

Trying to stop your body from moving when you're anxious is a bit like flooring the gas and brake pedals at the same time. Your anxiety creature may feel the urge to pace, punch a pillow, or just tremble. Let it. Movement, especially shaking, is a highly effective way to handle current or post-traumatic stress.

We often see shaking as a sign of weakness, but it's actually a powerful way for the nervous system to regulate into a state of peace. So, to the extent that circumstances permit, let your anxiety creature move your body however it likes.

AMYGDALA-WHISPERING SKILL NO. 4: ACCEPT YOUR ANXIETY CREATURE. IF YOU CAN'T MAKE YOURSELF DO THIS, ACCEPT THE PART OF YOU THAT REFUSES TO ACCEPT IT.

A frightened anxiety creature is like a crying baby who just won't settle: innocent but also exhausting. If we try to force it to stop feeling what it feels, it becomes more and more anxious. When we **accept** any anxious creature's anxiety, everything starts to cool down.

So, once again, picture your little anxiety creature, your chinchilla or marmoset or whatever, crouching verklempt and quaky in the center of your psyche. Imagine saying to it, "You know what? You can go ahead and stay scared. I'm not going to try to change you. I accept you exactly as you are."

Many people get indignant when I ask them to try this. They say things like "That is so bogus. I **hate** my anxiety creature! I just want it to calm down and shut up!"

If this happens, turn your attention to your own anger at the anxiety creature. Imagine telling this angry part, "You go ahead and stay upset. I'm not going to try to change you. I accept you exactly as you are."

At this, you may begin to fret: "But I learned in church that anger is dangerous and wrong! I've got to shut this down!" (This may be especially persuasive if you were raised in accordance with traditional female gender norms, just as "Stop being such a coward!" will likely resonate for those raised in accordance with traditional male gender norms.) Just notice the part that's protesting. Imagine telling it, "You go ahead and stay appalled. I'm not going to try to change you. I accept you exactly as you are."

Are you getting the picture here? **Accept whatever you're feeling, including any part of you that refuses to accept what you're feeling.** Keep this up long enough and you'll begin to connect with your genuine capacity for acceptance. At this point, your anxiety creature (who can't understand words but is extremely sensitive to your energy) will begin to calm down.

No matter how hard your psyche protests, you can always kindly outplay it by accepting whatever it feels. This is why Voss taught Benjie to listen attentively to Sabaya and then summarize his position. It's like a martial arts move that meets a high-force move, like a punch or a kick, by using no force whatsoever—simply stepping out of the way. Meeting no resistance, the attacker will topple over from their own acceleration.

All of this can happen in your imagination, silently. Now it's time to use your voice. Not words, just voice.

AMYGDALA-WHISPERING SKILL NO. 5: MURMUR, HUM, SING, OR CHANT.

When we're anxious, our throats tighten. Our voices go up in pitch as well as volume. Relaxing our breathing muscles by speaking in a low, slow voice is soothing both because it requires us to loosen this tension and because the physical vibration of a calm human voice helps regulate our nervous systems.

Voss trains hostage negotiators to develop what he calls "the late-night DJ voice." This is the calm, mellifluous tone you might hear on NPR or your favorite online advice show, airing live at three o'clock in the morning. Voss recommends imitating the deep, measured, thoughtful voice Oprah used while questioning her innumerable TV guests. If you haven't seen her do this, google it. Then spend a few minutes finding your own low, slow voice.

The amygdala is always tracking the tones and vibrations of human voices. It gets more anxious when someone yells or hisses and less anxious when it hears soft humming, singing, or chanting. In fact, research shows that chanting is one of the most powerful ways to help regulate an alarmed nervous system. After nearly getting his leg torn off by a crocodile, my friend Boyd Varty calmed himself and survived a trip to a distant hospital by repeating the yogic chant "Amaram hum madhuram hum" (I am eternal, I am blissful). Your amygdala doesn't care what words you use, but it will feel reassured by the sound and vibration.

AMYGDALA-WHISPERING SKILL NO. 6: DEPLOY KIND INTERNAL SELF-TALK (KIST).

Remember the Tibetan monk I mentioned in the introduction? The one who had a terrible anxiety disorder as a child and later became so calm and happy that researchers thought their brain-scanning equipment had broken? Well, he created much of the transformation in his own brain by using something called "loving-kindness meditation." Years before learning this term, I stumbled across something similar.

I call this process KIST, the acronym for "kind internal self-talk." I used it on myself for years before I told anyone about it. Frankly, I was embarrassed. I was pretty sure my intellectual acquaintances would sneer at the suggestion that we should all be kissing our own amygdalae. But then I had a client whose anxiety was so awful that I taught her my secret method and watched her start to feel better within minutes. Now I talk about the process all the time. It's helped me stop caring what my intellectual acquaintances think. Here's how to do it:

- Either silently or using your calm, soft, late-night DJ voice, remind your anxiety creature that you know it's there. Again, it won't understand the words, but it will feel your intention. By focusing on kindness, you'll wake up a part of the brain that lives in compassion and doesn't ever get stuck in anxiety. In order to get the effect, it's crucial to **frame your sentences as if you're addressing another being.** Don't call your scared creature "me," and speak not **about** it but to it. Say things like:

- "You're okay."

- "I see you."

- "I'm here with you."

- "I can tell you're really scared."

- "It's all right."

- "Everything's fine at this moment."

These words may sound inane to your intellect. But as you repeat them, notice that some of them help your anxiety creature settle, even if only a little bit. Repeat the phrases that work best.

- When you feel even a slight reduction in your anxiety, shift to silently offering yourself kind wishes, like these from Tibetan loving-kindness meditation:

  - "May you feel safe."

  - "May you feel peaceful."

- "May you be protected from all harm."

- "May you be happy."

- "May you feel free."

- You can use whatever compassionate "May you . . ." wishes that you can dream up. The longer you continue offering them to your anxiety creature, the more likely you are to regain a calm interior balance.

- Before going back to normal life, picture yourself tucking your creature into a comfortable padded box, then carrying the box in a small imaginary bag hanging from a strap across your shoulder. Promise the creature that you'll notice when it gets worried and help it calm down whenever it needs your attention.

- Keep your promise.

FEELING GOOD BY LOOKING WEIRD

You may be thinking that whispering to your amygdala sounds like a complicated process. But, actually, because it's instinctive, amygdala whispering is far more normal than detailing everything that ever went wrong in your childhood or listing all the religious vows you may have taken and then broken. Here's a summary of the whole process I've described above:

- Notice your anxiety creature.
- Sigh.
- Soften your eye focus.
- Move a little.
- Accept that you feel the way you feel.
- Make soothing sounds.
- Offer yourself kind wishes.

It takes Nicky about five minutes to master this during our first session. Once she's gone through the steps a few times, they come naturally to her, as they probably will to you. This is good, because you'll be reaching for this process often—your brain and culture will probably always have a negativity bias, so calming your creature is something you'll repeat many times until it becomes second nature. I ask Nicky to run through her self-calming routine first thing every morning and then again whenever she finds herself feeling anxious. We sign off until our next session.

What happens next is totally logical from the perspective of Nicky's nature, and totally illogical from the perspective of our culture. She starts farming.

"I didn't plan it beforehand," Nicky tells me in our next session. "It just kind of happened." One day, after calming her anxiety creature on the way home from work, Nicky found herself stopping at a flower shop. As she bought a small wooden planting box, some potting soil, a cherry tomato plant, and seeds for several herbs, she had the odd but pleasant impression that she was buying presents for her anxiety creature. Once back inside her tenth-floor apartment, she set up a little garden near a kitchen window.

"I'm not sure why I'm doing this," she tells me after carrying her computer over to show me her new plants. "I mean, is it normal?"

Culturally, not so much. Few people with expensive Manhattan apartments are cultivating vegetables in their kitchens. But physiologically and psychologically, gardening is one of the most normal things Nicky could do. Some of her happiest memories include helping her grandmother grow vegetables and herbs. Tending her little garden and cooking with her "crops" connects Nicky to nature, her grandmother, her Puerto Rican culture, and her body. The scents, textures, tastes, and simple actions help calm her whole nervous system.

Nicky doesn't mention her garden at work. Other lawyers—especially her bosses—would probably consider it a counterproductive waste of time. But with less anxiety and more inner peace, Nicky finds a new sense of balance. As she practices anxiety-whispering skills and lets herself enjoy her garden, she grows calmer about setting boundaries at work, taking on fewer projects, and creating more realistic deadlines. The quality of Nicky's work actually goes up—and the quality of her life is improving by leaps and bounds.

As you learn to whisper to your anxiety creature, you, too, may start doing things that are strange from the perspective of our culture but natural and healing for you. One of my loved ones calls this "feeling good by looking weird." And when you've got a little distance from your socialization, you'll be ready to calm your anxiety creature even in areas where traumatic experiences have left you most vulnerable. This high-octane creature calming is what we'll be looking at in the next chapter.

3

When Anxiety Creatures
Get Stuck

Long ago, when I roamed the fair halls of academia, I got a job working for a demanding, profane, aggressive professor I'll call Ervil Pondwater. Nobody liked Pondwater—I certainly didn't—but he liked me because I groveled to him like a damned golden retriever.

Pondwater often ordered me to do tedious tasks on short notice. When I'd try to say no or even "not now," I'd feel suddenly paralyzed. I'd just stand there, wanting to refuse but instead feeling myself getting sucked into the dreaded Vortex of Enthusiastic Agreement. "Well, **sure**," I'd say. "I would **love** to input four thousand questionnaires into a massive, bug-ridden computer data set! Of **course** I can finish it over the weekend!"

I'd smile maniacally at Pondwater, wanting to

whack him with a floor lamp. As soon as he dismissed me, I'd sprint back to my apartment, whispering "Run away! Run away!" (I wish I were exaggerating.) Then I'd try to rush through my new assignment, only to find that my mind and body had gone as limp as overboiled spaghetti. I'd slog onward, hating myself and Pondwater, wondering why, why, **why** I always got myself into this kind of situation.

One word: **anxiety.**

My relationship with Pondwater—and many other people—was dominated by a cluster of reactions technically known as a "defense cascade." Operating on directives that evolved long before cognitive thinking, parts of my nervous system were taking over control of my thoughts, perceptions, and behavior. Because I didn't understand what was happening, all the good intentions in the world didn't help me break the pattern. My conscious mind was overwhelmed before I had a chance to address my inner anxiety creature.

In this chapter, we'll talk about the ways **your** anxiety creature hijacks your thoughts, moods, and behaviors. Then I'll teach you some steps you can take to retrain your anxious self. Before I began using these steps, I felt like a skittish monkey, frequently overwhelmed by reactions I couldn't control. Now I feel like someone who owns that same skittish monkey as a pet. I have much more capacity to stay calm and relaxed, even when facing circumstances that once triggered intense reactions.

THE DEFENSE CASCADE

One of the baffling things about anxiety patterns is that they can lead to many different reactions, giving the illusion of having different causes when, in fact, anxiety is at the root of them all. You've probably experienced every part of the defense cascade, but you may favor one type of response over others. See if any of these stories sound familiar:

- Jim is enjoying a drink with his friend Leonard at their favorite watering hole when suddenly Jim feels a wave of rage. He's not sure why; he just wants to punch Leonard in the throat. Instead, he finishes his beer and stalks away from his baffled friend without explanation.

- Fred and Brita are having a terrific second date. Brita is great, Fred thinks: sparkling, smart, and funny. But then he begins to feel judged. He can't pinpoint why; it's just a feeling. Sadly, he realizes that Brita is just as judgmental as every other woman he's ever met. Their third date never happens.

- At a dinner party, Lindsay is seated next to Chris, a charismatic, opinionated extrovert. Lindsay leans toward Chris, asking questions, nodding in agreement, laughing at Chris's jokes. The whole time, she feels more and more disgusted—first by

Chris, whom she finds arrogant and obnoxious, and then, increasingly, by her own pandering, which she can't seem to stop.

- Fresh out of college, Emma lands a coveted internship at a TV news station, working for a famous anchorwoman. Emma desperately wants to impress her mentor, but whenever the woman asks her a question, Emma's mind goes blank. She just stands there, making small gasping noises. Her chances of getting a paying job do not look good.

- Kirby has been enjoying her new job at a home improvement store. In fact, she's just been promoted to floor manager. But instead of being thrilled by her new position, Kirby ends up calling in sick every day for a week. She spends those days lying on the couch, rewatching approximately forty seasons of **Survivor.**

If these experiences were one-offs, or if they only happened every blue moon or two, they'd be unremarkable. But that's not the case. Jim often has inexplicable swells of rage. Fred eventually ghosts every woman he dates. Lindsay perpetually fakes delight in the company of blowhards. Emma frequently freezes under pressure. And Kirby has never been able to go more than a few months without retreating to her Fortress of Solitude on the couch.

Each of them lives in the grip of the defense

cascade. Though their behaviors look completely different, they're all reacting to a hardwired sense of threat. I've already mentioned the famous fight-or-flight response, named in 1915 by Walter Bradford Cannon, who found that many animals secrete the same brew of high-action stress hormones when they're in danger. Since then, other scientists have added new **f** words to the complex of fear responses, including **fawn, freeze,** and **flop.**

For example, Jim had long-standing anger issues, going into "fight" mode without warning. When Fred ghosted Brita, he was unconsciously enacting a "flight" response. Lindsay's compulsion to flatter Chris came from an instinct to "fawn." This is a self-protective response often seen in social predators—that is, creatures who could easily kill each other, but also need to get along. Humans are such a species, as are dogs (google "guilty dogs" to see some adorable fawning).

Emma's tendency to "freeze" evolved to help animals hide from predators. Its goal is invisibility, and it works—even in situations where someone doesn't want to be invisible. Kirby's couch time may not look like self-defense, but it is. "Flopping" is the nervous system's Hail Mary attempt to survive inescapable danger. The body shuts down, hoping to help itself outlast the crisis and heal from any injuries it may have sustained. If you've ever suddenly lost all will-power, motivation, and energy, you were probably in an involuntary flop.

All of these reactions are brilliantly effective at protecting us in certain situations. Anger is a healthy response to injustice or attack. Running away helps us live to fight another day. A little reciprocal fawning—offering praise or help—facilitates many social encounters. When we don't know what to do, freezing can keep us from making fatal mistakes. And when we're sick or trapped, flopping can be the best way to conserve energy, rest, and heal.

The problem is that we may involuntarily experience these reactions when they're not helpful. Even worse, any part of a defense cascade can turn into an anxiety spiral. We may find ourselves going into fight, flight, fawn, freeze, or flop mode, then telling ourselves stories to justify that reaction, thus priming the whole thing to happen more easily the next time we feel threatened.

For example, my relationship with Professor Pondwater brought out every part of the defense cascade. I explained my fight, flight, fawn, freeze, and flop reactions as a response to my situation: clearly, Pondwater was an enormous asshat, but I needed the work, and it was politically smart to make the man happy. These explain-and-control arguments fed right back into my frightened left amygdala, deepening my belief that I **had** to behave the way I did. Like anyone stuck in an anxiety spiral, I unquestioningly accepted my own propaganda.

This is typical of people who develop repeating anxiety patterns. Jim tells himself his outbursts of rage are inevitable because people are idiots and everyone probably wants to punch everyone else most of the time. Fred firmly believes that women are inherently judgmental and sees himself as a lonely knight on a quest to find an accepting damsel. Lindsay will tell you she's just a good Southern girl, raised to use polite flattery. Emma blames herself for freezing up at work, thinking she needs to be more educated and better prepared. And Kirby often says she's just a hippie at heart: no matter what job she gets, she'll eventually turn on, tune in, and drop out.

All of these are very plausible explanations. But because they don't accurately track what's really happening, they reinforce dysfunctional patterns and make them even worse. What's really happening in each case is that someone's anxiety creature has picked up a signal of danger, grabbed the body's physical controls, and launched a defense cascade. Things start to make more sense when we identify the real triggers that are setting off our reactive patterns.

TRIPPING TRIGGERS

The concept of a psychological "trigger" has become very popular recently, mostly due to online discussions, which sometimes present a fuzzy version of the term. I know one woman who, while beginning a Zoom call with several colleagues, hit the "Mute" button and began bad-mouthing other people in the

meeting to the rollicking delight of some friends who
were in the actual room with her. She trash-talked
everyone on the screen—as they tried to tell her she
had accidentally **unmuted** herself and they could
hear every word she said. In a nimble defense, she
proclaimed that she'd been "triggered" by the hostile
appearance of everyone in that meeting and had to
honor her truth by insulting them all in the most
entertaining fashion possible.

This is not how "triggers" actually work. Scientists
use the term to identify moments when we truly
can't control our responses. For example, psychologist Catherine Pittman describes an army veteran
who started having panic attacks in the shower some
ten years after coming home from the Vietnam War.
Eventually, he figured out that his wife had started
buying the same brand of soap he'd used during his
deployment. It was the smell of the soap that triggered a trauma reaction, without his conscious mind
knowing why.

DECODING YOUR TRIGGERS

Human brains are masterful trigger-makers. They
do it by associating sense memories with painful experiences. The ancient alarm system in your brain
will take anything that happened in the instants
prior to a traumatic event and flag it as part of what
caused the problem. For instance, if you had a car

accident—even a fender bender—while wearing a red shirt and listening to a certain song, that shade of red or that particular song might forever send you into a defense cascade without your knowing why.

People who live in long-term danger end up pushing away their awareness of trauma day after day, year after year. If you're a member of a marginalized group—a person of color, a trans person, or a neurodivergent person, for example—you're well aware that you face constant threats of physical and psychological harm. You may live under a constant rain of injuries, small and large, that can happen anytime, anywhere. This can lead to long-term repression of normal defensive and self-protective instincts. This constant suppression of trauma responses often leads to many anxiety triggers—and complete exhaustion.

Whatever our situations, slowing down and talking about the times we get anxious can help our conscious minds "decode" our psychological triggers. This often doesn't happen until we're in safe places with safe people who can help us articulate our own experiences. A client named Angela told me she had no idea how angry and frightened she was growing up Black in a mostly white community in Montana. She'd simply never questioned the way she and other Black people were treated. She also believed that her many health problems—trouble sleeping, digestive issues, skin irritation, bouts of depression—were unrelated conditions.

Only after George Floyd was killed by a Minneapolis

police officer during the COVID-19 lockdown did Angela begin talking openly about the racial dynamics she faced every day. She quickly realized that her "unrelated" problems were all evidence of a healthy nervous system trying to respond within an environment where Angela usually had to hide her feelings.

As a coach, I've often watched people decode their anxiety triggers just by talking about times when they felt out of control. This is what happened with each of the clients I described earlier in this chapter:

- Jim remembered that right before he felt the urge to punch Leonard, Leonard had lifted his glass of Scotch and swirled it around—the same thing Jim's stepfather used to do when he was just drunk enough to start getting violent.

- Fred was raised in a puritanical religion. He wasn't religious as an adult, but years of conditioning had left him with unconscious shame about sexual feelings. Recalling his date with Brita, Fred realized that his sense of being judged had hit him just as he was starting to feel especially attracted to her.

- Lindsay was raised by two narcissistic parents who only offered approval when Lindsay treated them worshipfully. "All they ever really wanted to hear from me was 'Ooh!' and 'Aah!'" she told me. Later, when Lindsay encountered narcissistic behavior in anyone, her nervous system turned on the fawn response.

- As a child, Emma was shaping up to be a violin prodigy—until her parents hired a famous, expensive teacher, who scolded Emma viciously for even the slightest mistake. Emma began freezing up during music lessons, then in any situation where she felt scrutinized.

- Kirby's triggers formed during years of struggling along with undiagnosed dyslexia. If she worked incredibly hard, Kirby could keep up at school, but **barely.** The effort exhausted her. Constantly pushed to master things her brain wasn't designed to do, Kirby began to flop even when she meant to try harder. Eventually, any challenge could trigger an involuntary collapse.

Recognizing their triggers helped each of these people feel less insane, less afraid of their own defense cascades. Their reactions made sense in light of the painful experiences they had survived. But because anxiety spirals are so persistent, and our left hemispheres so prone to getting locked into their belief systems, just knowing about the event that originally caused an anxiety-based pattern may not be enough to dissolve it.

In fact, sometimes our triggers get created and pulled right out where we can see them—but we **still** can't stop our anxiety from going rogue and controlling us against our better judgment. The parts of our nervous systems that create these responses don't respond to logic and won't give up their habitual patterns just because we find them embarrassing. These anxiety creatures aren't just scared babies. They're more like powerful wild animals that effortlessly defeat our best intentions.

For example, a friend of mine—I'll call her Cassie—was born with a commanding personality and later developed a fear of flying. This combination became problematic when Cassie traveled. She used to call me from various airports after deboarding various airplanes and glumly report, "I did it again."

"It" consisted of Cassie washing down a Xanax with a glass of wine before the plane even took off. Once airborne, Cassie would take one look out the window, then grip the arm of whoever happened to be seated next to her. Eventually, when her anxiety had battled its way past the Xanax, Cassie would rip off her seat belt, stand up in the aisle, and shout, "LAND THIS PLANE **NOW**! WE ARE ABOUT TO **CRASH**!"

The flight attendants didn't have to physically struggle with Cassie to get her seated again—well, not very hard, anyway. And of course Cassie's fellow passengers didn't join her in panic—well, not all of them. Mind you, Cassie knew that her behavior was irrational. Before every trip, she vowed not to make a scene. But once her trigger got tripped, her anxiety creature followed its protocol with ruthless implacability.

I used to have a similar problem with medical testing. It started when my son was prenatally diagnosed with Down syndrome, and it got worse over the ensuing years as a series of autoimmune conditions rendered me disabled and racked with pain. I underwent countless medical tests, many of which were physically uncomfortable and led to disheartening diagnoses. Don't worry! I'm fine now! But even after my symptoms abated, I still had an epic fear of medical testing.

This phobia usually crouched in the back of my mind but lurched out of hiding every time I needed a routine health check, such as a mammogram. If you or a loved one has experienced this exciting procedure, you know it involves getting mostly naked, then physically embracing a huge cold metal machine and offering up some very special body parts to be squished. This process gives new meaning to the term **hard-pressed.** And once it's over, you can look forward to the possibility of a cancer diagnosis!

For years, I couldn't get a simple mammogram without turning it into a major production. First of all, someone else had to drive me to the exam, because I'd startle and shriek at anything I saw outside the car, including the sky. I could force myself to change into the little napkin the nurses called a "gown." But once the mammogram machine and I were cuddled up for our close dance, my body would begin shaking uncontrollably. As the Jaws of Life clamped down, I'd go into a full nineteenth century–style swoon. The one consolation was that I would never actually hit the floor. Instead, I'd end up dangling from the apparatus by a single anguished teat.

I was desperate to find some way to stop this pattern. And eventually I did. But first I had to learn a little about how my nervous system was actually creating defense cascades.

HOW TRIGGER REACTIONS TAKE OVER

Remember that when dealing with any form of anxiety, our task is not to fight our own nervous systems but to help them relax and enjoy cooperating with our conscious intentions, like sensitive animals that have learned to trust kindly humans. When we get hijacked by anxiety patterns, we're dealing with literal wild things: sections of our nervous systems that evolved long before cognitive thinking ever appeared. Understanding how our nervous systems switch on various defense reactions can help us tame even the most worried aspects of our anxiety creatures.

Some psychologists believe that the defense cascade is controlled by something called the "polyvagal circuit." This is a large collection of nerves that connect your brain to other parts of your body (**poly** means "many," and **vagal** means "wandering," so the polyvagal circuit is a bunch of nerves that wander all over your fine self). Some of this system evolved eons ago in organisms you'd never think to invite to your family reunions. Other parts of the polyvagal system first showed up in early mammals. Then there are the parts that are unique to humans.

These recently evolved nerve branches are essential for allowing us to communicate signals of danger or safety to one another. They connect our brains with the muscles of our faces and heads, creating facial expressions and head movements that send emotional signals without our having to think about it. This is why babies from all cultures smile when they're content, and why most adults automatically smile back. When we're not so pleased, even if we try to act happy, we flash involuntary "microexpressions" that last about a fifth of a second and reveal our true feelings. Our conscious minds may not see a microexpression of anger or fear on someone's face, but we track it subconsciously and may feel uneasy without knowing why.

Moving down from the head, we get to the part of your nervous system that connects your brain with your lungs, heart, and diaphragm. This part of your nervous system speeds up your heart and breathing rates when you sense danger. It evolved in prehuman mammals, and it triggers the fight, flight, and fawn responses we've just discussed. An activated fight/ flight/fawn response comes with physical manifestations like a flushed face, a sycophantic grin, floods of rage or terror, and a desperate desire to feel connection and approval from another person.

If a dangerous situation goes on long enough, or if we believe we absolutely can't escape catastrophe, the oldest section of the polyvagal circuit might take over. Here we find nerves that connect to the lower abdomen and gut. In good times, they help us rest and digest, two basic functions needed to sustain life. But in dire straits, this part of our nervous system causes the freeze and flop reactions that made Emma go blank and Kirby collapse on the couch. A so-called dorsal vagal collapse gives us that punched-in-the-gut sensation, the feeling of our stomachs dropping to our shoes. It can even make us pass out cold, like yours truly in the grip of a mammogram machine.

This entire alarm system is not only running our internal reactions but also constantly scanning the environment to see whether we're safe or threatened. Its perceptions are so subtle that we're often unaware of them. Polyvagal theorists call them "neuroceptions." I call them "spidey senses." These sensitive perceivers rev up the defense cascade when they notice anything that could possibly represent any form of danger (even when nothing truly dangerous is present). Then, when safety has been reestablished, they slow down our defenses and return us to peace.

This slowing down involves something called the "vagal brake," which, like the brakes in a car, lowers your heart rate and other fear reactions. This anxiety-braking system relies on the right hemisphere of your brain, which sends an all-clear signal down the right-side branch of the polyvagal circuit to your heart. If you get stuck in an anxiety spiral, however, spinning around in your left hemisphere's hall of mirrors, you can't activate this calming system. Your anxiety brakes literally fail, and you may go hurtling into self-destructive patterns.

GREEN LIGHT, YELLOW LIGHT, RED LIGHT

Some polyvagal experts compare this whole setup to green-, yellow-, and red-light situations. When our nervous systems feel safe, they give us the "green light" to proceed calmly and cooperatively. When we sense danger—even subconsciously—the "yellow light" goes on, blaring "Caution! Fight, flight, fawn!" And then there are the **inescapable** horrors, or at least what we **perceive** as inescapable horrors. (Some people can feel as trapped by a meeting with Ed from accounting as they would by a coal mine accident—the brain and body react to our beliefs more than our actual circumstances.) When we think there's no way out of a bad situation, our nervous systems give us the "red light." It's as if we've walked into a glass door. We feel stunned. We lack the energy to do anything, including give a damn. Of course, everyone's nervous system has been conditioned under unique circumstances, so what turns on your green-, yellow-, or red-light state may be different from what changes the lights for someone else.

These three states determine not only how we feel and behave but also how the world looks to us. When we're in a green-light state, everything seems as friendly and fine as the Emerald City of Oz. From a yellow-light vantage point, the same environment suddenly appears threatening: every dog is ready to bite, every business is trying to rip us off, and every pat on the back feels like an abusive blow. When we hit red-light territory, all positive energy flatlines. We may brood obsessively over huge problems like war or climate change while feeling so limp that taking out the trash seems like climbing Everest. If we're in a red-light state, receiving flowers is just a forced exposure to allergens. Adorable kitten videos? Mere reminders that all living things must die. Our lives— and we ourselves—become unbearable.

Sometimes we take rudimentary control over these manifestations of anxiety by using one type of nervous-system response to blot out another. When Kirsten's mother was dying of cancer, Kirsten avoided despair by raging at every doctor and nurse in the hospital. Marcus is inwardly terrified of conflict, so when his wife tells him that she's upset, he becomes fixated on work deadlines, worrying about tasks he can control as opposed to navigating relationship dynamics. Daniel is ashamed of his own anger, so when he's even slightly upset, he often smokes a bit of marijuana and falls into a red-light collapse, where he can trust himself to stay passive.

Once we understand that we may be stuck in a yellow- or red-light state, or using one response to avoid another, we can also begin to see that our terrified or hopeless versions of reality, however convincing, aren't accurate. They come from our triggered anxiety creatures, and we can do something about that. Instead of feeling overwhelmed by the oldest, most powerful parts of our own nervous systems, we can partner with them. We can depend on their instincts to keep us safe when there's real danger, then make sure they put us back into a state of joyful presence as soon as we're out of harm's way. The rest of this chapter will help you create this invaluable partnership.

PARTNERING WITH YOUR WILDEST ANXIETY: WAITING UNTIL NOTHING HAPPENS

Animal trainers often use a four-step process I learned from a veterinarian who worked at a zoo. He recommended it for teaching any creature to relax around something that triggers a defense cascade. It worked to calm my anxiety, so I started teaching it to clients. I call my own version of this process "Waiting Until Nothing Happens." Here's how to do it:

1. Establish a situation where the creature in question (an animal, your own anxiety creature) feels safe.

2. Very gradually expose the creature to something that triggers its anxiety. When the creature gets slightly edgy, but before it hits a true defense cascade, stop and stay. Just sit there.

3. Stay right at the edge of the creature's comfort zone, doing nothing until it gets bored and relaxes. Then edge forward a tiny bit.

4. Repeat as needed.

I've used this strategy to calm my own anxiety patterns in many situations. For example, while I can't say I enjoy medical testing, deliberately Waiting Until Nothing Happens has calmed me down considerably. I started by just thinking about an upcoming mammogram while sitting at home, reminding myself that I was okay at the moment until I could feel my anxiety back off a little. Then I began driving to the doctor's office early and sitting in my car until I got bored and stopped feeling anxious. Next, I used my early arrival time to hang out in the waiting room until my nervous system relaxed.

These days, I can drive myself to a mammogram appointment, chat amiably with the nurses, and walk up to the machine with barely a quiver. At that point, I still get a little tense—my retraining isn't complete—but it's nothing I can't handle. Yes, I have to focus on my breathing. Yes, I start chewing on the inside of my lip. But after the machine has finished, I can honestly say those three little words that can mean so very much: **I stayed conscious.**

So now let's help you veeeeery graaaadually connect with the parts of your system that spark **your** most intense anxiety. This is the only way to help your nervous system disarm the trauma triggers that may send you into an unwanted defense cascade. As you follow the instructions below, remember not to hurry. It may take many repetitions to disarm an anxiety trigger. That's okay. Persistence, not speed, is the key to success. When you're training a frightened animal, slow is fast. And I promise, the effort is worth it.

STEP ONE: Establish a Sanctuary

Your training sessions start with identifying a specific place where your creature self already feels relatively calm: your bedroom, your office, your comfy chair in a windowed corner. We'll call this place your sanctuary. If you don't **ever** feel calm anywhere, pick a spot where no one will bother you for a few minutes. Sit or lie down in your sanctuary for at least ten minutes every day, practicing the calming skills from the previous two chapters and letting your breath come naturally.

STEP TWO: Fill Your Sanctuary with Glimmers

Once you've established this safe place, make it more soothing by filling it with objects that help calm your nervous system. Author and clinical social worker Deb Dana, an expert in polyvagal theory, has a word for such things: she calls them "glimmers."

A glimmer is the opposite of a trigger; it's any object or experience that creates a moment of unforced ease or joy. It works the same way as a negative trigger: our spidey senses spot it, then immediately alert our whole polyvagal system—but instead of sounding an alarm, they turn on the green light. The sight, sound, smell, taste, feel, or memory of a glimmer automatically creates a little bubble of gratitude and appreciation.

Glimmers can be anything our primal instincts associate with comfort or delight: the smell of flowers, a shaft of sunlight through leaves, a cuddle. Remember Chris Voss's "late-night DJ voice"? It works because a calm human voice is a powerful safety cue to the human polyvagal circuit. Such a voice can soothe us even if we don't know why. Anything we've learned to associate with safety can have this effect. For instance, I have a friend whose parents used to calm themselves down by smoking. She knows intellectually that smoking kills, and she doesn't smoke herself. But the smell of cigarettes makes her feel instantly, dramatically safer.

Because of our brains' negativity bias, our nervous systems usually go through the world spotlighting every trigger while overlooking glimmers. When we're stuck in a yellow- or red-light state, this tendency gets worse. The whole world may appear to us as a sea of red and yellow triggers without a single green glimmer. **This is an illusion.** To break out of it, deliberately go looking for glimmers. Hunt for them, actively and insistently. At first, they may seem very thin on the ground. But once you begin finding them, they'll start to pop into your sphere of attention more easily. As your polyvagal state shifts toward green, you'll realize they're literally everywhere.

Look around right now, wherever you are, for ten things that "glimmer" you. I'll list a few of my own to show you how it works. Around me as I write this are the following objects, each of which gives me a bubble of joy and helps me feel safe (of course, these may not work for you; everyone's glimmers, like triggers, are unique):

- a warm, fuzzy blanket that feels like a hug

- a cup of tea with lemon

- a bottle of ibuprofen that just got rid of a headache

- a beautiful amethyst geode, which I originally saw in the home of a dear friend, and which she subsequently gave to me

• a TikTok video, sent by another friend, that features a bulldog who makes bizarre grumbling noises while a beagle looks on in obvious horror

Good Lord, I'm starting to feel **so much better**! Now I'm automatically noticing things like the smell of falling leaves outside my open window, a song I love playing in the back of my mind, and wonderful "paper friends" (books that have comforted and inspired me for years).

Okay, your turn!

Ten Glimmers That Are Near Me Right Here, Right Now:

1. _____

_____

2. _____

_____

3. _____

_____

4. _____

_____

5. _____

6. _____

7. _____

8. _____

9. _____

10. _____

Once you begin identifying glimmers, you can start gathering them as you go about your daily life and bringing them home to decorate your sanctuary. If a glimmer is intangible or too big to tote around, find a small object that reminds you of it (I like to find little quartzite pebbles in South Africa that remind me of the entire wild savanna). Or snap a photo of a glimmer—a tree in bloom, a friend's smile, your favorite restaurant—then print it out and tape it to your sanctuary wall. Keep adding glimmers indefinitely.

STEP THREE: Bask in Your Green-Light State

Each time you go to your sanctuary, focus on the glimmers around you and bask in the positive sensations associated with each one. If you feel yourself getting anxious, use KIST: gently tell your anxiety creature that it's allowed to feel anything it's feeling, but assure it that, for the moment, all is well.

Once you can feel even a few minutes of relative calm, begin closely observing what your nervous system's green-light state feels like. Slowly scan every bit of your body. Maybe you feel a slight hum of energy in your limbs, a sense of lifting in your chest, a warmth in your abdomen, or a comfortable drowsiness that makes you want to half close your eyes. Even if the sensations are subtle, tune into them and allow them to expand, filling your attention. Write down a description of these feelings here:

My Green-Light State Feels Like This:

_____

_____

_____

_____

STEP FOUR: Think of Something That Moves You into Yellow-Light Territory

Now it's time to begin connecting with the defense-cascade parts of your nervous system. Start by thinking about something that makes you feel the **beginning** of your yellow-light state. We're working as slowly and gradually as possible here, so don't dive into a huge mental horror show. Think about a small, everyday stressor, something that causes a tiny bit of worry, like the fact that you need to renew your fishing license, clean your sink, groom your sideburns, or whatever.

The objective here is to stay grounded in your green-light state while starting to explore the physical sensations of your yellow-light condition. (Deb Dana offers many ways to do this in her wonderful book **Anchored: How to Befriend Your Nervous System Using Polyvagal Theory.**) Observe everything that happens in your body as you begin edging up to a stress reaction. Feel your heartbeat get a bit stronger and quicker. Notice which muscles tense up. Don't try to control your facial expression; just notice what it does naturally. Consider your mood as well. Do you want to attack, escape, explain, disappear, or all of the above? Again, write a description:

My Yellow-Light State Feels/Looks Like This:

_____

_____

_____

_____

_____

If this sends you off into a full anxiety reaction, that's okay. You're not used to hitting your vagal brakes, so going slowly may not come naturally at first. You may get sucked into an anxiety spiral and find yourself in a full freak-out. Again, it's okay. Use your anxiety-whispering skills and you'll come back soon enough. Whether you manage to keep your anxiety low or lose control and watch it spike, move on to the next step as soon as you feel capable of deliberate action.

STEP FIVE: Return to Your Green-Light State of Being

Once you're in yellow-light territory, it can be hard not to follow your nervous system's pattern of fighting (getting annoyed, brooding about your enemies), fleeing (remembering you have to rush out and purchase a new foot massager stat!), or fawning (finding someone who wants something and giving it to them, no matter what it costs you). There's nothing wrong with these reactions, but right now we're focusing on retraining you to calm yourself without engaging in them.

To return from yellow-light alarm to a green-light state, stay in your sanctuary and use the following sequence of internal steps, which I call "going to SPACE." SPACE is an acronym for "surrender, peace, appreciation, connection, and enjoyment." Here are the steps:

Surrender

Whatever you're feeling, surrender to the fact that those sensations are there. Don't fight them. Instead, offer your yellow-light self some acceptance and KIST: **Go ahead and feel what you're feeling. I've got you. May you be comforted. May you be well.**

Peace

If you keep offering kindness and observing your internal state, you'll eventually feel some part of yourself relaxing. Focus on that bloom of peace, even if it's tiny. Breathe into it.

Appreciation

Savoring the sensation of peace, however small, look around your sanctuary at your glimmers. Touch a beloved object. Smell the books, or flowers, or coffee. Appreciate the small loveliness of each item. Offer them a silent thank-you.

Connection

Pick out a glimmer that reminds you of a connection with another being. This being may be a person, but it can also be a pet or even a plant. What matters is that you enjoy the presence of this beloved, and it enjoys you.

Enjoyment

Holding or contemplating this object, focus on only that one beautiful thing for about ten seconds. See if you can let enjoyment seep through your whole body.

STEP SIX: Move between Your Green- and Yellow-Light States

The idea of all this creature training is not to eliminate your self-protective reactions but to stop yourself from being triggered into a defense cascade when there's no real danger present and from getting **stuck** in a yellow- or red-light state after a difficult experience ends. So once you've gone from green to yellow and back again, repeat the process. Mentally approach your worrisome topic again, closely observing the sensations that occur as you go into yellow-light alert. Then return to the green-light state by going to SPACE, or just by enjoying your glimmers.

After a while, you may notice that although the fight/flight/fawn responses aren't comfortable, they aren't lethal. Meaning: **You don't have to be afraid of these sensations.** A surge of worry or anger isn't necessarily a sign that you're possessed by demons or that you should leave your marriage and start burying gold in the crawl space under your porch. Your yellow-light reactions aren't fun, but nor are they intolerable. Stay in the yellow-light state, observing it closely, until you get bored.

Wait until nothing happens.

Once you feel yourself calming down, pick up a glimmer and bring yourself back into a deep green state of peace and gratitude.

STEP SEVEN: Dip into the Red Zone

Once you've got some skill in moving back and forth between the green- and yellow-light states, you can begin using your sanctuary training time to think about what really scares you. Start with something that doesn't directly affect your life—something that might get you stuck in flop mode. If you need a handy red-light topic, glance at the news. Stories about children dying in war zones and the polar ice caps melting are enough to send anyone into a red-light state pronto.

A red-light state is sometimes called a "tonic collapse." As you contemplate something distant but terrible, notice how this collapsed state feels. You may lose all muscle tone and feel your body sag. Your blood pressure may drop until you get a head rush. You may feel nauseated. Emotional reactions may include despair, numbness, and indifference. How would you describe them?

My Red-Light State Feels Like This:

_____

_____

_____

_____

Notice that you can feel everything you just wrote down without being destroyed. Just like fight, flight, and fawn reactions, a physical and emotional collapse can be tolerated. It only gets truly unbearable if we fight it.

In fact, if you're in a red-light state and tell yourself "I must not feel this way," you're likely to call on dysfunctional manic energy or mood-altering substances to create a kind of override. I used to depend on things like public speaking and all-night emergency work sessions to squirt adrenaline into my system. Using yellow-light alarm systems was the only way I knew how to drag myself out of the red zone. (The use of one anxiety to block out another is common, as we saw with Kirsten, who used rage to block out grief when her mother was ill; with Marcus, who distracts himself from conflict by obsessing about work deadlines; and with Daniel, who uses pot to stay in a flop when he would otherwise get angry.)

I believe that this is how I ended up bedridden by all those autoimmune diseases I mentioned earlier (and the reason why I no longer have symptoms is that I learned to go back into my green-light state). If we frantically resist a collapse in the short term, we may get stuck in one for a long, long time.

On the other hand, if we can lovingly allow the ancient parts of our nervous systems to have their faint-and-flop reactions, we'll realize they don't have to destroy our lives. Give your red-light creature some SPACE, and don't push it to change too fast. Wait in the red zone until nothing happens.

STEP EIGHT: Come Back to the Green Zone, No Matter What

Some people think it's wrong to feel peaceful when terrible global catastrophes are in progress. Their (left-hemisphere) logic says that staying depressed, angry, and afraid motivates positive action. But all the horrors humans have perpetrated have come from people locked in panic or rage, grabbing for power, status, and stuff. The folks around them were often too collapsed in fear or horror to figure out solutions.

By contrast, when we're in a green-light state, our nervous systems automatically move toward positive connection and ingenious problem-solving. Inner peace isn't passive; it responds to hurt or harm calmly and intelligently. And acts of love are the only way out of the problems anxious humans have created.

With that in mind, heave a big sigh, shake the red-zone paralysis out of your hands and feet, and come back to this moment. Just rest in your sanctuary, right here, right now. Give yourself some SPACE. Be amazed by small, perfect things; celebrate experiences of joy and beauty. Find your way back to the green zone, over and over and over.

DEVELOPING A BUILT-IN WILDLIFE SANCTUARY

If a wild animal learns to trust you, and you trust it, the wilderness becomes a safer place for both of you. So instead of being blindsided by surprise attacks from the oldest, wildest parts of your own nervous system, you can let them warn and protect you with their spidey senses.

If you're privileged enough to live in relative safety, you can stop overreacting to situations where nothing is really threatening you. If you're a member of a marginalized group or live in a troubled region of the world—that is, if you face real threats every day—you can use your defense cascade wisely. You'll become more discerning about which people and situations are truly dangerous, which are triggering because they remind your system of danger, and which are actually safe. You can bring your nervous system into its green-light state more and more easily so that you can rest, connect, and heal.

I've watched many, many people partner with their wild anxiety creatures. Jim got therapy to deal with his memories of abuse and reclaimed his naturally relaxed, friendly personality. Fred stopped feeling sexual shame and blaming it on the women he dated. Lindsay, who can now see her own fawn reactions kicking in when she meets a narcissist, has learned that she doesn't need to pander. Emma's freeze reactions are slowly melting, making her more assertive and confident. Kirby got in touch with her anger at the system that attacked her because of her dyslexia. She has connected with others who share her experience, and she is starting to feel genuine self-esteem.

Dealing with our wild sides, our seemingly intractable anxiety responses, can set us free to feel calm and confident in parts of our lives that were once emotional minefields. Now that you've learned to calm the wild things within your nervous system, you're ready to take on the trickiest creatures of all: the divided aspects of your **uniquely human** psyche that may be trapped in anxiety spirals.

4

The Creature, United

The written word is addictive to me; if I'm not either reading or writing, it feels as if my brain is dying of thirst. However, I also wish I could draw or paint all day, every day, without a single verbal thought ever crossing my mind. It thrills me to explore unfamiliar places all over the world. On the other hand, I dread travel and try to avoid it. And while I want to dedicate every moment of my life to serving humanity, let me be honest: I do not like people.

Everything in the paragraph above is true. I am basically a walking clot of paradoxes. This once made any attempt to manage my anxiety very tricky. I'd feel anxious about getting lonely, then anxious about seeing people. I'd worry about taking time away from my children to work, then worry about taking time away from work to care for my children. I'd feel anxious that I wasn't getting enough sleep, then anxious because I thought I should be working all night.

"Do I contradict myself?" Whitman wrote. "Very well then I contradict myself, / (I am large, I contain multitudes.)"

Thank you, Walt, for claiming your internal contradictions, giving the rest of us implicit permission to do the same. I finally learned to do this when I encountered something called "parts psychology." The basic idea is that we're all made up of many selves, each of which can be seen as a whole person with their own opinions, history, and concerns. Therapy based on this concept has proved extremely beneficial for people with high anxiety, including me. In this chapter, I'll give you some helpful hints that I suspect will help you, too.

YOUR MANY ANXIOUS SELVES

You can probably identify several discordant parts of your own psyche. Maybe you have an ambitious self who would do anything to keep your job and a dreamy self who's sick of working. A nostalgic part that sees your grandma as a font of wisdom and a politically progressive part that disagrees with every outdated word she says. A loving parent who adores your children and an adult so starved for intelligent conversation that one more hour with those kids is going to physically destroy your brain.

I don't know which of your selves is reading this book, but I know there are others. Hello, part that's reading this right now! Who else is in there? Perhaps some selves who don't like self-help books—or any books at all? Maybe some parts that arch an eyebrow every time they hear the term "life coach"? Of course I'm not talking to **you,** dear reader. I know **you've** been following along. Maybe you've even done the exercises in the last few chapters and felt your anxiety ebb. In fact, you may have no discernible anxiety left!

But, of course, you may still have a lot of anxiety.

I mean the other "yous," who are also you. All of you.

My point is that even if some parts of your psyche may be perfectly calm, other parts may still be anxious. And you're not fully relaxed until every self in your inner community can access comfort and peace. To that end, this chapter will help you connect with your many selves and help them cooperate with one another. We don't want to make your whole inner community sing at the same pace and pitch—that would take away much of the beautiful complexity that is you. But we do want your selves to blend, to create the kind of gorgeous harmony that occurs only in an integrated human mind.

THE PARTS APPROACH: A NEW WAY TO LOOK AT YOUR SELVES

Almost every school of therapy acknowledges that we have different inner parts. Freud described our psyches as containing the id, the ego, and the super-ego. Jung pictured humans as clusters of archetypes. But my favorite kind of parts psychology was created in the 1980s by Dr. Richard Schwartz. When I first met Schwartz, in 2021, his approach, known as Internal Family Systems therapy, or IFS, was taking the counseling world by storm. Originally a family therapist who worked with groups, Schwartz noticed that often, an individual client seemed to have separate selves that worked like different members of a family. Using a systems approach, he was able to help these parts start communicating and cooperating.

"I could get the different parts into conversation," Schwartz told me. "As they listened to each other, they became less contentious. People started feeling compassion and acceptance for many different parts of themselves, and this was often very healing."

By the time I met Schwartz, I'd heard so many therapists and patients rave about his method that I signed up with an IFS therapist myself. I heartily recommend it. I also love the fact that IFS practitioners, including Schwartz, are very generous with their ideas. They'd love it if everyone were to learn and use the logic of the parts approach. So, by all means, find any resource you can (therapists, online information, other books) that will fill you in on the rich details of parts psychology. In the meantime, here's a brief primer that can help you connect and heal your anxious selves.

HOW AND WHY THERE ARE SO MANY OF YOU

If you grew up in a perfect environment where nothing ever went wrong, adored by caregivers who were absolutely happy with themselves, one another, and the world, you probably wouldn't notice that you have different parts, because they'd all work smoothly and harmoniously. You'd have little to no anxiety; your nervous system would move into defense cascades when they were needed, then immediately return to a balanced, happy green-light state the moment you were safe.

In other words, you'd be just like . . . pretty much nobody.

Our psyches begin to split apart when we encounter overwhelming situations, and there are countless ways this can happen to us humans, especially when we're small and helpless. Maybe there was a time when you got physically injured, sexually violated, screamed at, bullied, bereaved, uprooted, mocked, criticized, ignored, abandoned, or ostracized. Maybe you were repeatedly attacked because of your race, ethnicity, religion, socioeconomic class, neurodivergence, sexual preference, gender identity, body shape, or disability. Maybe it was the way you dressed or walked or laughed or cried or danced or refused to dance. Maybe it was because you had no dad or two dads or three moms or angry siblings or one weird kneecap or . . .

I could go on like this for the next thousand pages and never get near the end of it. But whatever happened to you, it really hurt. I have no doubt about that.

When you encountered any painful situation, you probably had a normal yellow- or red-light response: you went into fight, flight, fawn, freeze, or flop mode. If you had someone to turn to, someone who lovingly helped you articulate and integrate your emotional experience, you might have quickly returned to a calm green-light state. This pattern—a traumatic experience followed by a rapid return to well-being—can actually be a good thing; it's what makes people resilient. But if no one understood or cared about what you were feeling, it's likely that your psyche tried to protect you by splitting into parts that still haven't fully healed. And that can cause a lot of long-term anxiety.

THREE KINDS OF SPLIT-OFF PARTS: EXILES, MANAGERS, AND FIREFIGHTERS

The human psyche is incredibly resourceful. It's sensitive and easy to hurt, but it also has the capacity to deal with trauma by splitting off a part of itself to hold overwhelming psychological pain. It hides this part from your conscious awareness so that you can still function. In IFS, these banished pain containers are called "exiles."

The ability to exile parts of ourselves is a precious gift, but it comes at a high cost. As we go about our business, our internal exiles are stuck in frozen moments where they **continuously** experience the pain of the traumatic events. They need to surface so that they can be helped, healed, and reintegrated. They're always rattling their cages, sending out wisps of pain that make us intensely anxious. We may feel as if we're carrying a Pandora's box that will destroy the world if we ever let it creak open even slightly.

In order to keep the exiles out of consciousness, our psyches split off even more parts, whose job is to keep the exiles from surfacing. These parts come in two varieties. Schwartz calls them "managers" and "firefighters." Each of us may have many exiles, and the more exiles we carry, the more likely we are to have whole cadres of managers and firefighters. I'll describe each type here, after assuring you that **exiles, managers,** and **firefighters** are the only specific IFS terms you need to remember, and that having these labels can be enormously helpful as you calm your whole psychological system.

Managers are the parts of you that try to keep your life going by being virtuous. They obey cultural rules, reminding you to be a good boy or girl, or a hard worker, or a nice person, or a skilled athlete, or whatever other qualities your socialization favors. Managers remind us to tend to our health and finances. They like to track and list things, like any good left-hemisphere thinker. Though they mean well, they can be brutal, demanding continuous perfection and criticizing or shaming us if we can't measure up to their high standards.

Firefighters, on the other hand, are desperate to stop the exiles' pain. They'll burst through all kinds of boundaries in the attempt. They may try to keep from feeling the exiles' suffering by jumping us into anything intense and distracting: overspending, addiction, temper tantrums, illicit love affairs. Firefighters are always looking for someone to help them rescue the exiles, so they may join cults or become fanatical adherents to this or that philosophy. They'll do anything to drown out signals from exiles and prevent us from feeling what we don't want to feel.

Managers may rage at firefighters, pounding them with scathing criticism and terrible judgments. Your manager parts may hurl insults at you that you'd never say to another person. **What's wrong with you?** they may silently scream after you've eased your anxiety by smoking a carton of cigarettes or staring at the TV for nine hours straight. **Why are you such a weak-willed [pig/slut/moron/sissy/loser]?**

The firefighter parts feel the lash of these words, and they may briefly stop their behavior to baste in a stinging brew of self-loathing. But soon enough, the inner managers will get exhausted and the psychological stress will become too severe, so your firefighters will go right back to making you shoplift stationery or rifle through the medicine cabinet for anything that may bring on a few hours of oblivion.

Because the firefighters pop into action whenever our energy is low (this keeps our buried exiles from surfacing into consciousness), the managers can never achieve the perfect behavior they demand. As firefighters and managers oppose one another, they create a nonstop civil war inside us while our exiles stay in their hiding places, suffering and alone.

Doesn't that sound fun?

You are correct. It does not.

Along with the other painful effects, the dynamics of a system like this lead to sky-high anxiety. Exiles are anxious because they live in isolated pain. Managers constantly worry about staying in control. Firefighters are terrified that the managers may take away the tools they need to do their job, such as cow tipping and screaming at strangers who won't join their religion. We all contain multitudes, and if the multitudes aren't united, they're incredibly anxious.

YOU MAY BE YOUR OWN POLAR OPPOSITE

One goal of IFS therapists is to help managers and firefighters relax so that the exiles they're hiding can come into consciousness for comfort and integration. But managers and firefighters are reluctant to do this. Why? Because both are trapped in anxiety spirals. They invent all kinds of arguments to defend and reinforce their control efforts. Hiding great pain, managers and firefighters often spin out along separate anxiety spirals, creating stories to justify their behavior. To maintain balance, these parts tend to polarize—they go to opposite extremes.

This makes some people (and aspects of our entire culture) completely baffling. Mary, a sweet little octogenarian who once wanted to be a nun, is one of the most idealistic people I know. When I tell you she tries to be perfect, I mean **perfect.** But Mary sometimes gets so angry at certain politicians that her mind, slipping out of her control, conjures vivid images of ways she could kill them. Of course Mary never acts on these thoughts. She rarely even admits that she has them. But they're so graphic and persistent that some nights, instead of sleeping, Mary just lies there plotting fictional assassinations. Almost no one knows how much of her attention is consumed by her inner managers' constant struggle to stop entertaining homicidal fantasies.

Roland has a much less violent way to firefight: he daydreams about becoming rich and famous. Most folks do this from time to time, but Roland is so caught up in his fantasies that he's often dissociated from his surroundings. He's never been able to keep a job or finish the many projects that he thinks will bring him glory (a website, a screenplay, a motivational app). Every time Roland starts doing something that might actually move his life in the direction he wants to go, his inner managers shout him down, telling him he's a stupid, uneducated idiot who's bound to fail. Inevitably, Roland backs off from trying and resumes his addictive fantasizing.

When we're carrying many terribly wounded exiles, the contrast between managers and firefighters can be mind-boggling. Jack grew up in a house full of rage and physical violence. His mother, father, and live-in grandmother all abused him physically and often fought one another to the point of serious injury.

Jack struggled out of this hell to become a beacon of hope: a yoga teacher and motivational speaker who spent his time flying from city to city, helping people clear their chakras and achieve inner peace. Jack always ate organic food and used an expensive hyper-cleansing filter for every drop of water he drank. He also snorted prodigious amounts of cocaine, which, along with the ultrapure food and water, really helped goose up his energy for all that traveling, exercising, and speaking.

Unfortunately, Jack's split lifestyle was very expensive. He spent most of what he earned on drugs, then shuffled credit cards to pay his bills. His internal arguments must have become increasingly irrational. Then one day, Jack was scrolling online when he stumbled across a doomsday cult. It claimed that human civilization was about to be destroyed but saw this as a bad-news, good-news situation. On the downside, billions of people would die. On the upside, all debt would evaporate, and the members of the group—the only ones likely to survive the apocalypse—would have access to pretty much all the stuff they wanted.

Not long after connecting with this group, Jack disappeared. When his long-distance girlfriend flew to his city looking for him, she found his apartment empty but for a lot of abandoned paperwork, including financial records indicating that Jack had just purchased an off-road vehicle, an assault rifle, and a mountain of ammunition. On credit.

Even though I know how this kind of polarization can happen, I had trouble believing that Jack was both the serene yoga healer I'd met and a gun-toting conspiracy theorist. But this is what happens when a firefighter and a manager get stuck in anxiety spirals simultaneously, whirling one storytelling brain in opposite directions. Their stories don't have to be coherent or logical, because they're not based in logic—they're based in anxiety. And even the weirdest, most self-contradictory horror stories of the left hemisphere seem absolutely true to the part of the brain that tells them.

TALKING IT OUT

So far in this book, I haven't recommended a lot of **talking** as a solution to anxiety. Analysis and argument, favorite tools of the left hemisphere, tend to make anxiety go up, not down. But once we get in touch with the managers and firefighters that drive much of our behavior, it can help to work with words.

Exiles are like the wild things we discussed in the previous chapter, trapped in agonizing situations and sensations. They need to be **shown** that your circumstances are no longer dangerous—we worked on that. But as we've just seen, managers and firefighters aren't trapped in sensations. They're trapped in stories. Mary's internal stories about the politicians she hates help drive her inner conflict. Roland's fantasies of fame aren't physically present; they're projections of his storytelling mind. And Jack tells all sorts of strange stories to sustain his double life and his conspiracy theories. To get out of captivity, our inner parts need to learn more accurate stories, versions of reality that feel true at the deepest level of our being. Telling the truth is what allows our inner communities to reintegrate and heal.

In other words, we've finally reached the "tell" part of show-and-tell.

TELLING THE TRUTH TO OUR SEPARATED SELVES

As we've learned, our anxious parts are never grounded in the present moment. They're always focused on bad things that occurred in the past and horrors we may confront in the future. The stories they tell are stressful for any number of reasons, but especially because those stories are actually a tissue of lies, and at some level, we know that. Our frightening, shaming, or despairing thoughts come from an innocent place—they're really just well-meaning mistakes—but they're lies all the same.

Humans are the best liars in nature, but that's not saying much. Every time someone lies, their whole nervous system goes haywire. Most of us immediately hit a yellow-light state: our heart rates, blinking, and perspiration increase; our immune functions weaken. Even for a psychopath, who may be able to beat a lie detector, the amount of neurological energy necessary to keep false stories straight causes enormous stress. It's much simpler for the brain to stay grounded in reality.

That said, it's easy to see why our parts may tell false stories and mistake them for the truth. Exiles, terrified by trauma, live in a wordless, innocent lie that says, **The terrible thing that happened is always happening. I am still in it.** Managers and firefighters live in opposing stories but make the same false claim: **There is absolutely nothing wrong here, except that I don't have free rein to make my human do what I want all the time. I need to have absolute control. That is literally the only problem.**

In other words: **Nothing to see here! I am 100 percent fine! Please pass me my Bible and my crack pipe!**

CONVERSATIONS BETWEEN INNER PARTS

The genius of IFS theory is that it can get all the contradictory parts of a struggling human to communicate and cooperate. How? By treating each part as a whole, well-meaning person, asking it to tell its story, and letting each part listen to the stories of the other parts. When I heard this, I thought it was insanely simplistic. **This will never work,** I thought as I embarked on my own IFS therapy.

But then it did.

After I'd started working with my own IFS therapist and met Richard Schwartz, I learned how he discovered this surprisingly simple technique. When he worked as a family therapist, Schwartz would sometimes ask one person to leave the room so that another member of the family could feel freer to speak. Then he noticed that the dysfunctional patterns he saw in families were often mirrored within individuals. "One part of a person's psyche—for example, a highly critical part—might be very dominant," Schwartz told me. "So I thought, **Maybe I can just ask these domineering parts to step aside for a while and let me talk to other parts of the person's internal system.**"

When he tried this, Schwartz was amazed to find that the domineering parts usually agreed to step aside for a few minutes. Schwartz would ask the client to imagine those parts moving a few feet to the right or left. At that point, he'd begin speaking to other parts of the psyche, which now felt freer to express their own perspectives.

Once I started using Schwartz's approach, both in therapy and on my own, I was stunned by how quickly it left me feeling freer, happier, and, above all, much less anxious. I found that this was especially powerful when I did my "parts work" in writing.

A LETTER TO MY OTHER SELVES: WRITING TO AND FROM ANXIOUS PARTS

At this point, I can't resist mentioning another body of research that goes with IFS like bread goes with butter. In 1986, a psychologist named James Pennebaker ran an experiment in which he asked a group of college students to write for fifteen minutes about superficial topics. Another group wrote for the same amount of time, but Pennebaker asked them to focus on their most painful experiences. This wasn't analytical writing; he specifically asked the students to write **expressively.**

"Many students came out of their writing rooms in tears," Pennebaker reported, "but they kept coming back." Later, the group of students who'd written about difficult issues noticed enormous benefits. Hundreds of ensuing studies confirmed that people who used expressive writing to process painful experiences saw decreased anxiety, blood pressure, depression, muscle tension, pain, and stress. On the upside, they had enhanced lung and immune function, sharper memories, better sleep quality, happier social lives, and improved performance at work or school.

Nowadays, Pennebaker's studies might come with a trigger warning—even though the students benefited from writing in the long term, many experienced an upsurge of emotional pain in the short term. So, right here and now, I'm issuing my own warning: I'm about to recommend an exercise that could stir up your inner system and cause you to feel emotional pain. True, this is pain you're already carrying around in your exiles, but there's a reason you stored it away, and we need to respect that.

So before you start the following exercise, make sure you've practiced all the skills you learned in previous chapters. Make sure you can get your nervous system out of the yellow- and red-light zones and back into green-light territory. I'd also recommend that you identify at least one loving, stable person who can help calm you down if you feel very upset. If that person is a therapist, so much the better.

All of that said, this exercise contains its own safety device. You'll simply ask all your inner parts not to overwhelm you with emotion if you don't have free time or a safe person to help you process it. It's astonishing how cooperative most of our parts are, and how clearly we can feel them responding.

Here's the exercise in brief: You'll be writing to different parts of your internal system, asking them why they do what they do. You'll hear the stories your managers and firefighters use to justify their actions. You may also detect an exiled part that wants to communicate its pain. And as you converse with each part, you're going to **tell them the truth about your current situation.**

Each exile is stuck in one awful experience. The

managers and firefighters are stuck in anxiety spirals. They're all separated from the truth about **presence, power,** and **people:** your situation right here and now, your freedom and ability to choose your actions, and your connection to individuals who can help you regulate and integrate your conflicted insides.

New Skill

BRING ALL OF YOU HOME TO THE TRUTH

Take twenty minutes to go to the sanctuary you've created or another place where you feel safe. Bring a notebook and a pen or pencil. I've found that writing by hand is more powerful than typing thoughts into a computer.

Use all your self-calming skills to reach a relaxed state.

Once you're calm, write your way through the following worksheet.

I'll prompt you to write questions for your inner parts. To let them answer, write down whatever comes into your head. Don't worry about spelling or punctuation, and don't edit. If something doesn't seem to make sense, write it down anyway. This is for your eyes only.

Start by writing something like this:
"Hello, all my parts. I'm here to chat with you. Before we start, I'm asking you to help me release some of my inner pain, but not so much that I'll feel overwhelmed or flooded. Can you agree to that?"

Write down any answer that comes up:

_____

_____

If the answer says your internal system is willing to keep you safe, find a manager part.
Close your eyes, turn your attention inward, and locate a part of yourself that is perfectionistic and wants you to achieve all your highest ideals. Where does it feel like this part is located in your body? How does it make you feel?

_____

_____

Ask this manager part the following questions:
"What are you trying to do for me? Why are you so demanding?"

Write down whatever the part seems to say:

_____

_____

_____

_____

Now ask this manager part the following question:
   "What are you afraid will happen if you just stop doing everything you do?"

_____

_____

_____

_____

Go back to green.
   If connecting with the part has pulled you into a yellow- or red-light vagal state, stop, breathe, and use all your skills to return to the green-light state. Go back to the instructions in chapter 3 if necessary.

Thank the manager for talking to you.
   You might not love this part of yourself, but it's working very hard to keep you functioning. Acknowledge its good intentions.

Say thank you. Parts love to be treated respectfully.

Now find a firefighter part.
Close your eyes and connect with a part of yourself that doesn't want to follow the manager's rules. This part may do things you believe are bad or wrong, but you're not here to judge; you're here to listen. Where do you feel this firefighter part in your body? What does it do when it takes over?

_____

_____

_____

Ask this part a variation of the same questions you asked the manager:
"What are you trying to do for me? Why do you break the rules?"

_____

_____

_____

Now ask this firefighter part the following question:
"What are you afraid will happen, firefighter,

if you never get your way, or if you just stop doing everything you do?"

_____

_____

_____

_____

Go back to green.

If connecting with the part has pulled you into a yellow- or red-light vagal state, stop, breathe, and use all your skills to return to the green-light state.

Thank the firefighter for talking to you.

This may be hard to believe, but the firefighter also has your best interests at heart. Give it gratitude for the times it's kept you from unbearable pain by distracting you or numbing your feelings. Say thanks.

See if the manager and/or the firefighter can give you any information about exiles that may be trapped inside your psyche.

Say to them: "I know you're afraid to let go of control, and I think it's because you're protecting parts of me that have been through really bad things and hold a lot of pain. Please don't flood me with more information or emotion than I can handle right now, but tell me a little bit about the exiles."

Write down whatever comes up:

_____

_____

_____

_____

At this point, you may get a "visual" or another sensory cue that shows you an exiled part.

The exile may not be verbal. But you may sense its presence and possibly "see" it in your mind. It may look like a child, an animal, or even an inanimate object like a rock.

Write a description of whatever you sense:

_____

_____

_____

_____

_____

If the exile wants to express its pain or show you what happened to it, give it permission

to do so (after again asking it not to flood you with emotion).

Write what comes up:

_____

_____

_____

_____

_____

_____

Use every anxiety-soothing tool you've learned to comfort the exile.
Just to remind you:

- Sigh, shake, and move around.
- Soften your focus.
- Offer KIST in a low, slow, soft voice.
- Allow time for silence.
- Articulate what the exile is feeling.
- Connect with your glimmers.
- Bring yourself into a space where your calm green-light self can hold the exile in a warm pool of energy.

If the manager and firefighter become anxious, wanting to go back to protecting the exile, let them.

Often, the protective parts feel very anxious when the exile makes contact with your consciousness. They probably won't be ready to simply drop all protective behavior. Allow them to resume their roles, but let them know that there may be less exiled energy to contain, so they may not have to work as hard or be as intense.

Now, tell all these parts the truth about your presence, power, and people: your current life circumstances, your ability to make choices, and your access to those who can help you.

Write something like this:
"Here's the truth about **the present** (what's happening right at this minute). I'm now ____ years old. I live in_____. I'm not as small, defenseless, or confused as I used to be. There are glimmers all around me. Let me tell you about them."

Write anything positive about your sanctuary, the glimmers you see around you, and your present life.

_____

_____

_____

"Here's the truth about **my power to make choices**. I know a lot more than I used to. I don't have to ignore my exiled parts; I can listen to them and offer them love. I can acknowledge their suffering and validate that they deserve healing."

Add anything that feels true and useful:

"Here's the truth about **people who can help**." (NOTE: Some of these may be people you know. Others may be writers from past ages, or experts online, or songwriters who help you feel understood. If you believe in a higher power, put it on the list. And pets definitely count.)

Add anyone you like:

_____

_____

_____

Go back to green.
This is when you can really apply those green-light regulation skills. Use everything you've learned in this book so far to bring your nervous system back to a calm moment in your sanctuary.

Offer gratitude and end the session.
Thank all the parts for talking to you, and write:
"Is there anything I can do to help you all feel safe and supported?" (This may include imaginary acts, like bringing the exile to live in your heart, or acts of self-care, like wrapping yourself up in a warm blanket or listening to a podcast that always helps you feel better.)

Let your parts answer:

_____

_____

_____

If you've promised your parts any care or kindness, follow through.

Be extra kind to yourself after doing this exercise. If you feel stirred up, call your contact person. But also know that as the dust settles, you are likely going to feel considerably better and less anxious.

FROM DISSONANCE TO HARMONY

I've used this process over and over myself. It barely dips a toe into parts psychology, but I've felt it shift me toward calm faster and more dramatically than most other methods I've tried. I've seen it do the same for other people.

For example, Penelope is a successful entrepreneur in her midseventies who earned a large fortune by being smart, driven, and mean as a snake. When I met her, Penelope lived in perpetual yellow-light alert, entrenched in anxiety that came across as rage. She terrified her employees and had never been able to keep an intimate relationship going for long. Now Penelope feared she would die soon, and looking back on her life, she felt it had been lonely and meaningless.

"I would just like some peace," she said tersely during our first Zoom session. "And I'll do whatever you say. Hit me with your best shot. I'm a tough old bird. I can handle the hard stuff."

I was sure part of her could. But I suspected there were other parts of Penelope that felt vulnerable and wounded. Using my best Chris Voss tactics, I walked her through a version of the previous exercise. The manager Penelope called up was her disciplined, ambitious businesswoman self. Her firefighter was the part that tended to be cruel, snapping at people and keeping them scared as a way of controlling situations.

As Penelope talked to both of these parts, asking them why they acted the way they did and what other parts they might be protecting, a vivid scene popped into her mind. She saw herself as a baby sitting next to her mother's body on a bed, trying to wake her from a drunken sleep. The scene broke my heart, and Penelope, to her great embarrassment, began to cry. I asked her how she felt about her baby self.

"Well," Penelope said, trying to sound gruff, "to be honest, I would like to pick her up. No kid should have to go through that."

"Go ahead," I said. "Pick her up and see if she can let you know what else she might need."

Penelope fell silent, a steady stream of tears flowing from her closed eyes. After a few long, silent minutes, she said, with evident surprise, "Mostly the kid just wants to be with me."

"Can you think of a way to keep her with you?" I asked. "Maybe just in your imagination."

Penelope nodded and had another silent conversation with her baby self. Then we logged off.

The Penelope who appeared on my screen a few

weeks later was like a different person. She looked ten years younger, her face relaxed out of the pinched expression she'd been wearing when we met. True to her word, Penelope had been giving daily attention to her infant self, along with other "inner children" who'd shown up since we last spoke. She'd been showing and telling them how much her life had changed since her painful childhood. Then Penelope had found herself offering people spontaneous greetings and even compliments, something she'd never done before. Her employees were beginning to feel safer, and her company was functioning more smoothly.

"I'm just amazed that you could see those parts of me," Penelope said. "And know what to do for them."

But I hadn't seen Penelope's inner selves. Nor had I come up with a single idea about how to care for them. All of that had happened inside Penelope, with only the slightest bit of prompting from me. She continued to change, incredibly quickly, as she kept caring for all her selves. Her "empty, meaningless" life has grown rich with connection and kindness.

Since encountering parts psychology, I've spent less and less energy in coaching sessions, knowing that people's internal systems are the experts when it comes to healing and thriving. My own IFS therapist, who has all sorts of high-level skills in a variety of theoretical fields, says less than any other counselor I've met. She'll ask, "What does the part look like? Ask it what it would like you to know." And then: "Does that make sense to you?" The rest she leaves for my parts to work out.

Like Penelope, I've found this to be life altering. Now, whenever my anxiety rears its ugly head, I immediately go through the process above. I ask, "What's going on in there?" Then I connect with managers or firefighters and check for anxious exiles. At this point, I often use expressive writing to put the exiles' experiences into words, calling on my left hemisphere just enough to give a voice to the exiles' sense impressions and emotions. Then I write down a few true things about my present life, my power to choose options, and the people I can access for help.

I always find it comforting to talk to my selves like this. Because in doing so, I encounter an inner being wiser and calmer than all the rest. And if you persist in soothing your creature selves, you will meet the same energy. IFS therapists call it the Self, with a capital **S.**

MEETING YOUR TRUE SELF

Throughout this book, I've been asking you to do all sorts of healing things: imagine your creature self, call up memories of your best experiences, use a calm voice to offer yourself KIST, gather some glimmers, and make and keep promises to your creature self. Assuming you've been able to do at least some of these things, I have two linked questions for you:

Who's been doing all this? Who are you **really,** in your essence?

If you've been visualizing, caring for, and comforting your anxious parts, you aren't completely trapped in any of them. You are something that incorporates and transcends all these psychological splinters. According to IFS theory, this core part of you is the Self.

Richard Schwartz was surprised by the emergence of an almost identical Self in many of his patients. As he helped people reveal more and more aspects of their personalities, the same thing began to happen, as Schwartz put it, "out of the blue." Each patient would connect with a wise, peaceful core identity that was like none of the others. In his book **No Bad Parts,** Schwartz writes:

> [W]hen they were in that state, I'd ask clients, "Now, what part of you is that?" and they'd say, "That's not a part like these others, that's more myself" or "That's more my core" or "That's who I really am."

Over time, Schwartz observed that this Self eventually showed up in every person he treated:

> [A]fter thousands of hours doing this work, I can say with certainty that the Self is in everybody. Furthermore, the Self cannot be damaged, the Self doesn't have to develop, and the Self possesses

its own wisdom about how to heal internal as well as external relationships.

The goal of IFS therapy, as Schwartz told it to me, is not to expertly "fix" patients but to help them connect with this core Self, which does the deepest repair work. Your Self is available to you at any time. And it, more than anyone else on earth, knows how to calm your anxiety and access a joyful, peaceful life.

MOVING INTO SELF-ENERGY

As I've just hinted, every exercise in this book has been designed to align you with your core Self. After I learned to locate and access **my** Self, my IFS therapist talked even less. I'd often show up with a problem that had little to do with personal issues and a lot to do with the news. "Australia is on fire!" I'd say. Or: "Pandemic! Terrifying!" Or: "How the hell are we going to end racism?" My therapist would simply reply, "Okay, go inside and connect with Self-energy."

This was not what my anxious manager and firefighter parts wanted. They were after some high action, some strong arguments, some goddamn **control**! Instead, my therapist would remind me of the eight "Cs" that Schwartz identified as the characteristics of every human Self. These eight words begin with the letter **c,** because along with acronyms, alliteration is a fabulous tool for making things memorable. You can align with your Self by naming these values, in your mind or out loud. They are:

- calmness

- clarity

- confidence

- curiosity

- courage

- compassion

- connectedness

- creativity

You may be able to find your own Self-energy just by reading through this list, pausing after each word to find that quality in yourself.

Here's another method that works well for my clients. It's very simple: just recall and write about some situations where you exhibited each of the "C" qualities, and let yourself remember each situation. Remembering or imagining these situations will help you connect with Self-energy. Then you can picture that mood state growing like a pool of warm light that holds you and permeates your body. From here you can access all your parts, offering them love and liberation from anxiety.

As you practice this skill, remember that you don't

have to max out all eight "C" values; in fact, you may come up blank on some of them. That's okay. You only need to touch a "critical mass" of Self-energy to feel calmer and more connected to your green-light state.

New Skill

MOVE INTO THE SELF

---

1. Think of a situation where you often feel calm or where you felt calm in the past (e.g., "when I'm in nature," "when I'm knitting," etc.):

   _____

2. Think of a situation where you often feel **clear** or where you felt clear in the past (e.g., "when I quit my first job," "when I'm training my dog," etc.):

   _____

3. Think of a situation where you often feel **confident** or where you felt confident in the past (e.g., "driving," "tying my shoes," etc.):

   _____

4. Think of a situation where you often feel **curious** or where you felt curious in the past (e.g., "looking at the stars," "playing Dungeons & Dragons," etc.):

_____

5. Think of a situation where you often feel **courageous** or where you felt courageous in the past (e.g., "when I went to the equal-rights march," "when I stood up for my friend at school," etc.):

_____

6. Think of a situation where you often feel **compassionate** or where you felt compassionate in the past (e.g., "when my cat is confused," "when my friend is grieving," etc.):

_____

7. Think of a situation where you often feel **connected** or where you felt connected in the past (e.g., "when I heard that breakup song that expressed exactly how I felt," "when a newcomer talks at my twelve-step group," etc.):

_____

8. Think of a situation where you often feel **creative** or where you felt creative in the

past (e.g., "when I'm doing jigsaw puz-
zles," "when I planned my son's birthday
party," etc.):

_____

LETTING YOUR SELF ADDRESS
ALL YOUR WORRIES

Child psychologist Becky Kennedy contends that the best way to comfort a child is not by trying to "fix" them, which often feels forced and invasive. Instead, she suggests that parents imagine a field full of benches, each labeled with an emotion: anxiety, sadness, rage, despair, hope. Just go sit with the child, she says, on whatever bench they occupy. Be quiet, be patient, and let the child know that their feelings are valid.

Once you access your Self, let it sit down on any bench where one of your parts feels stuck. Don't push for solutions. Just stay there, linked to any calm, clear, confident, curious, courageous, compassionate, creative, or connected energy you can access. Allow the part to tell its stories to the Self. As the Self, gently offer truer stories to replace the wounded part's fictions.

This approach can work fast and persist indefinitely. It can be part of our internal way of living, permanently. We may always have brains prone to anxiety, but accessing the Self can also become almost automatic. It gently removes us from anxiety over and over, like a loving parent steering a toddler away from a busy street. One by one, we can relax all of our frightened, controlling managers and firefighters, as well as comfort and integrate each of our exiles. The frustrating, baffling polarities that once controlled us will begin to dissolve. Instead, our unique parts will offer their perspectives and ideas to help the entire community.

This shift to inner harmony, under the guidance of the Self, is how we stop being part of the world's problems and become part of the solution. In an increasingly anxious, polarized society, Self-energy flows like clear spring water after a terrible drought. And because it is inherently creative, it can devise new solutions to all the problems we face. If we are to thrive as individuals and survive as a species, we must start by soothing our creature selves. But then we need to keep moving into the territory beyond anxiety. We need to activate the curious, compassionate, infinitely powerful wellspring of human creativity.

Part Two

THE CREATIVE

5

Activating Your Creative Side

As I researched this book while deep in pandemic lockdown, I became so fascinated by brain function that I decided to run my own small experiment. Lockdown had given me a terrific opportunity. Any social scientist knows that in a situation where many factors are held constant, it's easier to judge the effect of something introduced into the scenario.

Well, my life had become an experimental condition. My days were more consistent and uneventful than they'd ever been. I did not go out, and no one unfamiliar came to see me. Every day, I wore my "pandemic uniform": a turtleneck, yoga pants, and a fuzzy bathrobe. My family and I were ensconced in our house on a densely wooded hillside in Pennsylvania, where we saw deer and foxes but no other people.

It was time to play with my brain.

I'd already been formulating and using the anxiety-easing methods you've encountered so far in this book. I was convinced that, oversimplification aside, there really was something to the localization of anxiety in the left hemisphere. So what would happen if I devoted myself to behaviors that revved up my **right** hemisphere? How would it affect my anxiety? My theory, based on much reading and pondering, was that engaging in tasks that called upon my right brain would pull me out of my left brain's anxiety spirals.

To find out, I designated a full month to cranking up the right side of my brain. With the generous support of my family, I set out to spend thirty days focusing almost entirely on right hemisphere–dominated activities. I'd always loved drawing, but as a young adult, I'd developed excruciating pain in my hands and basically had to stop. Now, free from symptoms, I decided that I'd start each of my right-hemisphere days by drawing something, anything. Then I'd just see what I felt like doing next.

As it turned out, I never felt like doing anything next. From my first hesitant sketches, I felt slightly high, fizzing with intoxicating little bubbles of joy. Drawing made me so happy that I—or at least my logical left hemisphere—became quite nervous. I had a feeling that my calculating mind was losing control of my behavior. But the experiment had to continue— in the name of science! So I used my anxiety-calming skills to quell my concerns and kept drawing.

Within a week, I was no longer losing control: I'd lost it. To use IFS language, the part of me that is writing these words right now had basically left the building. I was barely even verbal. Usually, I'm quite pragmatic: every day I make a list of things to do and then (usually) do them. Not that month. I'd wake up, brew a cup of coffee, connect with my family, and then sit down at a table with some paper and art supplies, which I'd use to disappear into the wordless part of me that makes pictures. Every few hours, my family would check on me to make sure I was still alive. I'd come out of my trance long enough to hug them, then notice that I hadn't touched my coffee. After a while, I stopped bothering to make it. Drawing all day was far more stimulating than caffeine.

To illustrate how this felt from the inside, let me refer to a scene from Kenneth Grahame's classic children's tale, **The Wind in the Willows.** This scene perfectly captures what happened internally as I turned my time and energy to right-brain pursuits. By the time you've gone through the exercises in this and following chapters, you may feel it, too.

At the pertinent point in Grahame's story, Mr. Toad has just escaped from prison by disguising himself as a washerwoman. An unsuspecting motorist gives him a ride, and when Mr. Toad asks to drive the car, the owner kindly consents. Toad starts driving very slowly and carefully, "for he was determined to be prudent." But then he goes "a little faster; then faster still, and faster" until the owner grows alarmed:

> The driver tried to interfere, but he pinned him down in his seat with one elbow, and put on full speed. The rush of air in his face, the hum of the engines, and the light jump of the car beneath him intoxicated his weak brain. "Washerwoman, indeed!" he shouted recklessly. "Ho! ho! I am the Toad, the motor-car snatcher, the prison-breaker, the Toad who always escapes! Sit still, and you shall know what driving really is, for you are in the hands of the famous, the skilful, the entirely fearless Toad!"

This is **exactly** how I felt when I allowed my right brain to steer my life. Anxiety? What the hell was **that**? The passage of time? News of the world? Other people's needs? They all disappeared into the rapturous struggle to make images on paper look the way they appeared to my eyes, or in my imagination.

The right-hemisphere life goes way, way beyond merely flattening our anxiety. It can take us on a wild, delicious joyride that leaves anxiety so far in the rearview mirror we can barely remember it.

YOUR TURN ON MR. TOAD'S WILD RIDE

I tell you this story as a fair warning. I've read many, many books and articles about how to overcome anxiety, but they all stopped at the point of achieving calm. To me, this is like bailing out a sinking boat without plugging the leaks: a good first step but not the best long-term solution—and a sad place to stop when we're within easy reach of a much, much more joyful way of life. Just dispelling anxiety means constantly bailing, working against the pull of our brain's negativity bias and the pressures of our anxious society. Moving further into the right hemisphere means sailing off on thrilling adventures.

In this chapter and those that follow it, we'll go beyond soothing your creature self, and activate your creative self. (Calm is a prerequisite for this, so remember that you'll have to calm yourself repeatedly en route to your creative self.) I'll give a more detailed description of the feedback system in the right half of your brain, the mirror of the left hemisphere's anxiety spiral. As I mentioned in chapter 1, I call this the "creativity spiral." The following section will look at what happens in our brains, bodies, and lives when we begin to ride this benevolent spiral away from anxiety.

This process may take you toward things that our culture typically calls "creative" work, like painting, dancing, or writing great literature, but it may not. We can use creativity spirals in everything we do: parenting, repairing cars, practicing science, leading a team, wearing clothes, having conversations, making sandwiches. And creativity is our **only** way of solving problems that are, like many issues facing our species in the twenty-first century, completely unprecedented.

When we're facing a situation we've never seen before—one that may have **never** existed before—there are no established rules for responding to conditions or solving our problems. We have to **create** those rules and responses, dream them up like a movie hero who's stranded on Mars, or a doctor facing a brand-new virus, or an engineer trying to build glass so strong that a building made from it—like the new World Trade Center—could withstand the impact of a passenger jet.

Unprecedented is the adjective for our age. Unprecedented situations are mushrooming around us. We live with an unprecedented amount of knowledge transfer, in an unprecedented escalation of technology, on a globe whose natural ecosystems we're destroying at an unprecedented scale. The world is facing a whole lot of never-happened-befores.

To deal with all this, we must—absolutely must— let our right hemispheres take the wheel.

As you learn to do this, you'll begin creating things, the way Nicky in chapter 2 created a vegetable garden in her Manhattan apartment. I have no idea what you'll make. But I do believe that it will leave your brain less anxious and more inventive. And I know that the most important creative project you'll undertake—the one you were born to complete—is the shaping of your whole life. As you become more creative than our society deems prudent, you'll make the choices that will lead to your own greatest happiness, and your best contribution to the world.

WE ARE CREATIVELY STARVED

I've asked you a couple of times if you'd be willing to act in ways that the people around you might not understand, or create a life that may not match cultural norms. Now I'm calling in that agreement. Conforming to our culture while trying to lessen your anxiety is one thing—**the** one thing most people are gunning for. But as you free your creative side, giving full rein to your right hemisphere, you may leave the bounds of our stressful, self-destructive, WEIRD society. You may start to look a little odd to the people around you, and even to yourself.

I speak from experience.

Within a few days of starting my experiment in right-brain living, my Art Toad floored the gas pedal by switching to transparent watercolor. It's a devilishly hard medium, one that caters to the right hemisphere's love of exploration and unpredictability. You never really know how watercolor will behave. You can't erase mistakes. And God help you if you sneeze on a painting, or if someone happens to touch the surface with grimy fingers. You have to just trash the whole thing and start over. Days of coping with this tricky, demanding medium drove me to distraction, swept me into obsession, hurtled me into bliss.

I began staying up late to paint after my family went to sleep. After hitting the sack around midnight, I'd rocket out of bed at 4:00 a.m., bursting with eagerness to paint some more. Whatever picture I happened to be working on became the only thing in the world—until I ruined it (which I usually did), threw it away, and started over. And over. And over. Once I was satisfied with a painting, I'd stash it in a closet and forget it had ever existed. My body brimmed with energy, my mind with enchantment. It was like being on some powerful psychedelic drug.

And as with many drugs, the problem was stopping. When my monthlong experimental period ended and it was time to go back to my usual lifestyle, Art Toad resisted mightily. Every time I opened my work calendar or my email, she'd throw silent tantrums. **NO, NO, NO!** she'd insist, penciling a faint image onto watercolor paper. **I'M NOT GOING BACK TO PRISON! I AM THE TOAD WHO ALWAYS ESCAPES!**

"But I have other things to do," I told her. "Normal life things."

THE WAY YOU WANT ME TO LIVE IS NOT

NORMAL! Art Toad would holler, splashing color onto a patch of wet paper. **THE WAY I LIVE IS NORMAL! GO AWAY!**

Another week passed, and then another. My left hemisphere was becoming quite concerned that I'd never get back to my potboiling activities: writing, coaching, and speaking. I work with teams of people who run my speaking engagements and online training. They needed me to show up at meetings, interviews, and the like. I had a strongly internalized (left-hemisphere) rule that said painting was a nice hobby but I had to put it aside and do "real work" most of the time.

I begged my therapist to help me reenter the left-hemisphere world.

"Okay," she said. "Find the parts of you that are in conflict. See what they have to say. Then connect with Self-energy and ask it what you should do."

I followed her instructions. After a few silent minutes, I reported, "It isn't working. My Self is on Art Toad's side. It's saying there's no need to live in stress and anxiety. It thinks I should choose bliss."

"Does that make sense to you?"

"No!" I shouted. "No, it doesn't! Because a lot of people depend on me to function in the real world!"

"Huh," she said. "Interesting."

Interesting? What good was that? If anything, I suspected that some version of Art Toad was rearing up in my therapist. And why not? Was Art Toad doing anything morally wrong? Why shouldn't we all just quit our jobs and spend our days painting, singing, writing, and learning to play the zither?

This was far from a new question for me. Many of my clients struggled with similar issues. "I can't just do whatever I enjoy," they often said. "I have to pay the rent. I have to feed my family." Remember, "premodern" humans actually did spend almost all their time doing things that balanced their brain hemispheres: interacting with nature; tracking animals; creating art, music, and stories; and otherwise engaging their right hemispheres as much as their left brains. But our culture has surrendered most right-brain activities to jobs that cater to the preferences of the left hemisphere, dampening our creative sparks so we can turn ourselves into cogs in the machine of material production.

By the time I started my right-hemisphere month, like many of us, I'd spent years favoring my left hemisphere—perhaps even more than most people. I came of age in one of the most competitive left-hemisphere environments on earth, starting at Harvard when I was seventeen and staying to get three degrees by the time I turned thirty. I spent the subsequent years totally focused on physically caring for my children and earning money to help support our family.

My Art Toad had been locked up tight, only allowed out for the occasional hour or two, then jammed back into her cell. When I offered my artsy self a whole month of total freedom, she reacted like a starving person on a binge, barely acknowledging anyone or anything but making art. I had expected that my month of drawing and painting would be followed by a return to my "old normal," a life in which art played only a bit part. Instead, that month decreased my anxiety and increased my joie de vivre so much that it became a major turning point in my life.

These days, I wake up early and literally go back to the drawing board. From five or six o'clock until eleven in the morning, Art Toad has the controls. I make art the way I did as a child, totally absorbed in pushing my skills, stunned by the colors and shapes of the world, completely outside time. Instead of bingeing for brief shining moments, Art Toad gets regular meals of drawing and painting. I've begun selling my work, and plan to sell more if anyone wants it, but that's not the point. The point is living a life free from anxiety, suffused with creativity.

I doubt you're as extreme as I tend to be, so amping up your use of your right hemisphere, in whatever way works for you, won't make you obsessive, sleep-deprived, or totally self-involved. If you find yourself feeling **desperate** to do creative work, the way I did, either find more time for creativity or set a firm intention to do so as soon as your life situation permits. Honor this promise—it's one of the most important things you can do to live according to your true inner nature. Whatever amount of creative activity you end up doing, I suspect it will make you saner than you've ever been. Let's see why and how this will work.

CREATIVITY IS THE OPPOSITE OF ANXIETY

By now you should know the elements of the anxiety spiral: an unfamiliar event causes a yawp from the left amygdala, which causes other brain structures to create control strategies and scary stories, which feed back to and cause **more** fear in the left amygdala, and so on.

The creativity spiral also begins in the amygdala when we see something unfamiliar. But if we're not actually in danger, our right hemispheres don't move into control. According to Jill Bolte Taylor, the emotional part of the right brain "instead of pushing things away . . . moves enthusiastically toward any experience that remotely smells like an enticing and juicy adrenaline rush." This curious exploratory response initiates a set of feelings and actions that are very different from those generated by the anxiety spiral—though this right-brain impulse may also form a self-reinforcing cycle: the creativity spiral. Instead of trying to control reality, it causes you to move toward inquiry and discovery. Let's look at some of the differences.

Anxiety spirals pull us away from the world. Creativity spirals pull us into it.

Curiosity, the sensation that begins the creativity spiral, is the force that tempts many young animals, including humans, to experiment with new experiences. Where anxiety makes us avoid more and more of the world, curiosity draws us forward, helping us get used to unexplored environments and unfamiliar experiences. Anxiety retracts; curiosity expands.

Anxiety spirals inhibit learning. Creativity spirals motivate learning.

According to one view of the brain developed by educators, our nervous systems are always asking three questions, in this order:

1. Am I safe?

2. Am I loved?

3. What can I learn?

It's only when the first two questions can be answered with yeses that we become able to use the parts of the brain that learn and remember. The anxiety spiral, with its fight, flight, fawn, freeze, or flop reactions, shuts down our ability to learn. Anxiety also makes us less able to feel and show love, and less receptive to love from others, darkening our emotions as well as our thoughts.

Creativity spirals, on the other hand, make us focus on the here and now, where we're able to evaluate situations and either take useful action or simply feel safe. They also impel us to learn about different perspectives and make us want to express ourselves to others. That's love in action. Once we feel grounded in safety and connection, the brain automatically asks, **What can I learn?** This makes us more inventive and intelligent.

Anxiety spirals show us only half the world. Creativity spirals show us all of it.

Remember that odd quality of the brain's left hemisphere that makes it unable to see or acknowledge anything but its own perceptions? Well, the right hemisphere doesn't share this peculiar solipsism. It's aware of **all** our perceptions, including not only creative ideas but also the logical, analytical thinking that happens mainly in the left side of the brain.

This means that while an anxious brain can gather and sort information, it can't put that information into a context of meaning, purpose, or mutual benefit. An anxious mind is like a ship with a very powerful engine but no charts, compasses, or destination. It just **goes,** racking up distance but never knowing why.

I once met a consultant who helps corporate leaders increase revenues—but first, she asks them why they would want to do such a thing.

"They look at me as if I'm crazy," she told me. "They say, 'Well, because that would mean more profits.' And I say, 'Yes, but what's the purpose of having so much money? What does it all **mean** to you?'" She told me that at this point, most executives either stop working with her (because she obviously "doesn't get it") or become wistful and then introspective. They begin activating the right-hemisphere search for meaning and context. "At that point," the consultant told me, "they begin finding their humanity, as well as the best way to make their businesses useful to the world."

This is the creativity spiral creaking into motion, beginning to carry us away from a viewpoint that sees only danger and wants only material things. It transports us to a place where we can take in both danger **and** abundance, and it holds the sense of purpose that moves us beyond mere survival into meaning.

Anxiety spirals make our lives smaller. Creativity spirals make them bigger.

As we twist along an anxiety spiral, our lives become more confined and more separated from sensory reality. Anxious people often avoid everything that doesn't feel safe, and as they pull back from more experiences, they feel more and more anxious.

This is how agoraphobia works: A person—we'll call them Pat—has a panic attack at a restaurant. After the attack, Pat avoids that restaurant. But since the panic attack didn't come from the environment, Pat soon has another one, perhaps while walking through the park. Now Pat associates parks with panic and avoids them. Anxiety that leads to avoidance (which doesn't stop the anxiety) makes Pat's world smaller and smaller.

The creativity spiral has the opposite effect. Each turn around this spiral entices us into more exploration and experimentation. As we push slightly out of our comfort zones, connecting to more people and experiences, we grow comfortable in more situations.

For example, our agoraphobic friend Pat may begin by creating a sanctuary and learning creature-calming skills. Feeling empowered, Pat may then get curious enough to start researching anxiety online and connecting with others who've had similar experiences. Hearing stories from people who've conquered their fears, Pat may feel emboldened to try some of their methods, like bravely taking the dog to the park and staying there, self-calming away until the anxiety backs off a bit. Feeling proud and excited, Pat may post a photo of this brave act for online friends to appreciate.

I've my own versions of both these stories. Looking back on my first cautious trips around the creativity spiral, I'm amazed by how much bigger my life has become since I first set out to expand my comfort zone. Gently but consistently choosing creativity spirals over anxiety spirals has made novelty itself less unnerving to me, and I've seen this happen for many clients as well. Following our creativity can introduce us to more and more unfamiliar experiences and help us feel confident enough to explore them until we feel safe. Instead of excluding and "othering" anything we don't understand (the left hemisphere's typical pattern), our right brains help us include people and things that once seemed strange. We feel safer and more peaceful, so we can help make the world safer and more peaceful as well.

BEYOND THE FEAR ZONE AND INTO THE FUN ZONE

If you were stranded in a wild environment, being skittish and hyperaware of danger (a.k.a. riding the anxiety spiral) would give you a survival advantage. But you'd also need to explore your environment and figure out how to thrive there, which would mean following creativity spirals. Because creativity, along with caution, is an essential survival skill, nature has imbued many ways of learning and experimenting with an emotion almost as strong as fear. The technical name for this powerful evolutionary necessity is **fun.**

Our left brains tend to think of fun as silly, unnecessary, frivolous. Merely **having** fun sets off storms of judgment in people who devote their full time and attention to grabbing more stuff. But nature doesn't seem to agree with them that fun is unnecessary. The more scientists explore animal behavior, the more they report that evolution has given a love of fun and play to almost every living thing.

For instance, it's obvious to anyone who's ever known a dog, cat, goat, or dolphin that mammals love to play. In Scandinavia, where cattle have to be cooped up in warm barns for the winter, entire towns gather to watch full-grown milk cows cavort through the fields when they're let out in the spring. Google it! It will make you happy!

While you're at it, search for "birds playing" to see crows sledding on their backs down snowy hills or cockatoos making up new dance moves as they rock out to human music. I once thought reptiles, which have much more primitive brains, would know nothing of play or fun. Wrong! Turtles and lizards play, as do crocodiles and alligators, which collect any small, flowerlike pink objects as playthings and have been seen giving otters "boat rides" on their backs. Speaking of flowers, some botanists believe that plants themselves are capable of play. And if you don't think of fungi as playful, you have never had a shaman-led mushroom journey. Fungi are indeed fun guys.

Once we've revved up our right hemispheres, our

curiosity and playfulness gain more neurological turf. Everything starts to seem interesting, and learning feels effortless. Since my right-brain experiment month, when I began deliberately moving beyond anxiety and into creativity spirals, I've found myself careening along on Mr. Toad's manic drive to more and more places, more and more often. I expect this will happen to you, too, as you work through the next few chapters and begin riding your own creativity spirals.

FROM FUN TO ART TO THRIVING

Of course, creativity spirals don't end with play. As you enhance your right-hemisphere capabilities, you won't just go beyond anxiety, and you won't just goof around; you'll find yourself making things. All sorts of things. Creativity loves problem-solving, so as you activate yours, you may find yourself engrossed in anything from Sudoku to songwriting to building your own airplane from a kit.

As I contemplated the creativity spiral during my right-brain month, I wondered why it felt so wonderful to push my watercolor skills, even though they have no survival value. To the left hemisphere—and most parts of our culture—the creative arts seem unimportant, or at least much, much less useful than left brain–dominated pursuits. This attitude persists despite abundant research showing that interacting with art improves our physical and mental health. For example:

- A study at Drexel University found that making art for as little as forty-five minutes reduced subjects' stress hormone cortisol, no matter what their skill level or experience.

- In another study, coloring for just twenty minutes reduced people's anxiety and stress. When subjects colored mandalas—circular designs revered in many wisdom traditions—the reduction in anxiety was even more significant. (For your coloring pleasure, I've included a mandala at the end of this chapter. If you enjoy art, try making one yourself. It's great fun!)

- A study in **The New England Journal of Medicine** reported that dancing reduced the risk of dementia in the elderly, while other activities, like cycling, golf, swimming, and tennis, didn't.

- As I've already mentioned, there's abundant evidence that writing expressively about a traumatic experience for just fifteen minutes had remarkable, long-lasting positive effects on volunteers' physical and mental health.

- Studies of trauma survivors showed that when these people used art to help them process their experiences, their risk of developing post-traumatic stress disorder dropped by a whopping 80 percent.

Clearly, there's an intimate relationship between our creative selves and our overall well-being. I believe this may be related to getting out of the anxiety spiral so that we're not always bathing our insides with stress hormones. If we can gently move our minds toward curiosity and problem-solving, we can enter the zone of our psyches where anxiety stops and we become totally present.

When I asked Jill Bolte Taylor whether the right hemisphere can feel anxiety, she said, "No, because anxiety is always about the future. No time, no future, no anxiety." She's still a scientist and an educator—but also a sculptor, a songwriter, a painter, and a performer. Jill's artistic pursuits keep her tied to the perspective she learned from living completely in her right hemisphere. And in other people who've damaged the left sides of their brains, we sometimes catch sight of the full, astonishing force of artistic creation.

WHEN CREATIVITY GOES FULL THROTTLE

One day in 1994, an orthopedic surgeon named Anthony Cicoria was standing near a pay phone when he was struck by lightning. Cicoria appeared to be dead—his heart had stopped—but a woman standing nearby, who happened to be an intensive-care nurse, was able to resuscitate him. He recovered almost unchanged except for one thing: suddenly, at age forty-two, Anthony Cicoria was a musician.

Prior to that lightning strike, Cicoria had never studied music. But after it, he began to hear tunes in his head. He bought a piano and started playing it for hours every day. By 2002—still a working physician—he was publicly performing difficult works by Chopin and Brahms. He debuted his first original piano composition, "The Lightning Sonata," in 2007.

Heather Thompson, a successful young entrepreneur, sustained a head injury when a car tailgate dropped on her head. During her recovery, a friend suggested that she try painting. Heather was skeptical, never having had any interest in art, but later said, "The first time I picked up a brush, I discovered my hands knew what to do. . . . It was as easy as breathing."

In Colorado, a young pilot named Ivan Schlutz got too close to an airplane propeller, and it carved away nearly half his brain. Amazingly, Schlutz survived, though he had some paralysis on his right side. Physical therapists gave him clay to work with his fingers, hoping to help him regain hand strength. Though he'd never done any art before, Schlutz grew obsessed with modeling the clay. He quickly became a successful sculptor whose works are sought by collectors around the world.

These people developed something called "acquired savant syndrome." This extremely rare condition sometimes appears when an individual with no artistic interest or training suffers a brain injury, typically on the left side of the head, and abruptly demonstrates prodigious creative ability. It's not anything to be envied—all these people endured a lot of suffering. But their experiences hint that artistic interests aren't things we **add** to our brains. They're already there. When the left hemisphere allows them some space, they emerge spontaneously.

I felt the unnerving power of my creative side during my Art Toad experiment. I can feel it pushing at me right now. When I have other work to do and can't make art all day, every day, I walk past my art supplies with averted eyes, like a recovering alcoholic passing a bar. If I were to start drawing or painting again right now, I suspect that Art Toad would pin me to the passenger seat of my life with one crazed amphibian elbow. I'd be off on another wild ride, and this book would never get written.

The bad news, I suppose, is that some of us really do become obsessed with art to the point where we stop eating and sleeping. The good news is that, unlike people who have had strokes or head injuries, we can invite our creative selves to arise gently and gradually. Once we've calmed our anxiety, we can tap into the thrill and fascination of creativity. Without anxiety, we're **naturally** artistic, communicative, fully present.

And one more thing: our creative selves can keep us forever young.

YOUR WHOLE LIFE CAN BE A HAPPY CHILDHOOD

The extreme human drive toward creativity—which takes us beyond playing with otters and into the realms of art, science, and invention—may be due to a genetic fluke called "neoteny." This is a mutation that happened sometime in the distant past, when our ancestors were just experimenting with walking on their hind legs.

All creatures seem to play more when they're young. Playing and having fun helps baby beasts learn the skills they'll need to forage, hunt, fight rivals or predators, mate, and rear their own babies. But in most species, the desire to play drops a bit as an individual reaches maturity. A newborn chimpanzee, for example, may play more than a brand-new human. But at puberty, as the chimp grows fangs, a brow ridge, and the willingness to tear off your arms, it will tend to play a bit less, though it will never stop completely.

In the case of humans, neoteny means that we

never stop looking and acting like **very young** apes. We have the delicate bone structure, flattish faces, small teeth, and—this is the key point—curious, inquisitive, creative drive toward fun that characterizes baby apes. If we decide to develop this drive, evolution has bestowed on us the inestimably precious gift of an endless mental childhood, with all the fun and wonder that entails.

A few days after I started drawing, my inner Art Toad zeroed in on her favorite subject: my two-year-old daughter. At some point almost every day, Lila and I would don galoshes and jackets over our pajamas, then just wander around the woods near our house, playing with everything. As we clambered over logs and splashed into puddles, I'd take photos of Lila with my phone. Then, using the photos as references, I'd draw her for hours and hours.

When I asked myself why Art Toad was so obsessed with drawing Lila, the answer arose immediately: Art Toad was herself a toddler. She was the part of me who'd spent countless days lying on the carpet in my parents' living room, drawing on three-by-five-inch note cards I'd nabbed from my father's office supplies. This part of me was barely verbal, stunned by the beauty of the world, and in a constant state of awe so overwhelming that I was perpetually on the verge of tears.

Along with this flood of perception and emotion came an astonishing amount of physical vigor. I could feel, very clearly, the kinds of health benefits that scientists have associated with artsy activities. I felt more like laughing (toddlers laugh about twenty-seven times more often than adults). I was more interested in other arts: I played music and audiobooks as I painted. Everything seemed so alive, so vivid, and, above all, so **connected.**

During my right-brain month, I didn't need science to tell me what powerfully good medicine creativity is. I just experienced it. And I deeply want you to experience it as well. The next three chapters will help you move into the joy of creativity that pulls us beyond anxiety. However—and this is important—the process of reviving your creative self might not feel the way you expect. You have some cultural biases to overcome as you build a stronger, denser, quicker neural pathway into your creative brain.

RELEASING CULTURAL EXPECTATIONS ABOUT YOUR CREATIVE SELF

When I coach people to use the skills in this book, I run into a few common cultural myths that tend to get in the way of awakening creativity. I'm going to list them here, before we go any further, so that you don't wander off in a suboptimal direction.

MYTH NO. 1: If I just do creative things, I won't need any other anxiety-calming skills.

I've worked with countless creative people, many of whom are also highly anxious, and I've asked all of them if they're ever anxious **at the moment** they're creating. The answer is always no. But if they have no other way of calming themselves, these people may get stuck in anxiety spirals and find themselves unable to "turn on" their creativity. If this describes you, stop trying to force yourself to create, and turn your attention to creature-calming skills.

Remember, our creative selves only become accessible **once we've calmed our anxious creature selves.** The truth is, you will always have to care for your anxiety creature. Using direct methods will take you to the point of calm; moving on into creative thinking will take you beyond it. So if you find yourself having trouble getting creative, go back to the first four chapters of this book. Use the skills you'll find there or any other method that helps you calm your anxiety creature. As you access Self, your creativity will return. It may begin to make meaning, even beauty, out of your suffering.

Ultimately, creative people can feel anxious when they're not actively creating, and the Self can use anxiety as inspiration, but anxiety itself isn't the creator.

MYTH NO. 2: If I have creativity, I won't need to work on my relationships with people.

Some of my clients who have social anxiety seize on the happy thought that just being creative will make them so joyful they'll never need to deal with the complex and challenging aspects of connecting with other people.

Of course, this ignores the whole point of all the arts, which is to express the artist's personal truth in ways that can be understood by the people around them. In other words, creativity is a way to love. But it's not the only way. We're fundamentally social creatures, so **creativity is not a substitute for safety and connection.** We can plunge into art, science, or exploring the world so deeply that we briefly forget other people exist. But we still need human connection.

One example of someone whose creative genius couldn't stave off loneliness is Alan Turing, who created the earliest computers in order to break Nazi codes during World War II. Turing was probably autistic and also gay at a time when gayness was a criminal offense in his native England. Heartbreakingly, one of his final products was an automated love-letter generator. Not long after inventing this, Turing was convicted of "gross indecency" for his sexual orientation. He died from suicide two years later. No matter how engrossed we get in creative work, we will always need other people. Every one of us.

MYTH NO. 3: The ultimate goal of creative work should be making money.

This is a biggie. I've been guilty of foisting it on people: "Wow," I'll say to a friend, "you're so funny! You should do stand-up." Or: "My God, those are beautiful drawings! You could sell those." Or: "You're so good on the ocarina! You should go pro!"

Now, it's true that some people become financially successful solely by doing creative work. But that doesn't mean every creative talent must be monetized. In fact, as I've already mentioned, research shows that you can kill a person's creative problem-solving skills just by offering to pay them a few dollars for the right answer to a puzzle. What was fun suddenly becomes filled with anxiety, and creativity flatlines.

This, by the way, is how I finally managed to stop my Art Toad's first manic, uncontrollable wild ride. A key part of my experiment was that I didn't set out to "do anything" with my pictures. I painted just to see what would happen to my mood, health, and anxiety levels. Then one day, three weeks or so after I'd totally failed to stop painting all day and most of the night, my partner, Ro, and I got an email from a designer at a children's book publisher who enjoyed our podcast. She asked if either of us had ever considered writing a children's book.

Aha! said my left hemisphere. **Redemption!** I wasn't just an Art Toad driving amok! My art had

Sales Potential! It could Earn Money! It could help me Grab More Stuff! Ro and I went to lunch with this lovely woman, who offered to help me get my work published.

And just like that, I stopped painting. Lost all interest. It was like the moment when Mr. Toad drives into a hedge: full speed to full stop in no time flat.

Being a professional creative—getting paid in the left-hemisphere world for the products of right-brain creativity—requires threading a very thin needle, balancing between pure invention and blunt pragmatism. We'll talk about this process more in later chapters. I'd love it if you became an artist, but this book is about learning to free yourself from suffering, broaden your world, and have a joyful life beyond anxiety. Once that's in place, we can talk career strategies.

MYTH NO. 4: Creativity is easy.

Because our culture tends to trivialize creativity, we think of it as either child's play, just sort of slopping around, or magic—something wondrous, conjured with inborn talent rather than elbow grease. In the late 1900s, psychologists who shared this bias set out to find where talent was hiding in the brains of child prodigies. They were surprised to discover that genius musicians and athletes start out with brains exactly like those of other kids. The prodigies just practice more. We'll discuss this in greater depth in chapter 8. For now, just know that while creativity will indeed take you beyond anxiety into joy, it's not like getting pampered at a spa. It may be the best hardest thing you ever do.

During my Art Toad month, my family was often confused to see me stomping around in frustration, muttering strings of four-letter words through clenched teeth.

"Isn't this supposed to make you happy?" they'd say.

It **did** make me happy, just not in a spa-day kind of way. It pushed me to the edge of my creative ability— an edge where our brains struggle to get things right but also flood us with dopamine and other feel-good hormones as we learn and grow. To get into the blissful state of "flow," we often go through moments when we're taxing our skills to the limit. It can be incredibly frustrating, but in a way that leads to growth rather than shutdown.

Michelangelo never actually said something I've seen attributed to him over and over: "I just took a block of marble and chipped away everything that wasn't David! Haha! Easy-peasy!" But he did compose a lot of doleful poetry about how much his back hurt while he was painting the Sistine Chapel's ceiling, and he also wrote, "If people knew how hard I worked to get my mastery, it wouldn't seem so wonderful at all."

But, of course, Michelangelo's mastery is wonderful precisely **because** he worked so hard to achieve it. A life lived to the full is splendid and difficult, and the splendor is often proportionate to the difficulty. It seems that our creative selves enjoy that combination. In fact, they'll settle for nothing less.

If you want to feel what it's like to bring your whole brain online by mastering a creative task, here's an exercise I learned as a teaching assistant at Harvard under the guidance of Will Reimann, one of the most talented artists and teachers on the planet.

New Skill

CALL ON YOUR WHOLE BRAIN

---

1. Get a sheet of plain paper, like printer paper or a lineless sketchbook page. Also grab a pen or pencil. Sit down at a desk or table where you can write.

2. Now call to mind a Troubling Topic, something that causes you a bit of anxiety. Think about this issue and feel the anxiety that accompanies it. Write about it here:

_____

_____

3. In the center of your blank paper, sign your first name, exactly as you usually do.

4. Now position your pen or pencil to the immediate left of your signature. Writing from right to left, replicate your signature **backward**, in mirror image. It will be scruffy, but it should be basically legible. Like this:

5. Now position your pen or pencil just underneath your first signature and "mirror-write" it upside down. Keep your eyes on the original signature, and try to let your hand follow the same path in this new direction. If you feel stuck, stop and relax your breathing, then start again. You'll eventually get something like this:

6. Finally—you knew this was coming—sign upside down **and** backward.

7. Repeat this a few times until it begins to feel a little easier.

8. Notice that although you might have become very focused or even frustrated while trying out this new skill, you are no longer thinking about your Troubling Topic.

So that, my friend, is one way to put your right hemisphere in the driver's seat of your life. It's not a substitute for self-calming or love; it's not simple and silly; and it's not instantly gratifying. Maybe you found yourself squinting and biting your lip like a toddler learning to use Legos. If so, congratulations. You just fired up some new neural connections, and they had to involve both your left hemisphere and your right. For a moment, you had to release your anxiety as you moved yourself along a tiny little creativity spiral.

Now let's help you steer further and further into creativity until you discover your most compelling creative processes, your true fascinations. We'll start by enhancing your powers of curiosity, the first impulse that moves you along a creativity spiral. Then we'll move on to the connections that the right hemisphere will form if you give it something to wonder about. Ultimately, you'll learn to master creative activities that bring you into "flow," flooding your brain with delicious hormones and the world with your best creative ideas.

"Washerwoman, indeed!" you'll find yourself shouting as you go faster, then faster, then faster still. "Ho! Ho! I am the Toad who always escapes!" You'll find it easier and easier to break free from anxiety spirals, moving your **creature** self to the point where it becomes your **creative** self. And always remember this: whatever else you do, going beyond anxiety into creativity will help you build the life you were meant to live.

6

Curiosity: The Secret Doorway

On the television screen, we see a montage of attractive young women, all expressing their delight at being left alone for the evening. "Finally, he's gone," one says as the door shuts behind her boyfriend. The other women add: "I have the whole night to unwind and do a little self-care—the only way I know how." Then, as one, the women burst into song:

Murder show, murder show,
I'm gonna watch a murder show . . .

They warble on, describing the relaxing delight of a true-crime story, hoping for a high body count to keep things interesting. This skit, from a 2021 episode of **Saturday Night Live,** gets big laughs from the audience because it's so paradoxical—and so true. Who doesn't love to pop some corn, pour a glass of wine, and settle in to hear about a day in 1987 that "started like any other" and ended in a nightmare of suburban carnage? The American Academy of Child and Adolescent Psychiatry reports that the average American child has watched sixteen thousand murders by age eighteen. And even when we turn off the TV, a huge percentage of books, movies, podcasts, and good old-fashioned campfire stories are all about homicide.

Why is this topic so incredibly interesting?

Because murder is one of the things that scares us most.

Fear and curiosity are closely linked. We take our first steps beyond anxiety when we're confronted with something unfamiliar and, instead of stepping into the spiral, stay long enough to relax and feel our curiosity rising up. That zap of intrigue pulls us into our creative selves. In other words, curiosity activates creativity.

You can see how tightly fear and curiosity are linked in many creatures. For example, when monkeys encounter a snake, they freak out, but they don't run. Instead, they stare fixedly at the serpent, gawking, jumping, and hooting—because the only thing worse than keeping track of a snake is **not** keeping track of it. In a similar vein, I once watched a bobcat kill a ground squirrel and carry it up a tree. Instantly, several deer bounded out of the surrounding forest, ran up to the tree, and stood staring up at the bobcat, emanating both horror and fascination in a silence-of-the-deer moment.

The connection between fear and fascination is what makes journalists say, "If it bleeds, it leads." It's why we rubberneck at accidents, hoping no one was hurt but grimly determined to see the evidence if they were. Evolution pushes curiosity in such situations because learning about crimes and catastrophes helps us avoid them. So don't be embarrassed if you can't peel your eyes away from a poorly written, badly narrated program that consists mainly of repeated zoom-ins on the same grainy crime-scene photo. You came by your curiosity honestly.

If you experience a lot of anxiety, you may be closer to creativity than you realize. Getting curious— for example, wondering why you always feel so anxious—can help you notice that little bit of intrigue. In her book **Big Magic: Creative Living beyond Fear,** Elizabeth Gilbert writes, "Curiosity is the truth and the way of creative living. . . . [I]f you can pause and identify even **one tiny speck** of interest in something, then curiosity will ask you to turn your head a quarter of an inch and look at the thing a wee bit closer. Do it."

This is like finding a doorway between the fearful and the inventive sides of your brain. It may be small and seldom used, the hinges rusted and resistant. But as you open that door and go through it, which is

what you'll learn to do in this chapter, it will take
you to a life beyond anxiety.

THE SWEET SPOT
OF CURIOSITY

When you see something strange, depending on how
dangerous the thing appears, you may feel almost
no reaction at all, or you may be instantly terrified.
Somewhere between indifference and terror lies the
sweet spot of curiosity.

For example, if you see a car swerving repeatedly
out of its lane a block away, you might not feel either
fear or curiosity—you're very familiar with cars, so
your attention may be better spent on other things.
On the other hand, if you don't spot the car until it's
very close and heading straight at you, fear will far
outweigh curiosity as you haul ass out of there. But
if you see the car coming slowly closer, maybe even
steering toward you on purpose, you'll likely focus
on it suddenly and intensely, estimating its trajectory,
peering at the driver's face, trying to figure out where
the car will go next.

Our curiosity sweet spot is so powerful that it can
generate elaborate ways of getting almost (but only
almost) too frightened. Horror movies, haunted
houses, and sports like BASE jumping and extreme
skiing pull in huge amounts of attention, not to

mention money. We love medical shows that offer dramatizations of people who've contracted horrible illnesses or gone through horrific accidents. And although humans are born with just two fears—loud noises and falling—people deliberately build very loud flying machines, then get in them and soar thousands of feet up **for the express purpose of jumping out.**

In other words, we'll do almost anything to experience that sweet spot where "almost scared to death" meets "I'll probably survive."

HOW HUMANS LOSE THEIR CURIOSITY

You were born with a level of inquisitiveness that fueled much of your early behavior, pulling you toward exploration, invention, and all sorts of learning. Leon Lederman, winner of a Nobel Prize in Physics, once said:

Children are born scientists. . . . They do everything that scientists do. They test how strong things are. They measure the falling bodies. . . . They're doing all kinds of things to learn the physics of the world around them. . . . They ask questions; they drive parents crazy with why, why, why.

The combination of innocence and intelligence makes children the curiosity champions of the world. Throw in neoteny, that "eternal childhood" mutation that keeps our brains young, and a human may sustain an extraordinary level of curiosity forever. Some people keep poking, prodding, measuring, and testing until they learn to send spacecraft to distant galaxies or build functioning human hearts using a computer printer and biocompatible plastic.

Some people.

So what happens to the rest of us?

In the early 2000s, a product designer named Peter Skillman devised a challenge to test the creative skills of teams. The challenge was to build a freestanding tower using several sticks of dry spaghetti, one meter of string, one meter of masking tape, and a marshmallow. Skillman administered the test to college students, engineers, lawyers, and several other groups. The worst performers on the task? Business school students. The winners by a country mile? Kindergartners.

This surprising outcome had everything to do with the way anxiety quashes curiosity. Business school students approached the task very rationally. They appointed team leaders, then had intelligent discussions about the best way to proceed. Finally, they divided up the work and started building—so slowly that they ended up with zero or near-zero scores. Five-year-olds, by contrast, seemed to have little social or performance anxiety, just a ton of curiosity. They dove right into the Skillman challenge, crowding together, snatching up materials, barely communicating. They said little, except for short exclamations like "Here! No, here!"

Adult teams failed the spaghetti challenge because they were more focused on social anxiety than on the actual task at hand. They worried about offending one another. They felt pressed to establish a social hierarchy. They weren't sure if they were allowed to voice their ideas. Author Daniel Coyle wrote that their "interactions appear smooth, but their underlying behavior is riddled with inefficiency, hesitation, and subtle competition."

These highly educated students had learned through hard experience the left-hemisphere biases of our culture: win group approval, express ideas logically, and calculate social dynamics . . . **or else.** They'd already spent decades being remonstrated for behaving like five-year-olds: standing too close, failing to explain their ideas verbally, picking up objects without asking permission.

Somewhere between toddlerhood and maturity, most of us get the message to be less curious about unfamiliar situations and approach them with anxiety instead. Our curiosity sweet spot shrinks until, for some people, it seems to vanish. Many of my anxious clients tell me they never experience curiosity—except, perhaps, when they're watching a murder show, wondering who killed that poor preacher's wife in Tennessee. (The preacher did it. The preacher always did it.) As we absorb the rules of our culture, many of us cut off our own curiosity at the root.

Socialized Out of Our Interests

In 2005, psychologist Jordan Litman found that there are two kinds of curiosity. The first, which he called "deprivation curiosity," is a worried need to know that stems from lacking enough information to feel safe—for example, not knowing how to get food or shelter. The second, which Litman called "interest curiosity," comes from a sense of wanting to know, the way children want to know what will happen if they put crayons in the toaster.

Children's curiosity is mostly interest based. But they swap it out for a lot of deprivation curiosity as they grow up. In school, we're supposed to learn all kinds of things we've never heard of and don't care about—but we'll be punished or shamed unless we focus on them. Once we're grown, we're supposed to know things like how to file seven years' worth of financial records, how to navigate complicated bureaucratic systems just to have a doctor look at a weird rash, and how to be just charming enough to get approval without eliciting envy. Failing to master such skills may result in anything from ostracism to prison time.

Interest curiosity feels good. You may remember

your childhood drive to find out what's over the next hill, or how it feels to bodysurf, or what will happen if you follow up your crayons-in-the-toaster experiment by dropping a pack of Mentos into a bottle of Diet Coke (google it!). This kind of curiosity is absorbing, compelling, and often exciting.

On the other hand, deprivation curiosity—how shall I say?—sucks. At best, it's like an itch you can't scratch: "I know I came into this room to get something, but what was it?" At worst, it creates a web of anxious wondering that's close to unbearable: "What's happening? Is that the fire alarm? What have I missed? What did I do wrong? Who's mad at me? Why?"

Our left brain–dominated cultural structures tend to push us toward deprivation curiosity so that we'll wake up terrified, like good Amazon employees, and unquestioningly support the present social hierarchy, thus helping the people at the top grab more stuff. We are trained to drop interest curiosity and tune in more closely to deprivation curiosity. In the early 2000s, when I had my own brain mapped, I realized just how committed we are to this process.

Using technology that was newfangled at the time, researchers at a clinic in Phoenix used adhesive goop to glue many sensors all over my head. Then they connected the sensors to a computer. After I'd sat there for several hours, doing various mental exercises assigned by the researchers, they gave me the bad news: I suffered from high anxiety and attention deficit hyperactivity disorder. The first diagnosis didn't surprise me, but the second one did.

"Really? I have ADHD?" I asked.

"Yes," the head researcher told me. "I'm sure it made school really hard for you." He added that for several thousand dollars, they could help me overcome my learning disability. I decided to spend the money on finishing my PhD instead. But I did ask him to tell me more about my disorder.

"Well, you have an abnormally interest-based nervous system," he explained.

"What does that mean?" I asked. "Interest based?"

"It means you pay more attention to things that interest you than to things that don't," he told me. "But don't worry—as I said, it's treatable."

I laughed heartily until I realized he wasn't joking.

"Wait," I said, "are you telling me that most people pay the same amount of attention to everything, whether they're interested in it or not? Good Lord, how would you even decide what to have for breakfast?"

"No, no, no," the researcher replied. "What I'm saying is that most people can allocate their attention in a way that's optimal."

"Optimal for what?"

"You know, school. Work. Functioning in society."

"Oh," I said. "I see."

I peered at him balefully, picking sensor gel out of my hair as I mentally clambered onto my favorite soapbox. Apparently, my brain was supposed to become a cog in the great stuff-grabbing engine of material production, to work for the man, to uphold white-supremacist patriarchy. A "normal" brain would do as it was told. It would punch the clock, abandon its interests, and have only the occasional murder show as a special treat.

Not for one moment have I regretted being born with a congenitally interest-based nervous system. For me, it feels like a navigation tool, one that's always guided me into life situations that feel meaningful. As I've said, interest-based curiosity is the doorway leading me out of anxiety and into creativity. It has helped me solve countless real problems in practical ways.

Up to now, this book has been about soothing your anxious self until it relaxes. Now we're going to gear up your energy and joie de vivre by helping you live with as much interest curiosity as nature intended. Whether or not you have ADHD, your interest curiosity is still hanging out in your brain, like a child who's been waiting to play for years and years. We'll start by revisiting that curious child, opening the secret door that leads you into creativity spirals, where you'll connect with your sense of purpose and begin building the life you were meant to have.

HOW TO GET YOUR INTEREST CURIOSITY BACK

No matter how hard you've been socialized to ignore your interests, and no matter how much your neuronal pathways to enchantment have been overgrown by pathways to anxiety, you can reignite your interest curiosity in an instant. Dr. Judson Brewer, a Yale-trained psychiatrist who wrote the wonderful bestseller **Unwinding Anxiety,** uses one simple, vowelless word to do this for some of his patients. Brewer describes running a retreat for an Olympic water polo team. He and his collaborator took the team for a hike in the Colorado mountains. They stopped at a particularly beautiful vista, and then, cued by a prearranged signal, both doctors said in unison, "Hmm!"

Immediately, all the athletes became intensely curious. And cheerful. Even when they were told that the doctors weren't curious about anything in particular—that the two were just **acting** curious— everyone's spirits lifted. The athletes started saying "Hmm" as a kind of mood-boosting curiosity practice from then on. As Brewer reports:

When they felt frustrated or stuck . . . **hmm** seemed to help them explore what that felt like in their body and mind (instead of trying to fix or change it). When they got caught in a habit loop of worry or self-judgment, **hmm** could help them shift . . . and step out of the loop.

You may recall times when you saw something unfamiliar, like a strange machine or someone behaving oddly in public, and felt all your attention pull away from anxious thoughts (**How am I going to pay that bill? What's this weird skin tag on my arm?**) to the question "Wait, what's **that**?" (**What is that strangely haunting music? What is that delicious smell? Who's that person wearing the fabulous outfit?**).

Everyone's interest curiosity follows the pattern of their own fascination. We share some fields of interest with other people, but each of us is unique. You probably have special interests you love to explore, from hang gliding to vegan cooking to basketmaking. If you aren't sure what activates your interest curiosity, try scrolling through the internet and seeing what makes you say, "Wait, what's **that**?" Feel how present you become, how your energy suddenly lifts when your interest curiosity is piqued.

Because being able to make things is an evolutionary advantage, watching people do it is an especially powerful trick for stimulating interest curiosity. If you love to make something—clay pottery, decoupage, avant-garde hairstyles—try doing it in public, and see how many people stop to gawk. The TV show **How It's Made** became successful by breaking the cardinal rule of captivating TV (include some conflict!). Instead, the program simply offers viewers a look at unnamed people fashioning everything from jukeboxes to trolley cars.

In short, experiment with your own interest-based curiosity by watching, learning, or asking about anything you find fascinating. Notice how anxiety takes a step back as curiosity blinks on.

THE ONE QUESTION THAT WILL ALWAYS PIQUE YOUR INTEREST CURIOSITY

This works best when you're not already feeling anxious—a condition that, as we've seen, can trap you in the hall of mirrors, where everything feels so dangerous that curiosity is inaccessible. If you're highly anxious, casual efforts, like saying "Hmm" or tapping into one of your particular enthusiasms, might not be enough to pull you out of the anxiety spiral and into curiosity. One of the worst things about being in a long-term red- or yellow-light state of nervousness is that we lose interest in everything. The world becomes more dangerous, but also duller.

Happily, there's one thing that reliably holds our interest even when we're deep in anxiety. This question can virtually always be an effective first step away from wretched deprivation curiosity and toward delicious interest curiosity. We always genuinely want to know: "How can I feel better?" Maybe you picked up this book hoping to answer that question. Let's capitalize on your curiosity by helping you get investigative about your own anxious state.

In keeping with our murder-show obsession, I like to frame this as a mystery story: "My joy is missing. I fear it may be dead. How can I find it?" This mystery plays out within the community of parts that make up your psyche. The "person" who has abducted your joy is often a manager or a firefighter and, even more often, a conspiracy between two of these polarized parts. The joy itself is what your exiles provide when they're released from their imprisonment and integrated, allowing the manager/firefighter parts to finally relax. And the genius detective who can solve the case? That would be your Self.

As you'll recall, curiosity is one of the eight "Cs" that Richard Schwartz uses to describe this Self (along with calmness, clarity, confidence, courage, compassion, connectedness, and creativity). This makes the Self an excellent detective, but compared with what you've seen on TV, this inspector is extremely kind. Its goal is not to put dysfunctional parts in prison but to get them out—to bring the exiles, managers, and firefighters into a state of calm, harmonious liberty. So right now, let's start following the clues.

When I use this exercise, based on a method that spiritual teacher Byron Katie calls "The Work," I always find that my anxious parts are: (1) doing their best, (2) inadvertently lying (because of what they've been told and what they've been through), and (3) very relieved to stop.

New Skill

HIRE THE KIND DETECTIVE

You can use your detective skills whenever you feel any kind of suffering or encounter any part of your life where you can't make things work. There may be places of great suffering, where you've truly abandoned or betrayed yourself, or just a small "disturbance of the peace" inside your mind.

Choose such a minor disturbance and write it down below. For example, "I'm so worried about money," or "I'm afraid Jessie is mad at me." We will call this place of worry or confusion "the crime scene" (any part of your life that's not at peace).

Just like Sherlock Holmes, the Kind Detective is highly observant, only its favorite saying is not "Elementary" but

"Hmm." You've seen enough TV (or read enough whodunits) to know that the detective must go to the crime scene, then observe everything and everyone around with close attention.

Right now, look closely at the part of you that's not feeling peaceful. Locate it in your body. Describe the way it feels. Write your observations here:

_____

_____

Once you locate it and listen for what it's saying, you'll probably hear it repeating disturbing thoughts, like **I'm not doing enough!** or **I'm not good enough!** or **There's not enough stuff for me!** Write down what your peace disturber is saying:

_____

_____

_____

_____

Listen compassionately to the part that's suffering. Then ask it some questions—the ones you'll find below. You don't have to be cruel to this disturbed part of yourself—the

Kind Detective never plays bad cop—but you do need to interrogate its claims. You have two tools for this: physical evidence and your nervous system's built-in lie detector. The first of these requires you to track your internal physical sensations. The second requires paying attention to the facts of your actual situation. Follow the directions below.

STEP ONE: QUESTION THE PEACE DISTURBER AND THE WITNESSES

Take one of the peace disturber's statements (e.g., **There's not enough stuff for me!**). Write it here, briefly:

_____

_____

As the impartial Kind Detective, see whether the peace disturber's statement is literally, physically true in your actual situation at this very moment.

After compassionately acknowledging any pain you're feeling, see if you can answer the following questions:

Is there any evidence whatsoever that the peace-disturbing statement could be untrue?

There may be only a tiny bit of evidence invalidating its claim, but a good detective will acknowledge that.

Example: "Is it literally true that there's not enough stuff for me? Hmm. Well, there's enough oxygen for me right now. And a safe place to sit down. And plenty of gravity. And I have clothes—not the clothes I wish I had but enough clothes for this very moment. And the love of a good parakeet."

_____

_____

_____

_____

Are there <u>multiple</u> reasons to believe that the peace-disturbing statement might not be true? How many can I find?

Once you start turning up evidence that runs counter to your disturbing beliefs, the right side of your brain will begin to make connections, revealing all sorts of evidence the peace disturber couldn't see. This may be a sign that you're passing through the doorway of curiosity, away from anxiety.

Example: "Actually, there are **lots** of birds who come when I feed them, not just my parakeet. There's so much birdsong! For that matter, so many songs, period. And jokes, and thoughts, and ideas—there's enough of all those for me."

_____

_____

_____

_____

The objective here is not to shame you for feeling bad but to show your nervous system a more balanced, realistic picture of your life. This kind of curious questioning can also move you into gratitude, the emotion that psychologists have found is most closely linked to happiness.

Time for the final logical question:

Could the extreme opposite of your peace-disturbing statement be true?

There may be several "opposite" thoughts (e.g., **There** is **enough stuff for me** and **There's not enough me for stuff**). Even odd-sounding opposites are worth a look. This step may not yield any convincing answers, but it might. See how creative you can get. Let your Kind Detective really work this one.

Example: "Could it be true that there's actually **too much** good stuff for me? Well, my hall closet is jammed with things I never even use. And I suppose the universe holds a lot of good things, more than I could ever need or use. Even this planet might offer me that. Or maybe I could create so many beautiful moments, or so much love, or so many interesting things to learn, that there would be more than I could ever take in."

_____

_____

_____

_____

STEP TWO: GIVE YOUR PEACE DISTURBER A LIE DETECTOR TEST

Your nervous system doesn't like to lie. When you say something that isn't true for you at the deepest level—even if your mind thinks it's true—your body reacts by getting weaker. If you're very attentive (and the Kind Detective is incredibly attentive), you'll feel a slight anxiety response whenever you say or think something untrue: rapid heartbeat, dry mouth, sweaty palms, tension in your muscles. You'll also feel negative mood states: increased anxiety, sadness, dejection, even hopelessness.

Taken together, all of these reactions indicate that the statement you're holding

in your mind is not true. Yes, the thought is unpleasant. But the reaction to a true statement is a clear impulse to act, like healthy fear. A whole-body tense-up is actually your system rejecting a lie. So, on with the polygraph:

Take your peace-disturbing statement (**There's not enough stuff for me!** or whatever else is bothering you) and write it down here:

_____

_____

Holding this statement in mind, check your lie detector. Observe these factors:

How does my body feel when I think this thought?

_____

_____

_____

How does my physical energy level change when I believe this statement?

_____

_____

_____

How old do I feel when I believe the statement? (It once may have been true, but it may not be true in the present.)

_____

_____

_____

How do I act toward myself and others when I believe this statement?

_____

_____

_____

Once it has finished its investigation, the Kind Detective deals with your inner peace disturbers by understanding them, thanking them, and gently asking what it can do to help them relax. It gives them lots of KIST (see chapter 2) and SPACE (see chapter 3). It makes an imaginary bed of soft, pure compassion and lets the peace disturbers lie down to nap and heal. Then it gives your whole system some self-care in the physical world. Like watching a murder show.

USING CURIOSITY TO LIGHTEN UP IN TOUGH TIMES

The kindness we show ourselves internally can give us a place to stand when we deal with others. It allows us enough calm to bring in one of the right hemisphere's most delightful capacities: humor.

Here's another exercise, one that can help you rev up interest curiosity about other people even when they're not people you enjoy. Because this new skill can be invaluable for handling predictably horrible social situations, I've taught it to many clients as they prepared for dreaded dysfunctional-family holidays or office meetings. I even showcased it once on **Good Morning America.** Try it if you're planning to go among people who are truly poisonous to your system.

New Skill

TOXIC SOCIAL GROUP BINGO

- Make a bingo card, a five-by-five matrix of empty squares. If you like, you can fill in the diagonal lines with the letters that spell out BINGO, like this:

B			O
	I	G	
		N	
	I	G	
B			O

- In each blank square, write down something awful or irritating that always seems to happen when your family (or work group or poker club) gathers (e.g., "Sally insults someone," "Jeff makes a homophobic comment," etc.).

- Have one or more of your friends make their own cards with their own awful expected events in their bingo squares. Each of you will take your card to the feared destination.

- When an event shown on the card actually happens, you get to mark off that square.

- The first one to get a bingo texts the others, wins the game, and later gets a free lunch.

My clients who play this game often have totally new experiences in dreaded, tediously familiar situations. When Grandma rears up to criticize someone, or Pat throws a bowl of popcorn at the televised football referee, or Alice punches a hole through the drywall, the bingo players no longer wince and clench their teeth. They lean forward, cards at the ready, thinking, **Go on! Oh,** please **go on!**

HOW ANXIETY CAN RUIN YOUR LIFE—AND CURIOSITY CAN SAVE IT

Your anxiety may try to scare you away from the exercises above, telling you they're just silly. Or it may insist that treating yourself compassionately is selfish and that dropping your anxiety in a tense social situation is dangerous. Remember, one of anxiety's most convincing stories is that **staying scared keeps us safe.** It takes only a bit of curious exploration to reveal just how wrong that is. Anxiety can destroy our whole lives, and if enough of us let anxiety take over, it may end up destroying the world.

As we've seen, a brain stuck in the anxiety spiral, like a person with right-hemisphere damage, may look straight at something and remain completely unaware of it. Hemispatial neglect, the left hemisphere's weird inability to acknowledge the reality of anything it isn't currently thinking, rears its weirdly haploid head whenever we spin off into anxiety. Again, unlike the sharp, useful focus we get from real fear, the attention blindness of anxiety, known as "inattentional blindness," can lead to devastating errors.

For example, a parent frantically trying to figure out a mistake on a credit statement might not remember that they have a toddler, let alone that this toddler has opened the front door and wandered into the great outdoors. A surgeon brooding about an insult from a colleague may lose focus and nick a vital nerve or artery. An air traffic controller, mentally replaying a doomsday prediction from a charismatic talking head, simply may not hear information coming through their headset, and unwittingly create disaster.

Because anxiety shuts down all curiosity about other people, it's also toxic to relationships. It not only makes us judge each other harshly one-on-one but also feeds into sweeping judgments about people or groups of people. Anxiety reinforces prejudice and makes us suspect evil motives behind the most innocent actions. It can lead us to embody the very attitudes we **don't** want to see in the world.

Research on diversity and equity shows that anxiety increases our tendency to "other" people who don't look, talk, or dress like us. Responding to unfamiliarity with fear, we create anxiety spirals that narrow our minds until virtually no one fits into our zone of acceptance. We also adopt any implicit biases that reflect our culture's overall discrimination against these "others," even if we truly value justice and equity.

If you feel like checking on your own hidden biases, click over to the Implicit Association Test, or IAT, and take the free exam (https://implicit .harvard.edu/implicit/takeatest.html). Bestselling author Malcolm Gladwell took it four times and kept getting the result that when it came to race, he had "a moderate automatic preference for whites," even though his mother is Black. Anxiety can literally turn us against the people we love—and even against ourselves—because of its drive toward social prejudice. In other words, when we hold unconscious biases that start with anxiety and are culturally reinforced, we don't just put ourselves in more danger. **We become dangerous.**

The cure for all of this is not more anxiety but more interest-based curiosity. In her powerful debut book, **See No Stranger,** lawyer and activist Valarie Kaur writes:

In brain-imaging studies, when people are shown a picture of a person of a different race . . . it is possible for them to dampen their unconscious fear response. . . . In these studies, **it was as**

simple as wondering what they like to eat for dinner [emphasis added]. Only then does fear dissipate.

The key word in Kaur's statement is **wondering**—in other words, getting curious. The only way we ever get used to something unfamiliar is by asking about it, exploring it, seeing it from different angles. And when the "unfamiliar thing" is a person, getting curious about that person's experience cuts through anxiety and leads to connection.

Interest curiosity, the ability to tune into the present moment and see the truth like a Kind Detective, the ability to laugh at frustration or annoyance, the physical sensations that let us feel the difference between an anxious thought and a true one—they all rely on the brain's right hemisphere. Wondering is among the right brain's favorite states of being, as are perceiving the present moment and noticing things about other people's outer and inner lives. When we were very young, wondering was one of our predominant pastimes, practically our lifestyle. Once we learn how to calm our anxiety creatures and begin moving our attention into the curiosity of our right hemispheres, we can get that childlike wonder back. For keeps.

THE CURIOUS LIFE

Once you begin turning on your interest curiosity, opening the secret doorway between worry and wonder over and over, you'll find that the door starts to work more smoothly. The hinges will creak less. The opening will feel larger. The neural pathways that abandon anxiety to go exploring will grow more abundant. Instead of living in anxiety and then digging around for curiosity, you may notice pulses of inquisitiveness popping up on their own, often displacing anxiety. Then curiosity may begin to **eclipse** anxiety entirely. You may start feeling younger as you return to the state of wonderment that fueled play and investigation during your childhood.

All of this leads to a different way of engaging with the world. When our curiosity is restored to its rightful place, we stop rhetorically wondering **Why is this** happening **to me?** and begin thinking like detectives: **Hmm. Why** is **this happening to me?** We aren't just defeating anxiety; we're making meaning out of all our experiences, even the painful ones. The beautiful minds of all great thinkers are so curious that they fix upon bewildering problems almost to entertain themselves.

This way of living turns anxiety into a catalyst for creativity. It repurposes the energy we've spent worrying, pouring it into inquiry and discovery. As the Irish poet and novelist James Stephens wrote,

"Curiosity will conquer fear even more than bravery will." Accessing curiosity takes us further than calm. It takes us into the courageous territory of the creativity spiral. At this point, we're on the verge of finding the solutions to all our problems. We're ready to imagine the most wonderful lives we can create, and to create the most wonderful lives we can imagine.

7

Making Your Sanity
Quilt of a Life

Frieda is one of the most anxious people I've ever coached, and boy oh boy, does she have her reasons! For Frieda, just breathing is a high-risk gamble. Allergies and chemical sensitivities mean that at any moment, she might have a fatal asthma attack. Her survival rests in the hands—er, paws—of her service dog, Griffin, a border collie who's been trained to sniff out any chemical that could trigger Frieda's asthma. If he smells danger, Griffin will alert Frieda or, in a pinch, even physically drag her away from the offending substance.

Frieda is participating in a three-day workshop where my fellow coach Boyd Varty and I are teaching around one hundred people. For the first two days, I don't even know Griffin is there. He sits so still that he blends right into the furniture. On day three of the seminar, Frieda raises her hand to ask a question, and we invite her to join us onstage for a little real-time coaching. Only then do I see the furry companion padding silently next to her.

Once onstage, Frieda sits down in the chair opposite mine, trembling visibly. Griffin is as calm as his human is anxious. He settles beside her like the Sphinx, perfectly balanced, absolutely motionless. I tell her I've never seen such a disciplined dog. Frieda pets Griffin's ears (he doesn't move) and says, "Yes, we only have one problem. He can't resist squirrels. He's always looking for them. If I let him, he'd chase them for hours."

Small talk over, we get to work dealing with Frieda's chronic fear. She is well and truly stuck in an anxiety spiral. Even though Griffin reliably keeps her away from problems, Frieda lives in constant terror, silently chanting the thought **Danger is everywhere!** and visualizing her own death. We try calling up her Kind Detective, which finds that the thought isn't **always** literally true; she's usually fine, and Griffin alerts her whenever she comes close to danger. When we look at how the thought affects Frieda, she says it's basically ruining her life.

Though she understands all this intellectually, the anxiety spiral has wedged Frieda into the terrible thought "Danger is everywhere" so completely that she can't even imagine any alternative ideas. Boyd and I gently prod her to consider opposite thoughts, like "Safety is everywhere." She can see the logic, but not feel it. All our word play hasn't even touched the sides of her anxiety.

In fact, as we talk, Frieda becomes more and more anxious, fidgeting, her voice gaining pitch and shrillness. I watch Griffin watch Frieda. He leans slightly toward her, clearly aware that her anxiety has risen, but he still seems completely calm. I ask Frieda to notice how peaceful he is, hoping she can use him to "co-regulate." We talk about the fact that Griffin can't scare himself with stories about things that aren't present. If and when he senses danger, he'll act. In the meantime, he just rests here, emanating peace, serene as a Buddha.

"You know," Frieda says, looking down at Griffin, "sometimes when he chases squirrels, I get this weird feeling that he thinks it's a part of his job. He looks at me like he's trying to show me something."

This piques my curiosity (key word), so I ask her to say more.

"It's like . . ." She gazes down at Griffin, stroking his motionless head. After a long moment, she slumps in her chair and says, "I don't know."

She seems to be in a full red-light flop response, so I decide to pitch in some energy by offering a guess. "What if Griffin is trying to show you," I say, "that even though there's danger everywhere, there are also squirrels everywhere? You know, fun. Play. Joy. Silliness. What if he's trying to get you to shift your attention to **your** squirrels?"

Frieda cocks her head a little, thinking about

this. "Well," she says slowly, "I guess . . . that . . . could be . . ." Her voice trails off. Then, for the first time in our conversation, she breaks into a genuine smile. "Yeah, that actually could be." She lets out a small chuckle.

And, suddenly, Griffin the dog completely loses his religion.

First he sits bolt upright and whips his head around to stare into Frieda's face. As her chuckle turns into a laugh, Griffin goes wild with delight, leaping into her lap, wagging his whole body, licking her face. Then he jumps into **my** lap and licks **my** face. Then he jumps into **Boyd's** lap. He covers us all with silky fur, doggy kisses, and pure joy.

I'm not exaggerating. If you were in that room, you'd swear Griffin were trying to tell his beloved human, **YES! YES! THAT'S IT! YOU GOT IT! YOU FINALLY GOT IT!**

Frieda says he's never broken protocol so dramatically.

I like to think he's dragging her away from something dangerous.

In this chapter, we'll talk about **your** "squirrels," whatever they may be. We'll see how by letting yourself be your Self, filled with calm and curiosity, you naturally connect with everything that nourishes your body, mind, heart, and soul. This is how creativity spirals work: once we've activated our curious right hemispheres, they go to work learning more about the topics that interest us most and finding innovative, unexpected ways to link them. The whole process pulls us further and further beyond anxiety into curiosity, where our right hemispheres will begin making new connections, coming up with unprecedented ideas, and heading deeper and deeper into fascination.

SQUIRREL INTERESTS

In the previous chapter, we talked about how you can rev up your interest-based curiosity by focusing on certain subjects. But within interest curiosity, we find a lot of variety. There are some topics that merely intrigue us and some that (once we're free from anxiety) **endlessly** fascinate us, as ever fresh and compelling to us as squirrels are to Griffin. The more we learn about these topics, the more we want to keep learning.

Some curiosity is brief and easily quenched. For example, if I run into a perplexing clue in a crossword puzzle, just figuring out the word fully satisfies my curiosity. That's not a squirrel-level passion. On the other hand, I've probably spent whole calendar years scrutinizing drawings and paintings, watched hundreds of online art demonstrations, and put in tens of thousands of hours experimenting with different techniques and media on my own. But I'm more curious about the visual arts now than I've ever been. That's how squirrel-level interests affect us. To quote from **Alice in Wonderland,** they make us "curiouser and curiouser."

If we follow anything that interests us far enough, we begin to encounter moments that fill us with awe, that give our whole existence more meaning. For example, Ram Dass, a spiritual teacher who started his career as a Harvard psychologist named Richard Alpert, used to give radical speeches about two of his favorite topics: yoga and psychedelics. One day, he spotted an elderly lady in his audience. She looked like just the kind of person who usually found Ram Dass appalling. Feeling a bit defiant, he gave a particularly outrageous speech about "experiences that I had had after using psychedelic chemicals, experiences that were very precious and far out." After the speech, the woman approached him. As Ram Dass put it:

> [S]he came up and she said, "Thank you so much. That makes perfect sense. That's just the way I understand the universe to be." And I said, "How do you know? I mean, what have you done in your life that has brought you into those kinds of experiences?" She leaned forward very conspiratorially and she said, "I crochet."

Now, a lot of people crochet. But this woman **crocheted.** For her, the art of the hook wasn't just making doilies; it was a true squirrel. I like to think that since crocheting requires the use of both hands, plus the ability to visualize beauty while also thinking in precise quantitative terms, it fired up this woman's entire brain to such a red-hot level that she made the same kinds of connections Ram Dass did through LSD.

My point here is that any interest might turn out to be a true squirrel passion if we follow it far enough. Climbing onto any creativity spiral that truly interests us can not only move us further and further away from anxiety but also deliver powerful, illuminating experiences that expand our ability to feel things like beauty and awe. But in our culture, these experiences tend to be tamped down. We don't follow our creativity as far as it can go, so we're surprised when a simple creative pastime like crocheting delivers the same powerful insights as a psychedelic drug trip.

Squirrel Passions Aren't Addictions

I think the limited permission we give ourselves to spend time following our passions actually leads some people to develop an internal hunger they try to satisfy with not only psychedelics, which typically aren't addictive, but also chemicals that are.

When I coached active heroin addicts, they told me they'd found their passion in life, and it was heroin. In fact, many of them said they had no other interests **at all.** I could tell that they believed this. But this obsession, though similar in some ways to the effects of a creative brain state, wasn't taking them toward peace, the way a real squirrel interest does. Addicts often told me that when they weren't high, they suffered from crippling anxiety, which they could only dull with heroin. In the process, they were losing things they valued: relationships, jobs, their own ethics.

Our firefighter parts may throw fake "passions" at us this way. They may discover that drugs or gambling or dangerous sex can blot out our anxieties for a while, and they mistake this for joy. But the effect of addiction is short-term pleasure followed by an intense sense of loss and need, accompanied by an onrush of horribly high anxiety. When we're addicted and can't **immediately** get that drug, or that rush, or that person's love, we panic.

Real interests have the opposite effect. The creativity spiral moves us steadily away from anxiety. Connecting with any genuine passion, we explore and learn, becoming more able to regulate our nervous systems into the green-light zone, where we stay for longer periods. Engaging with a true squirrel interest doesn't create growing dependence and anxiety. Instead, it powers a gradual increase in all of the Self's qualities: calmness, clarity, confidence, curiosity, courage, compassion, connectedness, and creativity.

IDENTIFYING OUR SQUIRRELS

Many people who come to me for help feel like service dogs in a world devoid of squirrels. They can't find their passions and often don't believe they have any. This used to seem strange to me, because passions, by definition, should be very noticeable. They are to my ADHD brain, at least (I once literally noticed a squirrel outside my window and left a business meeting to follow it). But as the folks who mapped my brain told me, neurotypical brains choose "appropriate" social behavior over interest curiosity. And, of course, many of us are stuck in anxiety spirals, which effectively lock us away from any trace of passion. We truly can't see what interests us—even though repressed, exiled parts of us still hold that knowledge in the secret corners of our psyches.

I've worked with hundreds of people who spend years slogging away at various chores, school assignments, and jobs that fill the time and pay the rent but never let them leave anxiety or experience their true passions. They've often spent most of their lives in a yellow- or red-light nervous system setting. From there, everything seems dangerous or depleting. They've felt anxious or flat for so long that they can't even remember true fascination.

Another myth that often plagues such people is the belief that finding a true passion happens in a blazing explosion of clarity and certainty, an unmistakable vision of one's whole future. That's simply not true. As I've coached hundreds of people, I've seen that finding our passions starts with a faint sensation of interest, then a slight willingness to investigate what interests us, then more curiosity, which motivates more investigation, which can ultimately grow into a lifetime's worth of purpose.

I believe we're meant to experiment the way we did when we were babies, dropping activities that no longer interest us and locking our attention on things that do. I've seen folks follow this steadily increasing creative cycle to careers, places, ideas, and relationships. Every once in a while, they may experience a big breakthrough (we'll talk about that in the next chapter), but each burst of insight is embedded in thousands of hours of growing curiosity.

Here's a sort of remedial exercise you can use to reconnect with your own passions—your own delicious squirrels—even if you think they don't exist. Start this exercise by calming your anxiety creature using the skills you've already learned from this book or any others that work. Then get something to write with and follow the steps below.

New Skill

NOTICE WHAT PUSHES AND WHAT PULLS YOU

This exercise will ask you to remember part of your education. If you grew up attending school, I'd like you to use that experience as the raw material for the exercise. If you never went to school, remember how you learned skills at home or in any job you may have had.

1. **Recall an anti-squirrel.**
   Think back on something you learned at school (or somewhere similar) that you didn't enjoy learning about. It might be a subject like math or social studies, or a dull textbook you were assigned to read, or lectures from a teacher with the power to put a turnip to sleep. Name this dull topic, book, or teacher here:

   _____

   Now remember the **feeling in your body** when you interacted with this person or subject. In particular, **notice what happened with your eyes**. Did you want to look at this person or thing, or did you want to look away? Play your memories like very short videos, and notice:

- how you felt when you saw it was time to learn more about the boring thing

  _____

- how it felt to enter the room where you encountered the boring thing

  _____

- how it felt when you forced yourself to pay attention to the boring thing

  _____

2. **Recall a squirrel, even a very vague or small one.**
   Think of something that you **did** enjoy learning about around the same time in your life: a subject, a sport, a song in choir. It may be your first love, about whom you wanted to know everything, or a car you longed to own when you grew up. Write your squirrel interest here:

   _____

Again, notice the **feeling in your body**, especially your eyes, as you remember:

- how you felt when you saw it was time to learn more about the squirrel interest

  _____

- how it felt to enter the room where you encountered your squirrel interest

  _____

- how it felt when you paid full attention to your squirrel interest

  _____

3. **Try switching back and forth between your anti-squirrel and your squirrel.**

   Notice that paying attention to something unappealing feels like a **push**, like walking uphill against a strong headwind. Going toward something that interests you, that piques your curiosity, feels more like being **pulled** forward, walking downhill with the wind at your back. Get familiar with how each sensation feels to you.

4. **As you go through a typical day, notice what feels like a "push" and what "pulls" you.**

   The next time you're driving to work, scrolling through social media, or mingling with a group of people, notice when something makes you want to lean in, look more closely, and learn more. Also take note when you want to look away and do something—anything—else. As you notice what you're feeling, just think, **That's a push** or **That's a pull.**

This little exercise can give you steadier access to your specific curiosities. You won't always be able to skip all your "push" activities, like answering emails, making dental appointments, balancing your checkbook, attending boring meetings, and endlessly soothing a sick baby. You may not decide to follow every squirrelly thing that "pulls" your interest, like jazz dancing, archery, stand-up comedy, or the art of spycraft. But you'll find that literally everything has a slight charge of either curiosity or aversion. You may not even know why something feels one way or the other. But like a good service dog, you'll begin to discern between what's toxic and what's part of your creative self.

WHEN CURIOSITY HAS BEEN CRUSHED

When I began coaching, I wasn't sure what to do for people who found the whole world uninteresting and showed no creative inclinations whatsoever. I'd go through lists of possible activities, asking what "pulled" and "pushed" them, trying to heave or drag them into the knowledge of what they wanted most.

It never really took.

Then I worked with a client who trained service dogs (like Griffin) for people with disabilities. One day, she mentioned that if a working dog doesn't get enough time to sleep and play, that dog will become joyless and burned out, just like an overtaxed human.

Damn, I thought to myself, **I've been serving the system!** My incurious clients weren't just devoid of imagination. They were **tired.**

Our left hemisphere–dominated society is so focused on economic productivity and keeping all the rules that it tends to leave rest and sleep out of the equation of a happy life. According to the Centers for Disease Control and Prevention (CDC), about a third of Americans don't get enough sleep. That single factor can kill our curiosity, ruin our health, get us into accidents, and lead to anger, despair, and, of course, anxiety.

If you feel no curiosity about anything, odds are you're simply exhausted. Here's a quick test to gauge if this is the case, which is so simple I won't even give it special formatting: Imagine that your fairy godmother suddenly pops through the wall and says, "Starting now, your whole life is going to be put on pause for a month. For that entire period, you must sleep as long as you can and spend the rest of your time just relaxing in a soothing environment."

Feel your internal reaction to this idea. What

happens to your body, heart, and mind? If a month of absolutely no activity sounds delicious, you're probably too tired to be creative right now. There have been many, many times in my life when just the thought of rest could make me burst into tears of longing (sleep deprivation makes this a likely reaction to absolutely anything, including brushing your teeth, but that just serves my point). On the other hand, if my fairy godmother had said this to me during my Art Toad weeks, I would have thrown a shoe at her and run away fast. A month of lounging when I could be painting? No freaking way.

It's true that when we live according to our passions, we may need less sleep, and that work and rest may come to feel like the same thing. But if you're **longing** for a month of empty time and rejuvenation, adding a bunch of creative activities is not a wise next step. The good news is it won't take you a whole month of absolute rest to restore your creative self. It will take about four nights of good sleep, four days when you're not pushed past your limits.

I don't know why four days is the magic charm that restores curiosity, but I've found this to be true for myself and my clients. Four days and nights of rest won't totally recharge your creative batteries, but it will get you above the "empty" line, with a bit of energy to go on. If you're serious about living free from anxiety and you're too tired to identify any interests, find a way—any way at all—to get four days of relative rest. Enact emergency measures. If you have insomnia, go to your doctor and get medical help. Take a sick leave from work. Do whatever will allow you to minimize your childcare responsibilities. Aside from oxygen and water, sleep should be your absolute highest priority.

Once you're rested, your brain will start looking for squirrels—and oh, it will find them. I've seen this happen over and over. Your childhood curiosity never dies; it just goes into suspended animation when rest is the greater need. As your "rest" meter rises above the "empty" line—not all the way to full, just above empty—your curiosity will begin pulling you toward your passions.

SEDUCED BY CURIOSITY

Living in the age of the internet allows us to dive right into rabbit holes that weren't available even a generation ago (caveat: some of these rabbit holes can get crazy, so don't believe everything you read). Learning more about a person, sport, science, or machine, you'll think, **Oh, wow, that's cool.** As you continue to investigate, the intensity will increase: **Oh, wow, that is** so **cool!** You'll feel motivated to spend even more time thinking, talking, and learning about it. At some point, you may go to the next level and develop a sense of longing: **I wish I could**

do that. Then the wish may become an intention: **I'm going to figure out how to do that!**

This is the point at which you may actually begin experimenting with the activities that fascinate you. After weeks of scouring the web to find videos of a certain comedian, you may start writing your own jokes and trying them out on your family. Or you may see a falling star, hear it's called a meteorite, start learning what that is, and then borrow your grandma's metal detector to start prospecting for interplanetary rocks. The topic could literally be anything. The point is that it's so cool you want to participate in it.

Here's a final point that will identify an activity as a necessary ingredient for your best life: when you focus on it, **you aren't aware of time.** In fact, you lose awareness of everything except what you're doing in that moment, which often means your thoughts won't flow out in language. Your attention will be dominated by your nonverbal, atemporal right hemisphere. This is the state that psychologist Mihaly Csikszentmihalyi famously labeled "flow," the maximum sense of joy and passionate involvement in life. I believe it's the way we are all meant to feel most of the time.

Just to help you remember, here are four spontaneous exclamations, sparked by snowballing creativity, that will take you from a boring, anxious life into your true passions:

- "Oh, wow, that's cool."

- "Oh, wow, that is **so** cool!"

- "I wish I could do that."

- "I'm going to figure out how to do that!"

Once you've found something that draws you seductively along this chain of interest, you're ready to start collecting things that remind you of it. These are glimmers that can pull you back into fascination whenever you need to feel inspired. I call them your "ragbag of curiosities."

YOUR RAGBAG OF CURIOSITIES

A literal ragbag is a sack of fabric scraps. When I was growing up as a good Utah girl, dressing in long skirts and sunbonnets to celebrate Pioneer Day and gathering windfall fruit to be canned for the winter, every woman I knew had a ragbag. When someone wore out the knees of their pants from hardcore praying or set fire to a floor-length gingham skirt while high on cough syrup, their mother cut out any usable fabric that remained and put it in the ragbag.

I like the idea of making a ragbag to gather our passions, because it's simple and slapdash, not lofty and impressive. Trying to be lofty and impressive is like aiming a gun at your curiosity—it will not work. It'll just scare you into anxiety.

Your "ragbag" might be any container, digital or three dimensional, where you collect cool things. Some ragbags, for example, might include lists of interesting internet links, a corkboard where you can pin up images of things that fascinate you, or a box where you can stash objects you've made and found.

New Skill

MAKE YOUR RAGBAG OF CURIOSITIES

- As you go about your daily life, set an intention to notice anything that makes you think, **Oh, wow, that's cool** or **Oh, wow, that is so cool!** or **I wish I could do that!**

- When you encounter such a thing, find or make something to remind you of it: a phrase, a photo, a recording, a computer link. These are your scraps of interest.

- Put all your scraps of interest in one place, physically or digitally.

The first, best reason for making a ragbag is simply to enjoy it. As a very small child, I would sometimes go through my mother's ragbag just to see pretty fabrics. The activity of perceiving these colorful scraps was enjoyable in itself—one mark of an activity that's truly part of our life's purpose. Once you get a ragbag going, take a few minutes every day to glance through it for sheer enjoyment. Eventually, you'll use your collections to start creating a new life, but right now, just enjoy them because they please your mind and senses.

My ragbag exists mainly in digital space, though I do have a largish stash of art supplies and a small one of sports equipment. Here are some things I have in my computer ragbag, just to give you an example:

- Photos of the cool people in my life doing their cool things: writing, teaching, performing service to the world.

- Videos of extreme skiers hurtling down near-vertical slopes.

- A folder containing the paintings of Hokusai.

- Videos of people doing Broadway dance routines, jumping on trampolines, and arriving at airports wearing **Tyrannosaurus rex** costumes.

- Many quotations from Taoist and Zen philosophy, written in the enchanting calligraphy of Chinese and Japanese artists.

- A Kindle and audiobook library that contains more volumes than I could possibly fit in my house. These are divided into categories, including but not limited to biology, psychology, animal tracking, physics, wilderness exploration, antiracism, anthropology, brain science, spirituality, ecology, and, of course, murder.

- An app that is boldly attempting to teach me Spanish.

- Many images of animals looking silly, with captions I added myself. I get the captions from online affirmation generators. (For example, one image shows an otter stealing an ice cream sandwich, with the caption "All my dreams are coming true in this moment.")

As I write this, I can feel the tide of squirrel-chasing joy rising up inside me, just from thinking about my ragbag. And it doesn't seem odd to me that I'm equally passionate about studying Asian philosophy and attaching New Age affirmations to silly animal photos. There is no ranking in my right hemisphere, no judgment based on financial productivity or efficient use of time. There is only curiosity, connection, wonder, and delight. This enjoyment is the primary goal of having a ragbag.

There is a secondary goal, however, and I hope to help you achieve it. That goal is to begin **making your**

life out of things from your ragbag of curiosities—all the coolest things that pull you into their orbit. At first, these things may seem to have no connection to something as lofty as your life's purpose. But as you play in curiosity, your right hemisphere will begin making connections you never dreamed possible.

For example, as a boy, Apple cofounder Steve Jobs found himself fascinated by the design of a certain food processor and also, on a different occasion, by the way a newborn calf could just get up and walk around. Surely these odd interests couldn't serve a person's life purpose, right? Wrong. The food processor gave Jobs the basic shape of what we now call a personal computer, and seeing the newborn calf made him commit to making machines that would come right out of the box fully functional, ready to use.

Again, finding and fulfilling your life purpose isn't something that happens in a single aha moment; it's a gradual process of combining things that genuinely light up your creator self. It's a bit like making a quilt from the bright scraps of fascination you've collected. The "quilt frame" in this metaphor is time—a day, a year, your whole lifespan. Filling it with an original patchwork of cool things is the way your creator self constructs the life you were meant to live.

SOCIETY'S QUILT PATTERNS

Though I've never made a quilt, I spent many childhood hours playing under stretched rectangles of
fabric, surrounded by the knees, calves, and sensible shoes of Mormon ladies as they stitched away. I
know that some quilts are meticulously planned to
fit patterns established centuries ago, patterns with
wonderful names like Lone Star, Jacob's Ladder,
Cathedral Window, and Bear Paw. The fabrics for
these quilts are purchased with the pattern in mind,
carefully laid out, assembled into pieces called
"blocks," and then sewn together with constant ad-
justment to keep the geometry perfect.

This is the way we're socialized to create our lives.
The process sounds simple: just stitch together activities seen as important, practical, and lucrative. We
can choose from several familiar patterns: Business
Tycoon, whose time is filled with making deals
and smoking fat cigars; Glamorous Influencer, who
spends every moment just staying beautiful and being
admired; or Perfect Parent, a pattern sewn from ten
thousand hours of prepping organic meals, keeping a
spotless house, and offering nonstop loving attention
to a child's every mood.

Growing up, most of us assume we'll replicate the
patterns we see on display all around us. Or maybe
we get a little wild and decide to combine patterns—
for example, create a patchwork from Successful

Entrepreneur and Perfect Parent. It all sounds like a wonderful idea until we grow up and start trying to make our lives fit the patterns of these expectations. Then we hit a number of snags.

Sometimes it turns out that the patterns we've chosen are so unattractive to our creator selves that just collecting the materials for them requires heavy "pushes," with no delicious, seductive "pulls." We drag ourselves through years of schooling toward professions that aren't inherently interesting to us. Then we try to make a life out of these materials, only to find that the quilts we've stitched feel stiff, grating, and unbearable. This is true even for people we see as madly successful. I've had many celebrity clients whose lives scratched at them like sandpaper, even as millions of people envied and admired them.

Making our lives out of fabric we don't like to match patterns we didn't choose is anathema to our creative selves. It's not just unfulfilling; it's actively depressing. It drives us out of the creativity spiral and into anxiety spirals. What we do manage to piece together is a quilt that looks bad, feels bad, and doesn't keep us warm.

This became crystal clear to me when I tried to combine the quilt patterns that make up Harvard Academic and Mormon Mother. The harder I worked to make a life following these patterns, the more the whole thing fell apart in my hands. I got physically ill and extraordinarily anxious making "quilt blocks" that didn't appeal to me on their own—and when

I tried to conjoin them, they actively repelled one another. My time was filled with a mismatched jumble of keeping house, working, finishing graduate school, and caring for three children under four—all of it stitched together with a ragged thread of sleep deprivation.

At some point, I realized that I was failing, every single day, to make a single quilt block that lived up to society's standards. There was simply no way to make my life look the way I'd been taught to think it should. In desperation, I decided to throw out all the patterns and make something my pioneer ancestors would have called a "crazy quilt." Except that once I got into the process, I realized I wasn't going crazy; it was making me happier and more balanced. I was making a **sanity** quilt. It worked better than I ever dreamed. I think it will work for you, too.

A DIFFERENT APPROACH TO QUILTING

Going against the careful, preplanned approach to quilting, some folks who have accumulated rag-bags full of pretty scraps decide to make up completely original patterns. There are no layouts in this method, no traditional patterns, no predetermined models. These quilters just sew together whatever pleases their eyes and hands, creating a design no one has ever imagined before. It's a very right-hemisphere way to sew. And in keeping with the left hemisphere's dismissal of right-hemisphere methods, people call the resulting masterpieces "crazy quilts."

The process of making a crazy quilt begins when quilters choose a piece of fabric they particularly love, one they want near the center of their finished product. Then they find another piece that seems to go with the first and sew them together. Then they add another piece, and another, working around the center, building outward in a rough circle—a literal creativity spiral. There's a lot of experimentation, eyeballing, and rearranging. Eventually, they have a patchwork big enough for the quilt they want to make. Then they trim and finish the edges.

Watching videos in which quilters teach this method fills my Art Toad heart with joy. They use phrases like "Just see what pleases your eye," "Let the shapes sort of flow," "If you don't like something, don't be afraid to rip it apart," "Spend a lot of time rearranging," "Wonky is good," "Hack at it wherever you need to," "You can always change it up," and "Be really forgiving of everything you do."

These are the words of people who, at least for the moment, have left anxiety behind, adopted an attitude of kindness toward themselves, and become fully engaged in the "connections" phase of the creativity spiral. They may still have anxious moments, but not while they're making these quilts (and video tutorials). They seem to be enjoying the process in exactly the same way that Frieda's service dog, Griffin, enjoys a good squirrel hunt.

Your left hemisphere may find this distasteful. "No wonder they call it 'crazy quilting,'" your order-loving self may think. "How insane to just take what appeals to you and sew it together!"

Or not.

I propose that most of the life patterns favored by our culture are the real "crazy quilts," the conglomerations of unappealing tasks that can trash our minds and hearts. Taking fabric we don't like and stitching it into unappealing patterns, filling the whole framework of our time with materials that feel uncomfortable and clash with each other—that's insane. It's insane to live on little to no rest, love, or joyful communion. It's insane to do things, day after day, year after year, that don't light us up. It's insane to look away from our interest curiosity and focus on only what we're told is "optimal." It's insane to serve systems that exploit humans, other beings, the planet itself.

Here are some quilting scraps that are actually sane: Knowing our own hearts' desires. Caring for our own bodies the way we'd care for any other priceless creatures. Spending relaxed time with our loved ones. Seeing ourselves as the children of nature, not its overlords. Staying out of anxiety spirals that poison our joy and make us feel justified in attacking, exploiting, and killing one another.

Exploring everything that makes us say, "Oh, wow, that is **so** cool!"

So now that you've got your ragbag of curiosities, let's keep making connections. Let's begin the process of turning your life into a sanity quilt.

A SAMPLE SANITY QUILT

For a shining example of a completed sanity quilt— that is, a truly sane life—I refer you once again to Griffin the dog. The "quilt blocks" that make up Griffin's days, weeks, and years include the job he clearly loves, the human he adores, good food, lots of sleep, daily playtime, and SQUIRRELS! Many, many squirrels! Possibly rows of squirrel pelts sewn together, tails forming a fuzzy fringe around an entirely squirrel-based quilt!

Of course, I'm not recommending that you use literal animal fur to make your own sanity quilt. I just want for you what Griffin the dog has (and seems to want for Frieda): a life where **most** of your attention is spent spotting things that fascinate you, getting closer to them, and putting them together in patterns of your own devising.

If your life is very regimented, sanity quilting may just be a bright spot in your day, a time when you get to go off leash for a brief dash around the yard. Over time, as "quilting" becomes a normal part of your routine, you can add other pieces from your ragbag, spending a bit more time each day stitching activities you love into your schedule. Your sanity quilt will start as a centerpiece, but it may end up covering your whole life with beauty and warmth.

For example, Evelyn was a human resources manager with a devoted husband and two lovely daughters. Her life was perfect, if you didn't count her crushing depression and monstrous anxiety. During our first session, Evelyn stared off into space, showing little interest in anything . . . except when she mentioned taking her daughters to a dance recital. For a moment, I saw some light in her eyes—not when she talked about her daughters per se, but when she talked about the way they danced.

I asked Evelyn to say more about dancing. She sat up a little straighter, telling me that as a child, she'd been obsessed with dance, endlessly practicing moves alone in her bedroom. She'd watched every dance performance, dance movie, or dance-related TV show she could find.

I asked Evelyn to gather a ragbag of dance-related items: photos, videos, music. The next time we spoke, she confessed with a huge smile that she'd started dancing alone in her bedroom again. She sheepishly called it "a wasteful time suck." When I told her that I thought it might be the most important thing she'd done for a long time, she laughed at me but brightened even more.

Long story short: after a few weeks, Evelyn signed up for jazz-dance classes, which made her so much happier that her husband, curious and intrigued, eventually agreed to join her in a ballroom-dance class. This breathed new life into their marriage, and the whole family began to dance through processes like making dinner or tidying the house. The next year, Evelyn began teaching dance to children at the little studio where her daughters had started. But the fact that she eventually made a bit of money with her dancing isn't the point. The point is that her depression and anxiety lifted, and her delightfully dance-mad family became a joyfully bonded little tribe of shared curiosity, creativity, and self-expression.

CREATE YOUR SANITY QUILT

Whatever sort of sanity quilt you make from your own favorite pastimes, you won't so much learn to fabricate a creative life as you will **unlearn** how to **keep yourself** from doing it. Your right hemisphere is a natural, almost automatic sanity quilter. Free from anxiety, fired up by curiosity, it automatically collects and connects things into unlikely units, much as I have just combined the metaphor of squirrel chasing and the metaphor of quilting into a larger—and, I hope, visually arresting—mixed metaphor. The image of a squirrel-pelt quilt fringed with fuzzy tails may have never entered your mind before. But it's there now, and I'll wager it's there to stay. You're welcome.

While you may not want to try literal quilting, piecing together your authentic passions into a wild and beautiful life will light up your creative self. In fact, I believe the process of sanity quilting is the fundamental task we're on this earth to undertake. And if we're not enjoying the process of shaping our lives—or at least feeling deeply absorbed by it—we're not making sanity quilts. So here are some succinct instructions.

New Skill

WORK ON YOUR SANITY QUILT

- **Choose something from your ragbag of curiosities that consistently pulls at your attention.**

  This **does not** have to be anything that brings praise or money. It might be a photo, a plant, a piece of music, an online cooking tutorial. The only criteria are that it seems really cool and you really want to focus on it.

- **Carve out between ten and twenty minutes of your day to learn more about this item.**

You may just read about your interesting item, or you may begin making something inspired by it. Either way, do this for the fun of it. You can always "hack at it" if it doesn't harmonize with the rest of your life.

- **Learn to think of this as the center of your day.**
  Even if your activity seems strange, and even if it doesn't fit into your life as you know it, this is not an "extra." **This is the centerpiece of the life you are beginning to create.** It isn't less important than "normal" activities. If anything, it's more important.

- **Include this item in your schedule every day for at least a week. Then consider what other item from your ragbag of curiosities might go well with it.**
  Writing books is the centerpiece of a quilt I started around the age of twenty-five. I had almost no time to write—only about ten to thirty minutes a day—but I felt strongly "pulled" to do it. Then I met a couple of other would-be writers and formed a writing group that met monthly. Then I started reading a few pages from "how to get published" books several times a week. And here we are.

- **Gradually sew more interesting "rags" into a bigger and bigger quilt.**

   I'm still sewing my "writing" sanity quilt. I'm doing it at this very moment, digging into my ragbag for ideas that help or interest me, hacking and shaping each sentence as I go. It's extremely difficult. It's a blast. I have no idea what time it is.

   I've coached other people as they built their own sanity quilts around all sorts of activities: raising chickens, making variations on spaghetti sauce, photographing insects, carving soap, filing coupons, dowsing, whistling, and piling rocks into interesting cairns, to name a few. Your interests may seem quite normal or completely bizarre to the people around you. What matters is that they stimulate **your** curiosity and make **you** want to keep playing with them.

- **Don't be afraid to rip out pieces that aren't working, cut apart pieces that feel too big, and rearrange, rearrange, rearrange.**

   In a part of my life that grew out of writing—coaching—I teach life coaches to think like quilters, sewing bits of passion into their lives' work and helping others do the same. Ironically, many aspiring coaches try to fit this into a cultural "job" mold. They talk about networking, getting business cards, going to conventions, and so on. If socially "normal" things like this are squirrel-level interests for you, use them. But if not, just find some weird thing you love and see how you can fit it into your life.

- **Let it look strange.**
    Remember, if you follow your creative self instead of social norms far enough, you'll end up looking weird and feeling good. Focus on the "feeling good" side. If you worry about looking weird, go back and calm your anxiety creature. In fact . . .

- **Calm your anxiety creature as many times as necessary.**
    This entire process is countercultural, and you're very likely to garner stern warnings and intense criticism from your own left hemisphere and the people around you. You will need to calm your anxiety and sort through your priorities many, many times. It is this repetition (falling into anxiety spirals, calming our creature selves down, moving into curiosity and connection) that builds creative resilience. Repetition will make you think less and less about whether or not you are afraid.

THE WEALTH OF QUILTERS

I've seen hundreds of metaphorical sanity quilters find enormous satisfaction and fulfillment by stitching their lives out of things they loved. Some of those people ended up making a living in the process, and a few succeeded beyond their wildest dreams. For example:

- As a young adult who loved animals, Zoe stumbled into a career training dogs to help veterans with PTSD. She was so good at it that the military recruited her to use her methods professionally before she'd even finished school.

- Claire has always been passionate about learning and teaching. In her thirties, she started an NGO to help build learning centers in rural South Africa where anyone, of whatever age, could learn literacy, numeracy, and job skills. The first meeting consisted of three people sitting on wooden crates. The organization now assists thousands of children and adults, many of whom have gone from dismal to brilliant scores on standardized tests. Claire travels the world, hobnobbing with donors when she's not encouraging teachers and learners.

- Xander is a professional gamemaster, so brilliant at concocting fictional worlds and retaining information in his head that groups of gamers pay him to run their tabletop games online.

- Georgia decided to homeschool her own children and loved it so much that she started a business teaching other parents how to homeschool their kids.

- Nonnelg started writing a blog about finding her way through marriage, child-rearing, and recovery from addiction. Over time, she added things to this basic quilt piece: writing books that became bestsellers, running a philanthropic foundation that raised over $45 million for women and children in crisis, marrying a world-champion female soccer player, and starting a podcast that became number one on Apple Podcasts' "Best of 2021" list.

Okay, **Nonnelg** is **Glennon** spelled backward. I refer to Glennon Doyle, and if that name isn't familiar to you, wait an hour. I've let her identity out of the bag here because I'm pretty sure she won't mind being identified as a person who chases her most interesting squirrels, and who quilts her life from the center outward.

Now, I'm not saying you have to become a famous blogger to live your dreams. Most of the people I just mentioned aren't wealthy. All of them have lived through many, many moments where they felt overwhelmed and terrified, and all of them have faced criticism from loved ones and casual observers who told them they should settle down and focus on ordinary jobs.

The difference between these folks and people who never stitch together a whole sanity quilt is that they insisted on trusting their joy over the norms of WEIRD culture. They found so little joy in noncreative lives that they were burning out, like service dogs who never get to chase a single squirrel. Their creative activities served them the way dancing served Evelyn—the more they focused on their real interests, the more they felt their curiosity returning. This sent them exploring for connections and questing for new ways to make new things, services, events, adventures. What they made was so full of joyful creative energy that other people took notice. This led to friendships, travel, business ideas, and the formation of entire communities that shared their passions.

Ironically enough, money is often a kind side effect of releasing the left hemisphere's obsession with acquiring wealth and instead focusing on intense commitment to our deepest creative impulses. If my clients and friends had set out to make money through their creative passions, they might have slipped into the "grab more stuff" mindset that fuels anxiety spirals. They might have killed the joy they felt. But instead, all these people began sanity quilting as a kind of medicine, which they initially sampled in small doses, then gradually increased. They eventually made money from their passions precisely because they did everything for the passion, not the money.

At any rate, most people who stitch together sanity quilts don't end up sitting on huge piles of gold. But they have another kind of wealth: the joy of squirrel chasing and permission to spend their time doing things that nourish their hearts and souls. The left hemisphere doesn't see this as reason enough to bound off the beaten path, following whatever squirrels we long to chase. But the right hemisphere—that is, the whole brain working in balance—does. King Midas, for all his riches, starved to death alone. A sanity quilter gets to cuddle.

When you see people who've spent years stitching away at their sanity quilts, people who may have even become rich and famous in the process, you might think they've followed some formula for success, something you need to emulate. But they didn't start with grand achievements. They started by doing something, usually alone, that held their curiosity. You can't get the results you want by replicating the particular **patterns** of their lives, only the particular **method** they used to make their "quilts."

That method requires absolute authenticity. It starts with identifying your squirrels, the things that seduce you into fascination. It revs up when you gather these things into a ragbag of curiosities. It begins to shape your life when you put the things that fascinate you at the center of your daily attention. And it grows as you connect, connect, connect these things together—making lots of mistakes, eyeballing and rearranging, and cutting things up and putting them back together.

After years of this, you'll achieve high levels of excellence in whatever weird and unorthodox interests you add to your life. And you'll do this not for power, wealth, or status but for the joy of exploring the outer limits of your inventive capacities. Your creative self loves a challenge—a really original challenge, even a visionary one, the kind that's enormously difficult and incredibly satisfying. So wrap yourself in your squirrel-pelt quilt and come along. In the upcoming chapter, we're going to delve into the next stage of the creativity spiral: mastery.

8

Mastery: Freeing the Magician

In the summer of 1949, a veteran firefighter named Wag Dodge headed out with a team of fourteen smoke jumpers to fight one of the worst wildfires in Montana history. As they hiked down a rift called Mann Gulch, a gust of wind caused the blaze to accelerate abruptly. Dodge looked up to see the flames much too close, racing toward the firefighters at seven hundred feet per minute. He shouted to his men, who dropped their gear and began running. But not fast enough.

In one horrible instant, Dodge realized that no one could outpace that fire. In the next, he did something he'd never been trained to do—something **no one** had ever been trained to do. Dodge stopped running, lit a match, and set fire to the grass in a circle around him. He shouted to his men, telling them to gather around him, but in the confusion, they continued to run away. Dodge threw himself down in the smoldering circle of burnt grass, covered himself with a blanket, and waited for the fire to pass over him. The flames raged all around him, but the burnt circle gave them no fuel, acting as a firebreak around Dodge's body. Thirteen other firefighters died. Dodge survived, basically unharmed.

What happened to Wag Dodge on that awful day shows a certain aspect of creativity, one that can serve us not just when we set out to do something original but even in the direst circumstances. This aspect of our creative thinking marshals our right hemisphere's ability to associate everything we've ever learned with whatever is happening to us in the present and come up with completely new ideas.

I call this "freeing the magician." Not because I believe in a fairy-tale brand of magic but because, as Iain McGilchrist says, magic is what the left hemisphere calls anything it doesn't understand.

If you decide to build your life on creativity rather than on anxiety, you may become so focused on turning your life into a sanity quilt—that is, filling your time with things you love—that you find yourself pushing all known limits. The creativity spiral will have taken you as far as most people ever go, but you'll want to go even further. In classic heroic sagas from many cultures, this is the moment when magical helpers arrive. In your brain, it's when you awaken the deepest genius of your right hemisphere.

If you allow this, your brain can do things like what Wag Dodge's did during the Mann Gulch fire. Working outside his conscious thinking, Dodge's right hemisphere evaluated the situation, combined memories of many previous experiences, devised a solution, and pitched it into Dodge's awareness as a flash of inspiration. He knew that once an area has been burned, it offers no fuel for an advancing blaze, so the fire skips it. When Dodge's brain perceived the speed and direction of the fire, realizing that he couldn't outrun disaster, it brought up all Dodge's stored experience working with firebreaks. Dodge knew, with sudden and perfect clarity, that he had just enough time to create an emergency safe zone where he could survive.

Again, this is not something Dodge did on purpose—it happened faster than his cognitive mind could think. His brain did it for him through a sudden burst of insight that psychologists call "the Eureka effect." **Eureka,** the word for "I found it!" in Greek, is supposedly what the ancient mathematician Archimedes shouted when he took a break from trying to solve a logical problem and suddenly saw the solution as he climbed into the bathtub. In other words, this phenomenon has been happening in the minds of creative thinkers for thousands of years. And it can happen to you, on the regular, if you know how to invite it.

Once you've learned to calm your anxiety creature, access your curiosity, and connect with more and more of your creative interests, stitching together a sanity-quilt life, you'll begin to live in a slightly different mood state, a consistent attitude of exploration and invention that differs from the usual tense energy of our anxiety-motivated culture. When my clients begin going deeper into their passions, making original, sometimes startling connections, they experience increased freedom from anxiety while coming up with ideas and life plans that they never before imagined.

Being psychologically lost in anxiety, in a culture dominated by left-hemisphere thinking, may not seem as urgent as a forest fire, but I believe it is. Individually, we're each confronted by the crucial issue of finding meaning and joy in life. Collectively, we're facing problems that are coming at us the same way the fire raced toward Wag Dodge and his crew: dramatic changes in almost all industries, political upheaval and polarization, wholesale devastation of the very ecosystems that keep us alive. Fortunately, we all have the internal equipment needed to solve problems in the same amazing, unprecedented way that Dodge did in the Mann Gulch fire. But because of our world's emphasis on anxiety-driven, left-brain thinking, many of us have forgotten how to use it.

THE MAGICIAN IN YOUR MIND

When I tell you there's a genius hiding in your head, I'm not just flapping my gums; I have data to back me up. For example, back in the 1960s, officials at NASA commissioned a study to identify "creative geniuses," folks they hoped to recruit for various space-related hijinks.

Just like the spaghetti tower challenge, the NASA genius tests turned out to be a breeze . . . for three-to-five-year-olds. A whopping 98 percent of sixteen hundred individuals tested in this age group scored as creative geniuses. But five years later, that number had dropped to 32 percent in the same cohort of children. Five years after that, it was just 10 percent. And as the researchers George Land and Beth Jarman noted, when the same tests were given to two hundred thousand adults, a measly 2 percent showed up in the creative genius category. The researchers blamed a school system and social environment that actively teaches us **not** to be the geniuses nature intended.

You're probably like the vast majority of people in the NASA study: you started life as a perfectly normal creative genius and grew into a person abnormally unaware of your own brilliance. I noticed long ago that when I start talking about using creativity to shape our own lives, my anxious clients often panic.

"Oh no, not me!" they say. "I'm not creative! I don't have a creative bone in my body!" Sometimes they even say, "I'm stupid; I could never do anything like that." It breaks my heart to hear how truly, madly, deeply they believe this.

The good news is that your creative genius can't be destroyed, only sent into exile. The essential Self you identified in chapter 4 has access to all those bits of abandoned genius. Every idea and exercise in this book is meant to help you reconnect with them. Now we've come to the point where you can learn to crank up your right hemisphere, free yourself from entrenched limitations, and start making a normal amount of dazzling magic.

HOW TO WAKE UP YOUR GENIUS

First of all, let me point out that if you want to live well **without** creativity, the way most of us have been taught to live, you're going to need a ton of lucky breaks. For starters, I'd highly recommend that you be born into a wealthy family. Make sure you're a white, straight cis male with no neurodivergence, no emotional trauma, and the buff, fatless body of an underwear model. Remember to have powerful people provide you with lots of money, pull strings to smooth your way through the educational system, and set you up in a profitable career.

There! Doesn't that work well?

We're so used to accepting this model of "succeeding" that most of my clients, having not been born with mouthfuls of silver spoons, can only imagine building lives they want by winning the lottery. Others drop clichés like "Maybe a rich relative I don't know will leave me a fortune" or "A celebrity will become my friend and then everything will be wonderful." They're joking. Kind of. But the jokes aren't that funny, and the fact is, these people really haven't been taught any other ideas for crafting a happy life. Their creative-genius selves are totally exiled. They live in the high anxiety of depending on factors outside their control to give them what they want.

If you aren't one of the privileged few, life may feel grinding, unfair, and incredibly hard. But you also have the motivation to approach success in a way that doesn't rely on a social pyramid of power; instead, it calls up your creative genius. To do that, you need four things: (1) circumstances that require you to grapple with difficult problems, (2) interest-based curiosity that prompts you to gather knowledge and experience, (3) a dollop of courage, and (4) an apparent impasse.

These are the conditions that trigger the Eureka effect. We can see them all in Wag Dodge's response to the Mann Gulch fire. Dodge had plenty of interest in fire: he'd spent years fighting it, studying it, and talking and thinking about it. He had the courage to enter a situation where his knowledge and experience would be tested. Then, when the fire blew up, Dodge found himself at an apparent impasse. He couldn't escape physically because the fire was closing in too fast. And he couldn't escape **psychologically** because he was the crew chief—there was no one else to look to or depend on. The buck stopped with him.

Ironically, it takes this kind of extreme situation for many of us to let our creative geniuses out of their cages. In the moment before he came up with the solution, Dodge probably experienced a moment of pure fear—not **anxiety** but the powerful call to action that arises in truly dangerous situations. At such moments, our verbal minds may go quiet and clear. Into the space that opens up when verbal thought shuts down, the right hemisphere can deliver an idea. This doesn't always happen, but when it does, it can change the way we approach a certain problem forever.

Dodge's men, perhaps not realizing how fast the fire was moving, couldn't understand what he was doing or what he was asking them to do. But faced with an impossible situation, the right hemisphere of Dodge's brain combined everything it knew with everything it could observe and flashed a solution into his consciousness. **Shazam!**

THE POWER OF IMPASSES

Approaching problems in this way is the opposite of an anxiety-based way of life. In fact, once I really understood that difficulties and impasses are necessary components our brains use to make creative leaps forward, I stopped feeling so anxious about all my problems. I even became less anxious about the problem of anxiety itself. I saw that it's only at the outer boundaries of our knowledge and resources that we genuinely need pure inventiveness rather than some other form of intelligence—due process, for example, or rationality, or even emotional sensitivity. To activate our inner magicians, we have to be highly motivated and completely stumped.

This is why creativity often emerges from people, or whole populations, who are in difficult situations. I have a friend I'll call Joe who works as a problem-solver for corporations. Joe has to be ingenious, because his cerebral palsy forces him to "think laterally" just to navigate a typical day. When doctors told Joe they could implant a device in his brain to lessen the effects of CP, he declined. He told me that having to deal with his differently abled body all day, every day, was what kept his genius sharp.

This is why creativity may surge in people— sometimes whole populations—who've lived in appalling circumstances. I'm not in any way suggesting that these folks were fortunate to be so unfortunate. But it's amazing to contemplate, for example, how the ancient Chinese, who lived in a huge floodplain and were devastated by flooding for centuries, invented an irrigation system so sophisticated it made them a world power—and is still in use today. Or the way the residents of central Turkey, plagued by war, figured out how to house twenty thousand people in a huge, eighteen-level underground city. (The array of ventilation shafts alone was an example of pure genius.)

Sometimes the most artistic kinds of creativity arise to help people in the worst pragmatic circumstances. Resmaa Menakem, a somatic therapist, remembered how his grandmother, her hands scarred from picking cotton, used to hum all day—not just a pleasant lilt but a powerful thrum that vibrated her whole body. Menakem said, "I don't think my people would have survived 250 years of legal rape—rape done for pleasure, rape done for profit, rape done to sell my ancestors and their children—if it wasn't for the humming and the rocking and the swaying and the vibratory glances across the land. That's an art form."

Art and problem-solving are linked in this way: to address the most basic practical problems, the human mind may reach for high levels of creative invention. The tougher the problem, the more ingenuity the right brain may call up to craft a solution. In my own life and the lives of my clients, I've noticed that cognitive leaps forward often occur during times of maximum difficulty:

- My friend Eva, a massage therapist, lost all her business at the beginning of the COVID-19 pandemic. She turned on a dime, learned to sew, and began making and selling very cool face masks to support herself and her young daughter.

- When my client Shane lost all his money to a pickpocket during a trip to Europe, he sat down on the street with his trusty guitar and busked his way into enough cash for food and a tiny room.

- When my cousin Lydia was a young working mom, she woke one winter morning to find the door of her car frozen shut. She stuffed newspaper into the crack between the door and the car frame, set fire to it, and got to work on time.

The point is that when we set out to build individual lives based on creativity rather than anxiety, **the problems we face help stimulate the creative process.** That's wonderful news, because though we may run out of many resources, our supply of problems never goes dry. If your life is problem-free, turn your creative attention to all those collective problems: war, injustice, and the threat of global ecological collapse. Pick a problem and wake up your inner magician. We need it.

COURTING THE
EUREKA EFFECT

In school, you were carefully taught to repress your creative genius by working through every subject in a logical, linear way. Whether you were doing math or writing an essay, you had to follow consistent procedures, and they had to be the same procedures used by everyone else. That's how the left hemisphere likes to approach any problem: describe the situation using language and numbers, consult experts who will tell you how this problem should be solved, and follow established protocol precisely. Whether the job is mixing chemicals, managing workers, or raising children, this is how the left hemisphere prefers to go forward. In fact, it believes that there is no other way. It would be **shocked** to hear that you've found another way.

Here's another way.

This approach to creative problem-solving doesn't directly apply known concepts and protocols. Instead, it creates the conditions that are most likely to wake up the sleeping magician in your right hemisphere. The magician will then solve problems **for** you in ways that will leave your left hemisphere agape in disbelief. I'll break down the process here, then spend the rest of this chapter helping you implement it. You've read about the initial steps already:

1. Calm yourself.

2. Wander around.

3. Catch fire.

4. Practice deeply.

5. Get stuck.

6. Trust.

Let's see how you can take all of these steps as you construct your most beautiful, practical, and magical sanity-quilt life.

STEP ONE: Calm Yourself

Part 1 of this book is meant to help you go from anxious to reasonably calm. I'm mentioning it again right now, repeating once more what I've been repeating ad nauseam, because **repetition is how you rewire your brain to get calm and stay that way.**

Calming your anxiety creature is like washing your hands: it doesn't take long once you know how, it should be repeated many times a day, and it's crucial if you want to avoid getting infected by the anxiety epidemic raging through our society. When our brains become entwined in the fearful stories and control efforts of the anxiety spiral, our creative geniuses are forced into deep cover. When we calm every aspect of ourselves, all our anxious creatures, we keep our left-hemisphere logic but combine it with the right hemisphere's insight.

When life gets difficult, choose your favorite calming exercises and use them, use them, use them. Just as fortune favors the prepared mind, creative magic favors the calm brain.

STEP TWO: Wander Around

Wandering and wondering are two things you did as a creative-genius child that you may rarely engage in as an adult. This is the ragbag-collecting mode we saw in chapter 7. Here I want to emphasize the power of **wandering** in stimulating your inner genius. If you have the mobility, nothing beats physical movement through new surroundings as a way to gear up your creative imagination.

If you love going to altogether new places, where you don't speak the language or know the customs, travel can fire up true kid-in-a-candy-store fascination, pulling your attention to things the local people don't really notice. If you can't travel abroad, try wandering daily for at least ten or twenty minutes. Pick a place that's easy to reach—a city street near your home, a museum, a bookstore, a farmers market—and ramble through it with no other goal than to notice what you notice. Allow yourself to be pulled toward whatever catches your attention. Investigate it. Listen, peer, sniff, and poke (if that's allowed).

If you can't walk or drive, you may still be able to wander. During the years I spent on crutches, when I was forced to slow down, I noticed things I'd never seen as I strode past them with two good legs. I also discovered how much strangers actively wanted to help me. (That, in itself, was a mind-blowing exploration.) And as a last resort, wandering through the internet—so long as you go to unfamiliar places and learn new things—is a way the brain can wander while the body sits still.

However you can manage it, wandering leads to wondering, and it deserves a place in your schedule. Never think that indulging your inner five-year-old's love of an aimless romp is a waste of time. In fact, it's one of the best ways you can go about solving your most urgent problems.

STEP THREE: Let Your Mind Catch Fire

In his book **The Talent Code,** Daniel Coyle uses the word **ignition** to refer to the moment we witness something that grabs our curiosity **intensely** and pulls us into deep exploration.

Ignition is what happened to Josh Waitzkin (the real-life chess champion featured in the movie **Searching for Bobby Fischer**) when he was six years old and saw chess hustlers playing in a park. By age sixteen, Waitzkin was an international chess grand master. But the story didn't end there. As a young adult, he had another "ignition" response to a Chinese martial art called tuishou (push hands), a popular sport in Taiwan. After years of training, Waitzkin reigned as middleweight champion in the Tai Chi Chuan Push Hands National Championships for five years straight. Genius can take you in all kinds of unexpected directions.

When a number of people get "ignited" at the same time, a wave of genius can surge through a population. Often, this wave becomes visible a few years later, after ignited viewers have had time to practice whatever skills they've seen. Coyle mentions the many top-notch Russian female tennis players who came on the scene several years after Anna Kournikova's semifinal match at Wimbledon. A similar batch of brilliant female golfers came out of Korea after twenty-year-old Pak Si-re won the McDonald's LPGA Championship.

If you want to actually **see** cohorts of geniuses rising in the wake of ignition events, binge-watch some televised competitions that require strength or skill. Try **American Ninja Warrior,** in which people of all shapes, sizes, and genders try to beat the same diabolically difficult obstacle courses. Or watch **So You Think You Can Dance,** where participants learn and perform a mind-blowing number of complicated routines in virtually no time. If you prefer cooking, go for **The Great British Bake Off** (known in the US as **The Great British Baking Show**), where strong men weep with shame over their soggy bottoms (again, please google it).

About five years after each of these shows debuted, the quality of the entrants abruptly skyrocketed. **American Ninja Warrior** once booked "walk-ons" in fanciful costumes who reliably face-planted right out of the gate. But after a few years, the show had to increase the difficulty of its obstacles, as viewers who'd watched early seasons began to display the agility of caffeine-crazed chipmunks. The dancers in later seasons of **So You Think You Can Dance** made the first crop of geniuses look like they needed walkers. And where a nice opera cake could once earn its maker the title of "Star Baker" on **The Great British Bake Off,** winning that honor in later seasons required feats like building a working combustion engine out of puff pastry.

In all these cases, a certain number of viewers were ignited by what they saw on the screen; they then set to work climbing and dancing and baking as if their (sanity-quilt) lives depended on it. These people were on fire. They had something psychologists call "the rage to master," an almost obsessive drive to learn certain skills. With a few years of practice, they were performing at levels inconceivable to those who went before. They also got wildly creative, making up new moves, new obstacles, new recipes.

And they practiced. Boy howdy, did they ever practice!

STEP FOUR: Practice Deeply

My martial arts teacher used to say, "Practice doesn't make perfect. Practice makes permanent." For this reason, he had his students perform every new move **very slowly but with perfect form** a thousand times. Then we'd move on to the next thousand repetitions, during which we were supposed to pick up speed. Finally, we'd do the move a thousand times using perfect form with as much speed as we could manage, and maximum force.

Coyle uses the term "deep practice" to describe this picky, relentless pursuit of mastery; other researchers have used "dedicated practice" to mean the same thing. Evidence shows that practicing this way—pushing hard for a lofty goal, as opposed to just routinely repeating exercises—shifts the brain toward mastery at supersonic speeds. Just six minutes of deep practice adds as much facility as a month of ordinary practice.

K. Anders Ericsson, the psychologist who came up with the idea that it takes ten thousand hours of work to become a master at any skill, discovered that this kind of practice works even better when it takes the form of something he called "dedicated play." Ericsson found that we learn best not when we're just doing drills but when we're really trying to **play** an instrument, **play** a sport, **play** chess, or do whatever (this process can happen in any activity that requires skill development). This means that even if the process is hard, it's also fun.

Having fun while satisfying the rage to master requires a delicate balance: striving for perfection but being very kind to ourselves—indulging in some KIST—if and when we don't reach it. According to a 2023 study, we feel maximum fun when we've been doing something creative for a long time, then **give up control** of the process. If you drive a car, you've probably experienced this. At first, it was hard and even frightening, but once you'd done it enough to stop thinking through every move, your driving became a kind of body memory that allowed you to stop focusing with your cognitive mind. That's how dedicated **practice** turns into dedicated **play.**

According to research from child psychologist Karyn Purvis, it takes approximately four hundred repetitions to create a new synapse in the brain with the sort of ordinary, grueling practice you were probably taught to do in school. But if learning takes place during play, it takes only ten to twenty repetitions.

Though "dedicated play" learning is rapid, there's nothing lazy about it. Unlike eating bonbons by the pool, this way of learning can be difficult and frustrating—even though it's also intensely rewarding. Dedicated play is probably necessary to reach mastery level at pretty much anything. I also believe it's the best way to wire our brains for creativity rather than anxiety.

To gain skills and open up access to the genius in your brain, start by finding some skill or activity that interests you so much you want to master it (this is slightly different from the intriguing things you put in your ragbag; it's a very targeted desire to achieve mastery). Next, strike the flame of ignition by watching examples of people who do this thing extremely well. Then take your absolute best shot at **replicating the highest level of performance you've ever seen.**

Spoiler alert: you will fail.

Then, instead of throwing in the towel, calm yourself. Apply KIST. Notice what you **did** do right and where you've improved, even just a little. Call upon your courage and curiosity as you acknowledge that you didn't achieve the perfection you were after, then figure out why. Ask yourself things like: **Why didn't it work the way I intended? What was missing? Where did I go wrong? What could I do better?**

Dedicated play goes against many of our cultural assumptions about creativity. For example, our left-hemisphere bias, which pushes us so hard when we're doing regimented, routine tasks, often equates creativity with a kind of ungoverned spontaneity that requires no effort or discipline. I know teachers of art or creative writing who encourage students to just let the paint or the words flow, without having an intended outcome or trying to do it "well." Of course this approach to creative projects is valid and useful—for example, the expressive writing I suggested in chapter 4 is a wonderful way to articulate feelings and understand ourselves. But when we set out to master something, "just do whatever" isn't a satisfying goal. It doesn't wake up the magicians in our brains.

When I was a child, possessed by the rage to master, I didn't just want to slap down some finger paint, as joyous as that can be. I wanted to draw the way my favorite artists drew. One of my clearest childhood memories is of sitting on the floor in waterproof potty-training pants, trying and failing, trying and failing, trying and failing to draw the human nose from the front. After days of effort, I came up with a sort of lame U shape. I remember weeping with frustration as I was forced to acknowledge it was the best I could do.

Ten years later, just starting to use charcoal, I was playing—deeply—by drawing a copy of the Madonna's face in Leonardo da Vinci's painting **The Virgin of the Rocks.** Having logged an estimated twenty thousand hours of drawing practice by then, I pulled off a pretty close likeness. Of course, my sketch was just a copy, not my own invention. But as I looked at what I'd just made, I burst into tears again. I had finally drawn a nose I could actually accept!

But the experience meant more to me than just that. When I looked at the beautiful face in da Vinci's work, I saw love itself. Being able to reproduce it meant that if I tried and tried, I might one day be able to put on paper what I felt in my heart. My Art Toad self, always on fire with the longing to express, felt a wash of incredible relief.

Four years later, I started my first college drawing class. It thrilled me when the teacher, the aforementioned Will Reimann, asked all of us students to draw straight lines and perfect circles. Not kinda-sorta straight lines and kinda-sorta round circles but **really** straight lines and **really** round circles. Draw the best circles we could, he said, and then check: Is that circle **actually round**? Does it have lumps, dents, bumps? Try again. See if you can eliminate the bumps and dents. Check again. Try again. Check again. And so on.

I was in hog heaven. I knew I'd found a great teacher, and I knew he'd push me to learn things I'd been yearning to master. That class freed my mind to approach **everything** as dedicated play, and I loved it. So I felt a bit shocked when, years later, I asked participants in a creativity seminar to do this exercise and was met with panicked resistance. Many participants began to grumble uneasily. One woman—I swear to God, I am not exaggerating—stood up and shouted, "I didn't come here for this kind of bullshit! I came to hear you praise me for everything I do!" (I refunded her money, sent her on her way, and chalked it up to my own "dedicated practice" in the art of running seminars.)

I believe that praising people for whatever they've made is a good idea when we're using creative activities to pass the time or heal emotional wounds. But just scribbling—or puffing into a bleating saxophone, or pounding randomly on computer keys, or writing down numbers that don't tell any sort of story— doesn't demand that we enter the creativity spiral. It isn't satisfying in the same way as mastery. And it most definitely doesn't keep us out of anxiety. In fact, it may make our anxiety worse.

In 2007, Stanford psychologist Carol Dweck reported that when children were praised for being gifted, smart, or talented, they got anxious. They sought tasks that would "prove" their brilliance and avoided tasks that wouldn't. Other students believed in developing skills, not just being talented. According to Dweck, they "underst[ood] that even Einstein and Mozart had to put in years of effort to become who they were." When these students took on challenges, they kept trying, failing, and trying again to come closer to the skill levels they wanted. They accessed the rage to master, then poured their energy into dedicated play—not into anxiously ensuring they wouldn't fall off their pedestals.

Praise yourself and others to the skies, but let that praise be for dedicated practice and deep play. Want to try it right now? Let's replicate that assignment from my favorite college course. Even if you don't aspire to be an artist, this will open your brain's connection to your creative genius. As art teacher Betty Edwards says in her classic original guide, **Drawing on the Right Side of the Brain:**

> Drawing . . . can provide a twofold advantage. First, by gaining access to the part of your mind that works in a style conducive to creative, intuitive thought, you will learn a fundamental skill of the visual arts: how to put down on paper what you see in front of your eyes. Second, you will enhance your ability to think more creatively in other areas of your life.

Whether you're trying to learn party planning, rocket science, parenting, or any other complex skill, your inner magician will use any dedicated practice you undertake to enhance your creative genius in all areas. Let's do it.

New Skill

A BIT OF DEDICATED PLAY

---

1. Draw a square and a circle freehand on the page below or on a different sheet of paper.

2. Notice where the square isn't exactly square and the circle isn't exactly round. Check it against a straight edge or a circular object.

3. Try again—freehand, please—and see if you can make your next square and circle more perfectly square and round. Make bigger squares and circles. Make them **perfect**.

4. If you can easily make perfect squares and circles of any size, draw a self-portrait. Not from a photograph but from a mirror. Be sure to get the nose right!

5. Continue to push yourself toward drawing something difficult and making it perfect until you start to feel so frustrated that you want to give up.

6. Try again after you've had some sleep. Your brain will have spent the night making new neural connections. You may notice a jump in your skill and comfort levels.

7. Try something even harder. Always work until you reach an **impasse**, the final necessity for awakening your creative genius.

A Perfect Circle	A Perfect Square

STEP FIVE: Get Stuck

An impasse is the feeling we get when we reach the limits of our ability in any endeavor. It's not the end of all options, but it's the end of all **apparent** options. This is the point where our brains' creativity spirals may come up with ideas we've never had before.

Most of us let our anxiety pull us back from the hard places where we're not highly skilled or sure how to go on. We learn basic skills for editing an online video but balk when the program we're using asks us to master a difficult technique by reading instructions or watching a tutorial. We write up our memoirs as a gift to our posterity but panic when someone suggests getting an editor to read through the draft and suggest improvements. We memorize three songs on the piano and play them reasonably well but decide that learning to read music, amazing as that would be, is simply beyond our capacities.

The moment we flinch like this, cringing away from a creative challenge, our lives start to shrink. But if we stay in the creative game, trying all sorts of possible solutions, messing up and trying again and messing up again (but messing up better), we can trigger leaps of insight and discovery in the mysterious depths of our right hemispheres. Hitting an impasse leads to a sensation I call "brain blisters," a raw feeling in our heads accompanied by emotional frustration. This isn't a signal that we should stop. It's a sign that we're awakening our creative genius.

This is what Zen students are doing as they sit with a confounding koan like "What is the sound of one hand clapping?" They stare at a blank wall, focused on the koan, not even thinking, waiting for the leap of insight that opens up a whole new way to see the universe. It's what Albert Einstein did in his spare time at the patent office, constantly pushing his mind to grasp strange truths, like his realization that time passes more slowly with increased physical velocity. It's what violin prodigy Min Kym did as she pushed herself to make incredible music and found that she, too, had to utilize relativity: at one point, Kym learned that since she couldn't possibly move her fingers fast enough to play certain passages, she needed to stretch time by slowing her mind. "[I]f you can see past time, let time elongate," Kym later wrote, "then you can play it all."

I would not have thought of that.

These wild leaps of genius are the perceptions we gain when new connections happen in our heads, joining neurons that were once far apart. Your right brain is actually a paler shade of gray than its left-side twin, because it contains much longer neurons, which are heavily fortified with a white substance called myelin (just as we use rubber or plastic to wrap electric wires, the body uses myelin to contain the electricity in a neuron). When we challenge our minds and bodies to go beyond our ability level, the brain begins joining these long nerves, connecting more and more bits of knowledge together in a process called "far transfer."

The ability to apply learning in one area to a completely different enterprise means that **everything we've ever experienced is material for our creative-genius minds.** That's why learning to draw a perfect circle really can help you be a better accountant, or songwriter, or deep-sea diver. When Josh Waitzkin became a martial arts champion, he made "far transfers" from chess that helped him strategize and think several steps ahead. Then he moved into investing, where he now applies skills from both chess and push hands to make a lot of money.

I've watched people make all sorts of far transfers, first inside their heads, then in their outward lives. Caroline used the skills she'd gained as a competitive skier to build a wildly successful consulting company. "To ski well," she said, "you have to throw your body down the fall line, which is the last thing your body wants to do. But taking that 'risk' is exactly what brings your skis under you and keeps you safe. Consulting is similar: I go directly to the issues my clients **least** want to hear. But as they 'lean into' these issues, they find out that carefully planned risk is the way to success—and it's exhilarating."

Bailey started college as an aspiring poet, then got ignited by science and brought to the study of botany the same precision he'd used in writing sonnets. Ezra worked for years as a computer programmer before writing and publishing a novel about a young hacker solving crimes. Olivia is a physician who makes a significant second income through creating and selling pottery.

It doesn't have to be art that awakens your magician, but any art you love offers an ideal place to start building superhighways in your right hemisphere. Will Reimann is a genius at helping people do this, very consciously forcing students into situations where they need the right brain's far transfers to gain new skills.

By the time I arrived at Will's studio and began

trying to draw straighter lines and rounder circles, I'd been deep-playing with pencils for years. Pencils allow for lots of sweet tricks: soft shading, lines that vary in thickness or trail off to nothing, high contrast between faint marks and bold ones. I relished all these techniques. I was using them one afternoon, sketching away in the studio, when an object landed on my sketchbook. It was a drafting pen—an instrument that makes a totally black line of unvarying width. Startled, I looked up to see Will grinning at me. "From now on," he said, nodding at the drafting pen, "use that."

OH MY GOD, how I hated that pen! You've got to understand, I had to draw. Had to. At the time, it was my only way of quieting my thermonuclear anxiety. But the drafting pen stole all my favorite techniques. No delicate shading. No varying line width. No faint sketches. I fought the pen all day and dreamed fitfully about it all night. I made many, many bad drawings. I got well and truly stuck.

Then one day, doodling to calm myself in another class, I noticed an interesting texture I'd accidentally created by building up differently shaped marks. A light flickered on in my brain.

Huh, I thought, squinting at it. **Well, yeah. That works.**

From that moment, I started using drafting pens in a new way. My methods came from my own brain and dedicated play, not from any example of pen-and-ink technique I'd ever seen. I sketched with dots and imaginary vectors and shaded with all kinds of differently shaped lines. Later, when I crossed off an item on my bucket list by winning a juried art show, I did it with that pen.

One day, after the pen and I had become besties, I once again traipsed over to the empty studio for some drawing practice. As I dotted and crosshatched away, something else landed on my sketchbook. A watercolor brush. I looked up to see Will sporting his best fiendish grin.

"Welcome to hell," he said.

I cursed him bitterly, and we both laughed. He was pushing me toward a whole new set of impasses. By aiming me straight at what he knew I couldn't do, he was teaching me how to draw, how to be creative, how to call up flashes of magic in my own mind. He was teaching me how to live.

STEP SIX: Trust

You can't kill your creative genius, but you can block it by anxiously trying to control the process of problem-solving. That's what you've been taught to do your whole life. Of course, I understand that if you're trying to achieve something difficult and you hit an impasse, you're almost certainly going to feel anxious. At this point, **you must climb off the anxiety spiral.** You may not be able to eliminate every pulse of anxiety in your brain. But you can end the spiral there if you use your creature-calming skills and then **stop trying to control the results.**

One way to do this is to let your mind go blank, the way Zen meditators stop thought, or the way Wag Dodge's brain might have gone blank when he saw the fire coming so close, so fast. A more reliable and enjoyable method is to use what I call "the Monty Python approach." **Monty Python's Flying Circus,** a comedy sketch show, was famous for linking skits with the elegant segue "And now for something completely different!" Push yourself to the impasse and then do something completely different. Go Rollerblading, work on a jigsaw puzzle, or train your hermit crab to know its name. Let your right hemisphere work.

I don't remember when I started using this approach, but I do remember noticing that when I'd drop a gnarly problem to do something completely different, I'd suddenly see a solution. I thought of it as my brain laying an egg. If you feel intimidated by working deep magic in the depths of your unconscious mind, imagine that your creative genius is a chicken. It drops ideas the way a hen lays eggs—plop!—and you don't have to know exactly how or why. This process is magical, but it's also humble and practical. Take it out for a spin with the following exercise.

New Skill

TRUST THE CHICKEN

---

1. Use the following process the next time you find yourself stuck in a problem: a disagreement with a loved one, a logistical conundrum, a tight deadline. Or, if you want to learn this process here and now (which will make you better at solving the problems that arise in the future), think of a small but persistent problem you'd like to solve, like how to stop losing socks every time you do the laundry or how to be charming at a party. Or, as a third option, you can try solving one or more of the problems I've listed below.

   - **How can I assemble a cool new outfit using only the clothes I've already got and whatever else is available in my home right now?**

   - **How can I make one dollar [or yen, or peso, etc.] from a completely new source today or tomorrow?**

   - **What game can I create for one or more children that will educate them, enthrall** them, and get them off my case for one damn hour?

- What meal can I make for my family or friends that's nutritious, delicious, and five dollars or less?

- What can I post on social media about a frustrating thing that's happened to me today, in a way that will make my friends laugh?

- What songs can I put on a playlist that will make someone I love feel [name your emotion: wistful, energized, inspired, angry, lovestruck, nostalgic, etc.]?

2. Think about your chosen problem until you run out of ideas. Then write a short request to your inner magical chicken. The request should go something like this:
   Dear Magical Chicken, I need new ideas to solve [write your problem here]. Please get to work developing one, and then deliver it to my brain. Sincerely, Me

3. Go do something completely different. Carry your phone or a notebook around with you to jot down notes if an idea/egg plops into your mind.

4. Continue doing completely different things until an idea arrives.

A MAGICAL LIFE

It's wonderful to watch people who felt lifeless and uninspired reawaken their creative genius. I've been privileged to witness this many times. I've seen that going around with your inner magician wide awake fills life with light, heat, and energy.

Once you learn to ride this part of the creativity spiral, you'll see many things that spark your interest. Some sparks will flare into a true rage to master. The dedicated play you do will then rewire the electrical circuits in your brain, combining flashes of connection and understanding from every part of your experience. And when you think you're stumped, sudden insight will blaze up in your mind, teaching you truths you've never known before—truths **no one** may have ever known before.

Compared with this, an anxiety-driven life looks so **boring.** Once you've lived as a creative magician for a while, you may start to see going back to anxiety as a choice. More and more, you'll feel able to simply refuse to enter the paralyzing, shrinking spiral of anxiety. You'll know that instead, you can deliberately turn toward curiosity and spiral up and out to new experiences and horizons. Creative genius is incredibly hard—and completely normal. It's the way you were designed to think and to live. It will take you right into fire, then deliver you to safety with flashes of inspiration. It may motivate you to find some way you can stay off the anxiety spiral forever.

And that's when the real fun begins.

Part Three

THE CREATION

9

Breaking Your Role Rules, Minding Your Mission

In the early 2020s, with Black Lives Matter and other social justice movements picking up steam, I went looking for someone to serve as diversity officer for the little company I run online. Since my work (coaching and training coaches) directly concerns helping people think differently, I wanted the values of equity, diversity, and inclusion (EDI) to permeate everything we did. My colleagues and I searched long and hard for the right person. Eventually, I found myself in a Zoom meeting with the three other people who make up my company's leadership team and an EDI consultant named Yvonne Jackson.

By this time, we'd all seen how the internet heightens all kinds of social tension. Online arguments can start with a few anxious people taking verbal stabs at each other, then almost instantly balloon into vicious fights that tear apart friendships and families. And that's when the topic is, say, how to groom a poodle. When it comes to discussing issues around violation, oppression, and murder, it's hard to see how anyone can even walk onto the field without taking a lethal amount of flak. We asked Yvonne how she might handle these unnerving situations, and how she could teach us to deal with them wisely.

"Well, what scares you most?" Yvonne asked me.

"I guess that I might make a mistake," I said. "I might do something wrong."

"Might?" Yvonne said, raising her eyebrows. "Oh, there is no 'might.' You're **going** to make mistakes. **Thousands** of them. And you're going to deal with people who are mad at you. I mean it. **Mad. At. You.** No way around it."

She beamed at us from her computer screen, and weirdly, I felt a bubble of happiness. This bubble didn't seem to come from Yvonne's résumé, though that was very impressive. It came from her sheer presence. She radiated calm, confidence, and compassion.

"And . . . you find this . . . enjoyable?" I asked, squinting one eye.

Yvonne laughed for a long time. "**Enjoyable** is a strong word," she said. "Enjoyable, no. But joyful, yes. Because I think joy is what you feel when you're 'on mission.' And if I'm not on mission, if I'm not in my joy, I won't last long. I think the same goes for everyone. If we all can't find our joy and our mission, we'll just end up repeating all the insanity that's been happening for centuries."

The interview ended. Yvonne logged off, and I looked at my three colleagues in their **Brady Bunch** boxes on my screen. "What do you say?" I asked Jennifer, my CEO. "Can we afford to hire her?" Always a financial ignoramus, I crossed my fingers, hoping against hope she'd say yes.

"I think," Jennifer said slowly, "that we can't afford **not** to hire her."

We broke into a unanimous cheer.

YOUR MISSION, SHOULD YOU CHOOSE TO ACCEPT IT

This chapter is about what happens when your quest to end anxiety takes you so far along a creativity spiral that you find yourself fully aligned with your true self, completely "on mission." The sense of purpose and fulfillment that arises at this point is so delicious that, despite any social pressures working against you, your curiosity will keep pulling you further into your own unique way of being.

This is the first hint of the sensation I call "commingling with creation." As I've mentioned before, it's an odd phrase, partly because in our culture, very few people talk about anything like it. We favor discussions about how to compete, produce, get ahead, and otherwise please our left hemispheres. But once you've followed your creative interests far enough to **master** a skill or project, there will be periods when even the hard work of mastery becomes utterly blissful. There's a sense of homecoming to this peaceful but intensely active state, a fierce delight in the process, a deep contentment that says you have found part of your life's essential purpose.

The most common reason people consult me is that they want this sense of purpose, even if they can't remember ever having it. "What's this all **for**?" they say, meaning their lives in general. "I just go to the office, come home, and get ready to do it again." Or: "I love my kids with all my heart, but is schlepping them around and doing their laundry really the way I'm supposed to spend my entire life?" Or: "I worked so hard to win an award for my work, but now that I've won it, I keep thinking, **So what?** It feels so pointless."

By contrast, people who are following their innate creative genius never ask, "So what?" The "so what" is innate fascination, which, as Emerson said of beauty, "is its own excuse for Being."

When Damion left his retail sales job to become a mechanic, he told me, "I used to look at the clock longing for the workday to end. Now I still look at the clock, but it's because I'm always wishing I had just a little more time to spend on a project." Carolina, an occupational therapist for children with disabilities, said, "I don't mind wiping little noses and calming tantrums, because helping kids develop life skills has always been the thing that fascinated me most." Because the sense of being "on mission" draws from the connective and interpretive skills of the right hemisphere, it pushes aside our anxiety, our mental chatter, and our sense of time. As Hesiod wrote about achieving any kind of mastery, "[W]hen you come to the top, then it is easy, even though it is hard."

To dwell consistently in this sense of being "on mission," we must do three things. The first is to detach from the social roles we may be following, unless they are perfectly fitted to our sense of mission. The second is to relax our mind's grip on everything we know—in the verbal, controlling, rote way the left hemisphere knows things (we'll talk about how to "let go" this way in upcoming pages). The third is to adopt a new way of getting things done, one that involves not **doing** anything at all. Or maybe I should say "not-doing" anything at all. Does this sound confusing? Don't worry. Once you've experienced it, you'll understand exactly what I mean.

So, let's get down to business. Which may or may not be business as we usually understand it.

TO FIND YOUR PURPOSE, BREAK THE MAIN DIRECTIVE

When people tell me that their goal is to be free from anxiety, or that they long for a sense of purpose, they rarely realize that these objectives are two sides of the same coin. As we've seen, living in a left hemisphere–dominated, overwhelmingly materialistic culture not only breeds anxiety but also shuts out the right hemisphere's ability to perceive context, connection, and beauty. As this happens, we lose our sense of meaning. WEIRD culture's main directive ("You exist to grab stuff!") motivates through fear and lack while draining us of purpose and joy.

Calming our anxiety and focusing on creativity can help us reconnect with our whole brains and bring us enormous happiness. And at some point, whatever our creative activity, indulging it also makes us countercultural. It connects us with the Mystery, with a sense that we're playing a part in a universal show that goes far beyond our individual lives. We may feel as if we're being guided, impelled, helped. Creation itself becomes our lives' work, and creation itself seems to be working our lives.

Many of my purpose-starved clients have had moments when they felt this connection with creation—but most of them have immediately backed away. For example, Pete loved traveling, meeting new people, and trading ideas that came from different cultures. He had an impressive job as an account manager at an international bank, but though it drew on the experiences he'd had while roaming the globe, it required him to stay in one location. Pete felt bored and lifeless. He asked me to help him find more satisfaction in his work.

Instead of giving Pete a new visualization exercise or method for goal setting, I asked him to think of a way he could travel around the world, starting **the next day,** without having to save up any money or dip into his savings. After a bit of incredulous laughter (he thought I was joking, but I assured him I was dead serious), Pete came up with the idea of traveling the world by teaching English on-site in various countries. He had several friends who had done this and loved it. Pete lit up like a neon sign as he discussed this "wild and crazy" possibility. Then, suddenly, the lights went out. Pete slumped over in his chair. "I can't leave my job," he said. "The money is just too good."

Lynette, a yoga teacher, was getting frustrated with teaching the same classes month after month. "I want to teach people to do yoga in a way that realigns their **lives,** not just their bodies," she told me. "I've figured out my own way to do that. I know how it works. I'm dying to share it." When we talked about the possibility that she could start a new series of classes, adding her own take on traditional yoga instruction, Lynette got so excited that she said, "I have to slow down—I'm hyperventilating!" Then her anxiety reared its ugly head. "But what right do I have to teach stuff I just **made up**?" she asked. "If I do this, everyone will think I'm so into myself. And maybe it won't even work for everyone!"

I've had variations of this conversation with literally hundreds of people. They begin to connect to their real curiosities, their inner genius, their rage to master, and the whole world feels like a fabulous adventure. Then, suddenly, their joy collapses and they fold back in on themselves. Then they always say some version of the same thing.

"Of course I'd love to live that way," they say gloomily, or angrily, or anxiously. "It would be incredible. But the bottom line is, it's too risky. I have to make as much money as possible first. Then maybe I can have some fun."

This is our materialistic, productivity-obsessed, left hemisphere–dominated culture's favorite story about each of our individual lives. **You don't get to go all starry-eyed and purpose driven! You don't get to feel yourself commingling with creation, whatever the hell that means! You have to grab more stuff!**

Now, of course I agree that we all need material things to sustain ourselves and our families. But our conventional wisdom makes this a package deal: to survive **at all,** we must accept the whole catastrophe of WEIRD thinking and behaving. We must serve a system that has no point beyond creating wealth, that treats us like cogs in a machine, that has no room for our creativity or uniqueness.

I've found that people who seek purpose first tend to find ways to support themselves. But those who are focused on getting "enough money" before they go looking for a sense of mission never feel they've got quite as much wealth as they need. I've coached people with no money in the bank who've managed to fund big life adventures, and people with millions of dollars who kept saying they needed just a little more before they could feel free to go looking for their real purpose.

The key to breaking this cultural pattern is to remember that when we devote ourselves to our life missions, we tap into an enormous amount of internal motivation. If we set it free and let our right hemispheres work on the issue, it can help us see new ways to fund our lives. We also free up our creativity to help us do old jobs in new ways. "Once you know **what** you want to experience," says one of the most adventurous people I know, "the **how** is easy to work out."

This goes against the left-hemisphere canon. The First Commandment of WEIRD culture is "Thou shalt make much money before thou thinkest about thy life's purpose." But that's not the truth. It's just been force-taught to all of us by a society that truly believes it and never considers creative alternatives.

You can see the power of this particular bit of socialization when people suddenly come into a lot of money and still don't find themselves feeling free to follow their bliss. In a 2010 study, Scott Highhouse of Bowling Green State University found that 85 percent of Americans who won the lottery stayed in the workforce. Some cut back to part time, but 63 percent just kept doing what they'd always done. Why? Though it's possible that they just loved their jobs, that's not the reason they gave when they explained their decisions to the researchers. Instead, they said:

- They had "work-based identities." This meant that they defined themselves by what they did for work—they felt they **were** their jobs. The idea of quitting felt like annihilation.

- They had a "narrow stimulation bandwidth." Their jobs were their main source of stimulation. They couldn't think of anything more interesting to do on their own.

- They feared the unknown. They were terrified by the thought of having to fill their time without formal jobs.

- They had "work ethic–induced guilt." The researchers found that these folks felt they could only justify their existence by working. As Highhouse put it, they lived by the "produce-or-at-least-feel-guilty" social rule.

All these explanations go back to anxiety: the dread of losing identity, getting bored, facing the unknown, or feeling guilt. Even with a lot of money on hand, most of the lottery winners said they were still motivated by these anxiety-based rules. There's nothing wrong with having a job, and if you feel "on purpose" at work, I hope you never quit. But when people tell me that only money stands between them and the creation of a meaningful life, I wonder if the real problem is being stuck in anxiety.

WORKING "ON PURPOSE"

Just as some people have lots of money or enviable jobs but can't find their purposes, we can find our purposes without needing to accumulate more money or have jobs that are tailor-made for our missions in life. We only need to detach from the money-obsessed anxiety of WEIRD culture, calm ourselves enough to feel what stirs our interests, and then find ways to spend time developing our interests as they grow into true passions.

Again, people who live like this become enormously creative about making a living. They shatter typical social roles, often inventing career identities that have never existed before. They figure out how to support themselves and their dependents but focus most of their mental effort on creating experiences that make their lives rich and abundant in many ways, including but not limited to financial ones.

For example, after Chuck was laid off from his management consulting job, his family had to downsize by moving to a smaller house and dramatically cutting their spending. Then Chuck's teenage son, Ben, decided to enter a contest that involved making a model rocket. This reawakened Chuck's own love of creative engineering. Together, he and Ben poked through salvage yards and the local dump in search of materials. They posted about their project on social media and began receiving crowdsourced donations from other model-rocket fans.

"Before I lost my job," Chuck said, "I would have just assumed I had to budget extra money to help Ben with a project like this—and I **never** would have offered my time to join him. Instead, we were able to make the whole thing totally cost neutral, have a blast together, and make some real engineering breakthroughs. It's the most joy and purpose I've felt in decades." Later, Chuck began working as a coach for engineers who felt stuck or unmotivated, which got his income flowing again.

I've seen this kind of joy and creativity in people with all kinds of life missions. Leah, a nurse who had suffered from insomnia, teamed up with two other medical professionals to run retreats that teach exhausted people how to sleep better. Laura became a drop-in vegan chef for health-conscious professionals who were too busy making money to cook their own healthy food. Barney consults with home and business owners to streamline their use of energy, often saving them enormous amounts of money while contributing to his passion for lessening the imprint of fuel use on the planet.

Once you start living on the creativity spiral, you'll find yourself coming up with ingenious solutions to all sorts of problems, from the most individual to the most universal. And this work—or, rather, deep play—will feel intensely meaningful. Yvonne calls her prime directive joy and insists on doing nothing that doesn't feel joyful to her. You can call your sense of purpose fascination, absorption, your happy place, or your own superhero quest. Whatever the label, this way of problem-solving and sustaining your life means that you're virtually always "on mission." You are Toad in a motorcar, enraptured, feeling the wind on your face.

Go wherever this feeling takes you, and there will be moments when you forget all about your socially programmed reasons for doing things. You'll forget to worry about the usual suspects—money, your work-based identity, your limited experience, your fear of the unknown, and your "work ethic–induced guilt." You may actually forget **all** identity—at least your identity as one small, isolated, vulnerable being. Instead, you'll get swept into the flow of creation by becoming entirely your Self—the Self that is calm, clear, confident, curious, courageous, compassionate, connected, and creative. And other people's Selves will want to play along.

This may lead to a totally new way of making a living—we'll talk more about that in chapter 10—or make you uniquely valuable in the job you have now, or capture the attention of people who recognize something extraordinary in the quality of your work.

When you're living on the creativity spiral, many people will realize they can't afford **not** to hire you.

YOUR MISSION VERSUS YOUR ROLE

Remember, this radically creative, mission-driven way of adding value to the world isn't condoned by left-hemisphere thinking. People will tell you that it's weird, because WEIRD cultures are designed to turn out humans who perform well in school, do "productive" work whether they enjoy it or not, raise their children to do the same thing, and then die. They want us to fit into rigid, socially prescribed roles. They want us all to be mold people.

Let me explain.

If you want to make a clay sculpture of a human form, you might go about it by getting a mold, then pushing clay into that mold until it fills every curve and crevice. Another way is to build an armature—a sort of stick figure, usually made of wire. Using this method, you pack the clay around the armature, gradually fleshing it out into the right shape. Using a mold, you can make an endless number of almost identical sculptures. Using an armature, you'll never make the exact same sculpture twice.

A social role is like a mold, designed to make many people into virtually identical copies. Each role requires specific tasks, characteristics, and ways of dressing and speaking. Every culture assigns roles, and the members of that culture try to fit into a few of them. My clients constantly reference their roles and the responsibilities adhering thereto: the good girl has to stay sweet and compliant, the tough guy can't break down and ask for help, the hotshot executive must never let underlings get their way, the perfect parent must never run out of patience, the self-sacrificing hero can't complain or demand justice, the glamorous influencer must not get old, the generous do-gooder can't afford self-care, and the cutthroat overachiever never shows—or even feels—mercy.

We all recognize these roles—they're cultural tropes. Everybody knows that a minister isn't supposed to act like a rock-and-roll singer, who isn't supposed to act like a soldier, who isn't supposed to act like a nanny, and so on. The fact is, most of us could play **all** those roles, or go outside any role ever devised. But this is not an approved practice in most cultures.

Role rules may be strange, pointless, and completely arbitrary. But they're upheld by a critical mass of people who believe that **things must be done a certain way.** For instance, I just saw a Twitter (now X) post by someone named Noah (@NoahDoNotCare), who wrote, "i accidentally said 'big' instead of 'grande' at starbucks n they took me behind the store n shot me in my leg." (Point of clarification: This is a joke. The people at Starbucks did not shoot Noah in the leg. They just wanted to.)

The reason why people react so negatively when someone breaks a role rule is because they're obeying the overall social rule that says, "We must all stay in our roles!" They're trying to play specific social roles themselves. Most of them have experienced a lifetime of the "push clay into mold" approach. It probably started before they were even born. I've had clients whose parents filled their childhood rooms with posters of the Ivy League schools they were expected to attend, or sports equipment they were expected to use at a professional level, or religious paraphernalia. Especially religious paraphernalia.

If you want to push someone into a mold, **hard,** use religion. Choose one that adheres to the old left-hemisphere motto "Our way is the **only** way!" If they show curiosity, kill it with righteous dogma. It helps to live in Utah.

There's just one small problem with using intense social rules to make mold people: if you push too hard, you might break the mold. You might actually—horror of horrors—set someone free. Any role that maximizes pressure can do this, whether it's religious or not. Once the mold breaks, the person shoved into it is at liberty to access their deepest sense of mission, the armature around which they can build a totally unique life. After that, the role rules are basically screwed. That person is never going to act exactly like anyone else, ever.

BREAKING THE MOLD

This is what happened to Yvonne. One day, after she'd become my personal and professional EDI coach, I asked her how she managed to work in an incredibly volatile field with such persistent, obvious delight. I mean, didn't she ever get anxious?

Yvonne laughed even harder than usual. "Oh, believe me," she said, "I could be an anxious wreck if I didn't have coping mechanisms. But I've learned how to take myself in a different direction. Because I know what low is. And when you know what low feels like—intimately—you have no other choice but to find your joy."

And then she tells me a story.

Flash back a couple of decades. Yvonne, age twenty-two, sits numbly in a tense, silent church meeting, waiting for the elders to come out of the room where they are deciding her fate. Yvonne has just finished publicly confessing her "sins," most prominently the fact that she started a relationship with another man while separated, but not yet divorced, from her ex-husband.

The elders file back into the chapel and gravely announce that God has told them Yvonne is insufficiently repentant. She is disfellowshipped, a process similar to excommunication. From that moment, she is to be shunned by the community, including her friends and family. Just talking to Yvonne is now a sin for which other people may be punished.

"They told me," Yvonne remembers, "that I walked into that room alive and I walked out dead."

"Dead" is an interesting social role. On the one hand, it's good practice for accepting the impermanent nature of all things. On the other hand, it means receiving **no** social support. That was the whole point of ostracizing Yvonne. By taking away everyone who might love and champion her, the church maximized the social pressure that might force any of us to behave exactly as we have been told. Yvonne was expected to crawl back into the mold, push herself into the desired shape, and keep her religion's role rules forever after.

But that's not what happened.

The next few years were incredibly hard. As a Black woman, Yvonne had always faced the exhausting daily grind of racism and sexism. Now her friends, her acquaintances, and even her family had rejected her. "I was told I was nothing, treated as if I was nothing," she told me. Then she broke into her infectious smile. "And I'm so glad, because otherwise I might still believe what I was taught growing up. Instead, I got obsessed with finding out what was true for me. Once I was free to gain that inner clarity, I was **free.**"

Slowly, Yvonne began to find an identity deeper than any role. Instead of going back to her church, she began patching together a sanity-quilt life. She took a series of jobs, guided by the intuition that came to fill the space once reserved for religious dogma.

For Yvonne, this guidance came in the form of joy. Unconstrained by social roles, she turned toward anything that gave her a sense of that inner warmth.

Yvonne felt especially drawn to helping eliminate injustice and discrimination, which she'd suffered in more forms than most people ever even have to think about. Reflecting on her own experiences, she developed methods of helping people connect across cultural, ethnic, religious, and other boundaries. Yvonne revived her love of design—she had once gone to art school—and created her own website and training manuals. She took and then quit several jobs, gaining skills and competency in running organizations. "I didn't know what I was doing **consciously**," she told me, "but I always had a sense of where I needed to show up."

Eventually, Yvonne felt drawn toward the task of getting officially trained in EDI. "That did not sound good to me!" she said, laughing. "I did **not** want to go into this field. This stuff is **hard**!" But strange as it seemed, that's where Yvonne's joy seemed to be steering her. She described it to me as an insistent, inexplicable knowing, a magnetic pull from her heart that defied all the protests in her head. So off she went, breaking the role rules of corporate America by quitting one more job (a lucrative, prestigious position at Apple) to launch her own consulting firm.

That's what led to the Zoom meeting with me, my teammates, and Yvonne. We still haven't stopped celebrating. We can't believe how lucky we are to have found her, this person who was told she was nothing and treated like nothing, this person uniquely suited to help and teach us, this creative genius we couldn't afford **not** to hire.

There's never been a better time to break whatever social mold constrains you and create your life on the armature of curiosity and joy. We live in a time of incredibly rapid social change, which is continuously speeding up. Whole industries are collapsing as others spring up—for example, the venerable book-publishing business has been completely transformed by the easy availability of online information. The hotel industry has been shaken by Airbnb. Retail malls, once humming with crowds, have turned ghostly as almost everyone shops online.

In the meantime, the constant communication and sharing of experiences made possible by technology means that individuals can find people to support them in leaving the social roles they were mold-made to fill. People who are exploring different gender identities can now find friends who share their experiences. Artists in any field can meet and interact with others who share their interests. Parents raising neurodivergent children can get together and think of ways to change society to meet their children's needs, instead of forcing those children to serve the culture's definition of "normal."

My point is that virtually all existing social roles are being stressed, changed, broken, or opened up.

New ways of living and serving our purposes are arising everywhere, as we'll see in the following chapters. But to take advantage of these opportunities—even to notice them—we first need to start breaking the rules we're keeping merely to stay aligned with socially approved roles. Approval seeking is an anxiety-based behavior fueled by a left-hemisphere belief that there is only one way to live. Here's an exercise to help you abandon anxiety as your basic role motivation and imagine who you might be if you follow your sense of curiosity, creativity, and connection.

New Skill

BREAK YOUR ROLE RULES

---

1. Complete the sentences below by writing down some things you always do, **not because you really enjoy them but because you want to be thought well of by yourself and others.**

    Write this thing in the first blank. In the second blank, write what people would think about you if you failed to do it. (As you fill in the second blank, you may actually hear the voices of the people who socialized you.)

EXAMPLES:
I always [activity] **get up at sunrise**.
If I didn't, people would think I'm
[judgment] **a lazy piece of crap**.

I always [activity] **wear expensive,
uncomfortable shoes**.
If I didn't, people would think I'm
[judgment] **no better than a barbarian**.

I always [activity] _____

_____.

If I didn't, people would think I'm [judgment]

_____

_____.

I always [activity] _____

_____.

If I didn't, people would think I'm [judgment]

_____

_____.

I always [activity] _____

_____.

If I didn't, people would think I'm [judgment]

_____

_____.

Now write down some things you **never** do even though you'd like to. You refrain from doing these things **not because they are illegal or immoral but because you're afraid of how people would judge you if you did them.**

EXAMPLES:
I never [activity] **speak up for myself.**
If I did, people would think I am [judgment] **selfish and demanding.**

I never [activity] **complain.**
If I did, people would think I am [judgment] **weak and whiny.**

I never [activity] _____

_____.

If I did, people would think I'm [judgment]

_____

_____.

I never [activity] _____

_____.

If I did, people would think I'm [judgment]

_____

_____.

I never [activity] _____

_____

_____.

If I did, people would think I'm [judgment]

_____

_____.

2. Next, fill in the left-hand box below by copying the things you've just written down. Once you've done that, go to the right-hand box, and think about what you'd **really, truly prefer to do**.

COLUMN A: THINGS I DO TO SERVE MY ROLE	COLUMN B: THINGS I'D PREFER TO DO
Examples:	**Examples:**
• I always get up at sunrise.	• I'd like to sleep until I feel rested.
• I always wear expensive, uncomfortable shoes.	• I'd like to wear Birkenstocks.

COLUMN A: THINGS I DO TO SERVE MY ROLE	COLUMN B: THINGS I'D PREFER TO DO
Examples: • I never speak up for myself. • I never show sadness.	**Examples:** • I'd like to demand more gruel at lunchtime. • I'd like to cry on someone's shoulder.
1.	1.
2.	2.
3.	3.
4.	4.
5.	5.
6.	6.

3. Now think of something you could do today from column B (in other words, an action that fits within the range of what you

find moral but falls **slightly** outside your role rules). Said another way, you don't honestly think there's anything wrong with doing or not doing this thing, but the people who socialized you wouldn't think well of it.

EXAMPLE:
Today I could break my role rules by:
taking a nap in the middle of the day / wearing Birkenstocks to work / telling my teenager to stop playing the drums at night / complaining to everyone I meet about how much I hate snow / et cetera, et cetera.

YOUR TURN:
Today I could break my role rules by:

_____

_____

_____

4. Do what you want. Break the rules. You will probably feel very anxious about this. Just breathe, calm your creature, and stay the course.

5. Repeat daily.

The payoff from learning to live this way is that we become more and more aware of the beautiful things we want to stitch into our sanity quilts. At the same time, almost as an afterthought, we find ourselves enlarging our comfort zones, changing our behavior in ways that nourish us, and leaving anxiety far behind. Activities that come from our cores (rather than from social molds) fuel our interest, increase our physical and mental vigor, and calm our hearts. The more we break our role rules, the more likely we are to combine the precise elements that make up our most purposeful life missions. Nobody can give us the maps to these missions. We must draw them for ourselves by joining with the energy of pure creation.

JOINING WITH CREATION TO MAKE YOUR MISSION

Now that we've seen how social roles keep us from finding our purposes, and have begun considering ways to break free from our particular molds, let's see how life might look out beyond the world of mold people, where each of us is creating according to our own unique sense of purpose.

Most people who know they aren't living their souls' missions go looking for new roles that will fit them perfectly, right off the rack, requiring no alteration or imagination: a different job, a home in a nicer climate, a new partner. If you've made a change like this and landed in a life perfectly aligned with your life mission, I could not be happier for you. Stop reading! Go back to your great life!

But most people are more like the checkout clerk at the grocery store where I went to stock up on supplies after a trip. She asked me why I needed so many groceries, and I told her I'd been running a change-your-life safari in South Africa.

"Wow!" she said, wide-eyed. "How did you get that job?"

"Um . . . I didn't really **get** it," I told her. "I kind of . . . made it up."

Driving home with my groceries, I remembered how nervous my friends and I had been as we made a sanity-quilt block from our love of animals and wilderness, our commitment to restoring ecosystems, our respective attempts to find happiness, our love for one another, and our sense of mission. Each one of us had helped create this "quilt block" (the change-your-life safari retreat), and it became a beautiful component of our individual lives. And though it's incredibly inconvenient for most of our clients to travel all the way to the African bush, there seem to be a lot of people who feel they can't afford **not** to sign up for it.

The philosopher Frederick Buechner defined vocation, or life mission, as "the place where your deep gladness and the world's deep hunger meet." My client Pete found such an intersection: he loved to travel, and he knew he could teach English to people who really wanted to learn it. Yoga teacher Lynette told me, "I **know** I could help people be healthier with the practices I've invented," and she knew that many people desperately wanted to feel better. Only Pete's and Lynette's fears of leaving established roles and creating somewhat original alternatives kept them from stepping into this powerful intersection of joy and service.

When my friends and I set out to run safari retreats, we had no idea whether we'd be able to earn money. We were running on faith, frequently succumbing to bouts of terrified anxiety. You'll probably be scared, just as I always am, when you begin moving away from cultural norms by creating a more direct way to follow your mission. But this won't be due to a literal physical threat in the room, like a fire or an enraged platypus (platypuses are only about two feet long, but they can stab the crap out of you with their poisonous heel spurs). In other words, this isn't true, healthy, useful fear. It's just anxiety. When it arises, address it directly with the skills you learned earlier in this book, and forge ahead.

Live this way and you may end up finding a mission that no one else has even imagined. Use the previous exercise—the one that helps you identify unrewarding things you're doing out of social convention and encourages you to choose rewarding alternatives—over and over. Seek and shift every role convention that feels toxic or exhausting. Exchange them for anything that interests you, and I mean **anything.** Quilt block by quilt block, you'll find that you can stitch many of these things together until you've made a way of life that gives you deep gladness and helps nourish other people in the places where their bodies or souls are hungry.

Once you've created this sanity-quilt life, you can give your way of living a name. I've heard Leah, the nurse who helps insomniacs, call herself "the Sleep Lady." My friends in South Africa call their job "restoring Eden"; others may call them habitat healers. It's not uncommon for people to start calling folks by titles they never expected. I still cringe at the label "life coach," which didn't exist when I was growing up, or even when I was getting my doctorate. "Life coaching" is **way** outside the role rules of academia; it's the kind of title that makes traditional scholars want to take you out back and shoot you in the leg. But the "Harvard academic" role made me an anxious mess. When I decided to leave it and follow my curiosity into joy, I finally felt "on purpose."

Most of my friends live this way. Some of them have had great success by not playing socially defined roles. In fact, they never stay in any recognized role for very long, and most of what they do for the joy of it doesn't earn money. They follow curiosity, allow it to grow into the rage to master, and end up making completely original things.

So I'm about to do something that people have

advised me not to do: I'm going to describe some **very successful** people. "Don't go there," I've been advised. "Big success isn't relatable. Keep it simple." But I'm going to describe these people, without disguising them, so that you know great success is very possible once we break our social molds and begin building our lives from our deepest senses of meaning.

- Liz, miserable in her role as a suburban wife and not wanting to take the next socially approved step into the role of mother, threw all her energy into the one thing that sparked a tiny flame of curiosity in her brain: the desire to learn Italian. If you want to know what happened next, read **Eat Pray Love.**

  When I met Liz, she told me that she pretty much always went where curiosity took her. She'd recently become obsessed with gardening (this later showed up in her novel **The Signature of All Things**). Later, during my Art Toad month, I texted Liz a photo of a picture I'd drawn. She got so enthusiastic that she stayed up the entire night creating a full seventy-two-card deck of tarot cards. Liz didn't plan to publish or sell her new card deck. She just loves to create.

- Alex grew up in South Africa under apartheid. During his childhood, his family hit rough financial patches so intense that the only way Alex could eat was to follow a chicken around until it laid an egg.

As a young man, Alex broke with his white ancestors' racist social norms by apprenticing himself to Renias Mhlongo, a brilliant animal tracker from the Shangaan tribe. The two became best friends and such legendary trackers that they're recruited to help conservationists locate and protect large predators all over the world. Alex and Renias founded a "tracker academy" to train young people from rural areas so that they could get jobs using ancient tracking skills to help guide safaris. Then Alex launched a company to create high-nutrition porridge to be served at schools so that every child could get a full day's nutrients from school lunch, motivating their parents to help them access education.

- I met Susan when she was appointed editor in chief of **O, The Oprah Magazine.** The buzz around the office said she was a "triple threat" who'd already succeeded as an art designer, journalist, and editor. As one of the magazine's monthly columnists, I went to New York to meet with her. We were expected to talk about our work. We didn't.

I'd just read **The Devil's Teeth,** Susan's gripping book about great white sharks, and I wanted to hear more. After our shark discussion, we went on to contemplate rogue ocean waves, the intelligence of dolphins, and Susan's dream of diving in a deep-sea submersible (she would turn each of these topics into bestselling books). When we realized our time was up and we hadn't even mentioned work, we considered meeting again for lunch the next day. But Susan couldn't make it. She would have had to miss her sword-fighting class.

Again, I'm using these extremely successful people as examples because I want you to know what can happen when we commit ourselves to living creatively and designing lives that fill us with a sense of purpose. None of these people started out with a clear map of their missions. None of them succeeded financially right out of the gate. Alex never forgets what it's like to be chronically hungry. Liz remembers gently kicking a mouse out of a hole in her family car's floor as they drove through the freezing Connecticut woods. When I commented on how humble and down-to-earth Susan is, she laughed and said, "I never set out to be anything impressive. I'm just happy to be in the room."

These folks have always had rich, abundant lives, **whether or not they were in the money.** They've all had many jobs and relationships as they created their sanity quilts. But they never expected any single job or relationship role to **be** their mission. Over and over, they had the courage to leave the comfort of established convention, to face criticism and push-back. They all felt as if they were jumping off a series of cliffs. They all felt the fear of the unknown. And at some point, they all felt themselves entirely disappear. In fact, that was the big payoff.

Again, let me explain.

WHEN EGO DISSOLVES INTO CREATION

On the morning of Jill Bolte Taylor's stroke, she stood in the shower and watched her hand resting on the bathroom tiles. As her left hemisphere flickered on and off, these objects kept changing their appearance. First Jill would see the tiles and her hand, as usual. Then her left brain would tune out, and she'd see the tiles and her hand become clouds of intermingled energy. There was no separation between them—between anything. Reality was just one interconnected field of vibrating energy.

Jill wasn't hallucinating. Her brain wasn't "making up" what it saw from her right hemisphere. She was simply observing reality without the **editing** and **simplification** of the left hemisphere. The "clouds of energy" version of the world matches the description of reality we get from modern physics. But **seeing** that with our actual eyes is deemed weird in

WEIRD societies. And you'd think it would hamper practical performance. In the case of a massive stroke, that's true. But when we call on our right hemispheres by creating our way through life, we get tantalizing hints of what it feels like to intermingle with creation—and this is often associated with **maximum** performance.

This is what Jill tells me she experiences when she's sculpting: a sense of unity with the stone, with the figure she's carving, with the act of creation itself. Yvonne feels herself becoming an embodiment of joy, even as she navigates explosive emotional territory. Liz says that when she doesn't want to write, starting anyway soon takes her to a place where "the walls fall away," and she dissolves into the creation of story. During a tracking expedition, Alex's mind is so quiet and focused that it vanishes, becoming an indistinguishable part of the landscape and the animals. And when Susan got her wish and traveled miles below the surface of the ocean in a tiny transparent submarine, she told me she wasn't scared at all. She felt held, safe, part of the sea and some compassionate universal force, completely unconcerned about her individual existence.

I doubt that you were educated to find ways of disappearing into creation. In WEIRD cultures, that's not really a thing. But many ancient traditions have taught people to deliberately dissolve their identities as they perform any task. They cultivate the feeling that arises when we go beyond anxiety, disappear to ourselves, and feel something unfathomable using us as a tool of creation.

The closest thing WEIRD societies have to this cultural trope may be the image of the Force helping Luke Skywalker shoot his proton torpedoes into the underbelly of the Death Star (I believe our need to name this experience, to "trust the Force," is part of what made **Star Wars** so successful). Ancient Chinese Taoists describe this as wei-wu-wei (doing-without-doing). Their intention was to allow "doing-without-doing" to arise in every part of their lives. It's like Luke allowing the Force to steer **all** his actions, from flying a rocket to eating lunch.

There's no easy English translation of **wei-wu-wei,** because the experience is ultimately indescribable. But this can and does happen to all of us, if only in tiny ways, because our nervous systems have the inbuilt capacity to do it.

An example I've already mentioned is the skill of driving a car. Experienced drivers don't have to consciously think out a strategy every time they tap the brakes or turn the wheel. And you may have had the experience of reacting to a sudden problem—an animal darting into the road, for example—before your conscious mind even knew what was happening.

If you do any sort of three-dimensional work that calls on right-hemisphere thinking, like gardening, building, or cooking, you may sometimes feel that the soil or the hardwood or the food in your pan is "asking" for what it needs in a way you can't describe. Novelists may find their characters saying unexpected things. Painters talk about canvases "wanting" certain colors and shapes. A heart surgeon once told me, "There's a moment where the patient's body begins letting me know what it wants my hands to do. I have no idea how to describe that feeling, but I make damn sure I follow its instructions."

Doing-without-doing arises primarily when we've put in a lot of hours to achieve mastery at some creative skill and then **stop trying to control** what we're creating. This is a paradoxical feat, a razor's-edge balance between integrated skills and complete relaxation. But we were designed to achieve it. Here's an exercise to help you get started.

New Skill

DO WITHOUT DOING

---

1. Choose something you want to make. It could exist in space, like an object, or in time, like a piece of music, or both. It might be doing something like line dancing, reconfiguring your van, or any creative activity you enjoy.

2. Find some examples of people making this sort of thing **masterfully**.

3. Commit to some deep play by trying to make your own thing—your object, your music—as well as the masters do.

4. If this thought makes you anxious, calm your creature, connect with curiosity, and move on. Refuse to be deterred.

5. **Now shift your attention four times: go up high, go down deep, go away, go back in.**

GO UP means mentally zooming back in your mind, like a hawk circling higher and higher, until you can see the ultimate purpose that you're trying to serve by making this thing.

For example, when I'm working with Yvonne, we're constantly "zooming up" to look at our ultimate goal of creating a company that will help catalyze a more just society.

GO DOWN means dropping back to the task immediately before you. Become completely focused on making that small task take you toward the purpose you've just seen from up high.

My team and I go from lofty aspirations

to practical tasks: writing a bit of copy to put on our website, taking a single photo, whatever tiny step we must take to follow our broadest mission.

GO AWAY means exactly that. Get up and walk, or read a novel, or swim in a river, or play Dungeons & Dragons with your friends, or see how your living room looks when you're upside down. Do something that forces you to stop thinking about your mission-based tasks.

GO BACK IN means returning to that string of tiny tasks that lead to your highest purpose while holding the relaxed, open mindset of a wanderer. The tasks may seem different now. You'll see them from new angles. You'll connect new things. You'll transfer ideas that emerged while wandering to solve problems that once confounded you.

Yvonne's insistence on joy is one such stroke of genius. "Come on, now," she'll say. "You can find a way to do this that lifts you up. Enjoyable? Not always. Joyful? Absolutely."

6. Do this again and again until you begin to feel a sense that something is think-ing, speaking, or moving **through** you,

without your having to labor at it. This may be only a flash at first, but each time you practice, you should feel more moments of doing-without-doing. Gradually, your brain will wire in this state as its favorite way to move forward.

THE PLAY OF CONSCIOUSNESS

I can't make you feel this strange and wonderful sensation of dissolving into creation, so again, **please try the exercise above rather than just reading it.** Compare the sensation with how it feels to keep the rules of your social role, whatever that is. For most of us, living by rigid adherence to the roles available in our left-brain society leaves us with no objective except to "justify our existence by working." But mingling with creation, allowing ourselves to follow the right hemisphere's curiosity and creativity, is delicious enough to be an end in itself.

If you can recall any moment of relaxed mastery— an inspired move on the playing field or ski slope; the first time your fingers automatically found a chord on your guitar; the strange boldness that pushed you past your shyness, making you say just the right thing to the person you were soon to fall in love with; the sudden bloom of a new idea, gadget, group, or event—remember what that sensation felt like. Imagine feeling it more often, feeling it **all the time.**

Is this constant river of blissful discovery common? Hell no! Is it possible? For thousands of years, people have been proving that the answer is yes.

In some Indian philosophies, the universe itself is seen as a product of this kind of absorbing, delicious energy, which is known by the word **Lila** (pronounced **Leela**), or "divine play." The conscious cosmos, feeling its own identity through various forms, is creating reality for the sheer joy of it. When we become conscious of this feeling, and notice the force of creation steering our actions, we feel a jolt of awe that Indian sages call "the splendor of recognition." The Force inside us sees itself as one with the Force around us: the divine meeting the divine, playing in a new form.

Liz Gilbert likes to tell the story of a dancer she met who was chosen to play Joan of Arc in **Seraphic Dialogue,** one of the most iconic works by the great choreographer Martha Graham. At the time, this up-and-coming dance star was only eighteen. She was both ecstatic to have been cast as Joan and intensely anxious. On opening night, waiting for the curtain to go up, she had a true panic attack. "I prayed for the floor to open up and swallow me," she told Liz. "And then . . . it did. I disappeared. And Joan of Arc stepped out onto that stage."

This dancer didn't mean that she was literally

possessed by the spirit of a long-dead French heroine. She meant that the Force—whatever force drove
the real Joan of Arc, as well as the fictional Luke
Skywalker—seemed to gently take over the controls
of her body and mind.

When Andrew Newberg and Eugene d'Aquili
studied people who felt a sense of unity with all creation, they found that these meditators dropped into
bliss when two parts of the brain went quiet: a part
that gives us a sense of being separate from the rest
of the universe and another part that makes us feel
a sense of being in control. Losing our sense of self
and our sense of control? Yikes! That's the left hemisphere's worst nightmare! You've been socialized to
avoid it throughout your life!

But oh my, how it can dance.

When we begin breaking away from social roles,
surrendering to the energy of universal creation by
following whatever lights us up, we feel this transcen-
dent experience. It doesn't only happen when we're in
front of an audience. It can be just as intense when
we're watering our plants, or running a meeting, or
learning a language, or playing with our children, or
writing an email to a friend.

If you calm your anxiety and walk away from the
roles you've been given toward the actions that bring
you joy, you'll end up in more and more places where
your deep gladness meets the world's deep hunger.
That will motivate you to strive for mastery because

it is indescribably absorbing, the furthest extreme of **fun.**

At some point, when you've gone up, then down, then away, then back into a task, you may forget to control anything at all. You may just slip into trusting the Force. And then, to adaptively paraphrase Eleanor Roosevelt, you will do things you think you cannot do—because you aren't the one doing them. There will be no difference between you and the rest of creation. You will have come home to your selfless Self.

10

Constellating an Ecosystem

If you happened to be driving in West Sussex, England, sometime in the 2010s, you may have seen a small, unassuming man walking along the road, picking up trash and putting it into large plastic bags. If you drove the same route frequently, you might have seen this man on multiple occasions, especially given that he often walked more than twenty miles a day, gamely lifting and bagging everything from dead animals to broken toaster ovens.

Knowing nothing more about the trash-picking man, you might not have been surprised to learn about his difficult history. He was one of six children, small for his age, afflicted by tics and compulsions that today would probably be diagnosed as OCD or Tourette's syndrome. Even as a child, he knew he was gay and lived in terror of being found out—a fear that proved justified later on, when his father discovered his homosexuality and banished him from the house. As a young adult, the trash picker drifted from one interest to another until he found something he could commit to: drugs. Almost anything mind-altering would do, though he favored crystal meth. He funded his addiction and eked out a meager living by doing menial odd jobs, mostly cleaning houses and apartments.

Poor thing, you might have thought, hearing all this. Your heart might have ached for the man, now in his sixties, as you watched him trudge along, hands scratched bloody from reaching through brambles to pick up soda cans and plastic bags of dog feces. What you probably wouldn't have guessed is that he also owns multiple houses, decorates them with original paintings by the likes of Picasso, and hires the occasional private jet when he hits a travel snafu. Cleaning roadways day after day is just his hobby.

The man's name is David Sedaris. He's famous for writing humorous essays, which he reads aloud to sold-out crowds all over the world. Now, this is not typically an easy-money gig. The folks at the unemployment office won't ask you, "Have you considered writing humorous essays about your life and then reading them out loud?" Even for successful authors, who are very rare, most book readings draw tiny audiences. The only person I can think of who had a career anything like Sedaris's is Mark

Twain—but Twain had no competition from television, the internet, or audiobooks. And he certainly never gave readings in China or Romania. Sedaris packs venues everywhere he goes, from the Sydney Opera House to Carnegie Hall.

This success didn't come from following the rules, flattering the right people, and clawing up the success ladder. Sedaris broke rules right, left, and center. He did what he liked, from drugs to housecleaning (an obsessive neatnik, he chose the work not just because he needed the money but because he enjoyed it). Most of all, **he refused to stop creating.** Over time, Sedaris wrote so much strange, funny prose, and got so good at reading it aloud, that more than fifteen million people bought his books. And even after achieving fame and fortune, Sedaris kept doing exactly what he wanted—including cleaning roadways, mile after mile.

A NEW ECONOMIC ECOSYSTEM

We could see Sedaris's career as a mere fluke, a one-in-a-million story of someone who happened to succeed despite indulging in his eccentricity. But after seeing firsthand how hundreds of clients and friends have found success on unlikely career paths, I don't see it that way. I believe that Sedaris is rich and famous **because** he indulges his eccentricity. He's become the center of a supportive, abundant network of people, ideas, events, and financial wealth that naturally forms around people who live creatively. I call the process of connecting with such a network "constellating an economic ecosystem," and I believe we can all do it.

This chapter will discuss how you can constellate a new way of living—and of making a living—as you spend less time tapped into anxiety spirals and more time following creativity spirals. When I say "constellate," I mean gather together, the way bees gather around flowers, or tourists gather around street performers. The more you allow yourself to embody your unique creative genius, the more you can become the center of a system that not only feeds your soul but also makes your fortune. Without even meaning to, you can create a way to thrive that has never existed before.

NATURAL ECOLOGY VERSUS THE WEIRD ECONOMY

But, first, what exactly do I mean by "ecosystem"? An ecosystem—for example, a jungle or a coral reef—is a network of living things in which each component is constantly responding to all the other components and the surrounding environment. For the vast majority of human history, we as a species have lived as cooperative components of ecosystems. The Khoisan, who have occupied southern Africa longer than any other humans have lived anywhere, survived for **hundreds of thousands of years** in this way. When the rains came, they foraged for edible plants. In the dry season, it was easy to hunt animals at watering holes.

Virtually all "premodern" people we know of saw the logic in cooperating with their local ecosystems. There were exceptions, like the folks on Easter Island, who cut down all the island's palm trees, disrupting the ecosystem so much that many ended up eating each other, starving to death, or both.

But most traditional societies were made up of intelligent people who understood that it's not a good idea to plunder and destroy an ecosystem when you're part of it. As a Peruvian shaman once told me, "Give me a fish, I eat for a day. Teach me to fish, I eat for a lifetime. Teach me to keep fish alive and healthy, and my descendants eat forever."

I believe that we can live by creating miniature cooperative systems wherever we happen to find ourselves in the world, in society, and in the economy. Most of this chapter will explain how you can do that. In fact, at our point in history, constellating your own economic ecosystem isn't just a nice idea; it's a way to steer clear of danger as the economy that dominates our planet collapses under its own creations.

THE IRON CAGE OF THE WEIRD WORLD

"Look, I don't like the faculty meetings, either," says a colleague I'll call Dr. Delmer Fancyhat. He offers me a smile, the tolerant smile a kind professor bestows on a thirty-year-old lecturer like me.

"But if you can grit your teeth and hang in there for just a few years, you might get tenure, like me." Fancyhat gestures around his office, which is filled with books, papers, a picture of his wife and children, and the fossilized dinosaur turd he once received as a gag gift. "I'm set for life here. It's worth the misery."

"Uh, okay," I say. "I . . . hear you."

This is true, in the sense that I can hear sounds coming out of Fancyhat's mouth. As for his argument, it makes no more sense to me than the brain mapper's offer to "treat" my interest-based attention. The thought of spending the rest of my life fighting tiny intellectual battles, writing papers that will be read by an average of seven bored and contentious colleagues, makes my flesh crawl.

"I just . . ." I fix my eyes on the dinosaur poo. "I just can't."

Fancyhat settles back in his chair, exasperated. "Well, then," he says, "I guess you'll never be anything but a lowly faculty wife."

It's such a gift, having him put things just that

CONSTELLATING AN ECOSYSTEM

way. In the verbally cautious world of academia, you don't often hear things expressed so bluntly. Fancyhat's words have given me a story worth telling over and over, as I'm doing right now, and I'm filled with gratitude.

I'll think of Fancyhat often in the years to come. I'll think of him as I worry and budget, trying to get my first book published. I'll think of him when I hear he's been fired, tenure or no tenure (I never will learn exactly why). And I'll think of Fancyhat the year I realize that I just paid more in taxes than the total amount I'd earned during my years in academia.

But at the time of that conversation, I wasn't so confident. I actually agreed with Fancyhat that I should keep my sensible job, struggle for tenure, the whole package. But I was physically and psychologically burned out. My autoimmune diseases made it physically impossible to sit, stand, or use my hands for long. What little energy I had needed to go to my three young children. And even on that scary day, I knew that the economy of the modern world was changing, and that even "secure" jobs wouldn't stay secure forever.

As a person near the top of the economic pyramid, Fancyhat didn't share my uneasiness about job security. He expected his current financial setup to support him forever. He overlooked uncomfortable realities, like the fact that tenured professors were getting fired more often and that huge parts of our economic systems were beginning to crack, fragment, and dissolve. I doubt he'd ever imagined a world without the social system he'd always experienced—the one designed to put a few wealthy, privileged people at the top of an economic pyramid.

These privileged few—property-owning white males—were the "all men" Thomas Jefferson had in mind when he penned the words "all men are created equal" while being waited on by people he looked upon as his property. The economy of the WEIRD world, including the institution of slavery, was designed to keep men like Jefferson rich by exploiting the labor of others.

And it worked. It worked like a charm. In the centuries that followed Jefferson, the rich got richer, and the poor kept creating more and more wealth they weren't allowed to keep. Oh, sure, this led to revolutions in places like China and the former Soviet Union. But these uprisings simply propelled a different group of people into the exploiting class, shoving many formerly privileged people into the starving masses. As they said in China when I did research there in the 1980s: "Under capitalism, man exploits man, but under communism, it's the other way around."

This situation is still working for you if you're among the 1 percent of humans who, at the time of this writing, own **half the wealth in the world.** In fact, the system's pretty great if you're among the richest 10 percent of adults, who hold 85 percent of all earthly wealth. Things get less exciting if you belong to the other nine-tenths of the human population, who have to split the remaining 15 percent of the world's economic resources.

Way back at the turn of the twentieth century, all of this was predicted by the "father of sociology," Max Weber. He described what modern jobs would look like long before such jobs were widespread. Weber was fascinated by the American economy because the people who created it, he noted, were driven by a religious belief that God always bestowed wealth on the righteous. So they constructed an economy obsessed with maximizing wealth. This would one day lead to narrow, specialized jobs that maximized efficiency and profit.

Weber called this "the iron cage of rationalism" and stated that it would one day suck all humans into itself, crushing their individuality. Then he went to lie down for a few years, crippled by depression, insomnia, and anxiety. In other words, he did an excellent job of foreseeing a future in which almost everyone would end up in a left hemisphere–crafted cage, then got swept up in the emotional problems typical of someone stuck in that very prison. He died in 1920 at age fifty-six, possibly succumbing to a worldwide flu pandemic, which he hadn't predicted. Nobody can think of everything.

HOW AND WHY THE IRON CAGE IS COLLAPSING

In fact, while Weber's brilliant mind correctly en-
visioned the development of machinelike jobs, he
didn't mention the most glaringly paradoxical feature
of the iron cage: it wasn't designed to support life.
Its mechanistic focus on money ignores the fact that
humans aren't naturally built to depend on money;
we're built to depend on biological systems. Because
we **are** biological systems.

This fact was flashing like a neon light in my mind
as I listened to Delmer Fancyhat and thought about
my lousy health and my three kids. I knew that a
professor's career description, like most iron-cage
jobs, rested on the assumption that each academic
would have an invisible asset the system doesn't value
at all: a "lowly faculty wife."

Without Fancyhat's own lowly faculty wife doing
unpaid full-time work to sustain his family, his whole
way of being would break down. The iron-cage job
couldn't exist without lowly wives, because there's
nothing in it that actually takes care of people: raises
children, comforts the sick, helps the elderly, creates the emotional bonds we all need to stay sane.
Mrs. Fancyhat, like millions of other unpaid "lowly"
folk, was doing all of that for free. But her husband
(and she herself) had been taught to value only jobs
that earn money in the iron-cage fashion. Most of

those jobs can't be done while simultaneously taking care of our bodies, one another, or the earth.

So here's our ironic situation: billions of people have forced themselves to do miserable jobs, thinking this is necessary to stay alive and raise families. In the short run, that looks true. It's certainly what any self-respecting anxiety spiral would recommend. But in the long run, we'll either start using our brilliant creative minds to **care for life** or end up like Easter Islanders, destroying the conditions needed for our own survival.

In short, we don't need to do iron-cage jobs so that we can all survive; a lot of us need to **stop** doing iron-cage jobs so that we can all survive.

When this first dawned on me, I felt like I'd been sprinting along a racecourse, giving it all I had, when I suddenly realized that the finish line lay in exactly the opposite direction. It was confusing at first. It flies in the face of our conventional wisdom, and there's no clear path toward it within the left hemisphere–dominated logic of our current society. But already, more and more people are escaping from their iron cages, either because they can't tolerate the conditions or because social change and technological advances are tearing apart the whole iron prison that dominated the last century.

As I write this, industries our grandparents saw as permanent and stable are disappearing or fundamentally changing. They include old stalwarts like agriculture, manufacturing, postal services, hotel services, taxi driving, financial advising, publishing and all print media, and hundreds of others. I recently got an email from a minister who told me that all the other ministers are now using artificial intelligence to compose sermons—**really good** sermons. "How can I compete?" she asked. Before hearing from her, I wasn't even aware that ministers have to compete, but of course, in our social system, they must. And those who use the latest technology are winning the competition.

Functioning in this situation doesn't require robotic, factory-job repetition. It requires creativity. If we step away from anxiety and nourish our creativity, we can use emerging technologies to do almost anything.

WHAT THE WORLD NEEDS NOW IS CREATIVITY

In 2005, Daniel Pink published **A Whole New Mind: Why Right-Brainers Will Rule the Future.** The basic idea presented in Pink's bestseller was that the methodical, analytical aspects of the business world would increasingly be mechanized, and that the most valuable assets in the future would be right-brain-focused qualities like the ability to play, show empathy, create meaning, design things, and tell stories. Pink's work was criticized for oversimplifying the functions of the brain. The same can be said of any book that essentializes the right-hemisphere/left-hemisphere disparity (including this one), even though I obviously think this can be a very useful simplification. However, nobody criticized Pink's predictions for **not going nearly far enough.**

For example, Pink proposed that "MFAs are the new MBAs," that people who got degrees in the arts would become hotter commodities than people who got degrees in science. He didn't predict that any academic degree would become less and less useful for getting jobs—that college could become irrelevant to people's careers. But in 2016, Charles Sykes, a senior fellow at the Wisconsin Policy Research Institute, wrote that "sending a child to a private university now is like buying a BMW every year—and driving it off a cliff." He cited astronomical costs and the fact that, instead of guaranteeing a job, a college education leaves many graduates utterly unprepared for the real world.

Pink also said that big companies would hire more and more "right-brainers." He didn't say that big companies would start collapsing as new technology allowed small businesses or even individuals to outcompete and undersell them. And like Weber, Pink couldn't have predicted that global pandemics would become increasingly likely as people invaded natural ecosystems and came into contact with new microorganisms. Pandemics, as we all know by now, accelerate many social transitions, permanently changing industries like travel, clerical work, casinos, fitness centers, grocery stores, restaurants, and many others.

All these lists delight my little Sociology Toad, so please allow me to hit you with just one more. (Of course I have a Sociology Toad! Do you think I'd be writing this if I didn't?) Here are a few of the jobs that rose up out of nowhere as many big companies began to flounder:

- online community management
- website and app development
- three-dimensional art
- online marketing analysis
- game development
- Airbnb hosting
- freelance research
- online tutoring
- user interface design
- video editing
- DoorDash food delivery
- humorous-personal-essay reading, a lucrative industry made up of David Sedaris

Many of these jobs are stopgap parts of a gig economy, where people scrape by without things like health insurance or paid leave. They aren't ideal, but they are a sign that the big companies once necessary to performing services like food production and delivery are being supplanted by smaller, more nimble providers.

For many families, earning enough cash to care for children, the sick, the disabled, and the elderly now requires at least two people working full-time jobs. And remember, these "normal" jobs were **designed for people who were assumed to have stay-at-home wives.** That's why one of the fastest-growing sectors in our economy is "home health and personal care aides." As we biological organisms thrash through an economic system that assumes we function like machines, our physical and psychological needs are glaringly unsupported. We desperately need the kind of support that "premodern" people offered one another simply by living and working in close connection.

By the time you read this, even more good old-fashioned industries will be gone, replaced by people who need nothing but their phones and their creative-genius interests to make a living. Their actions don't fit the pattern of an iron-cage job, where a man punches the clock, works like a cog, and receives a steady drip of wealth to take home to his lowly wife.

This is all very bad news if you're planning to depend on the iron-cage economy to support you forever. But if you're willing to put your energy into designing your life and career as a fundamentally creative being, the news is actually wonderful.

For the rest of this chapter, we'll look at ways we can return to nature's ecosystemic model to replace our culture's wildly unfair, inhumane, and collapsing pyramid of wealth. Start with this: as you imagine making a living, don't think factory. Think forest. Let me give a few examples to show you what I mean.

HOW ECONOMIC ECOSYSTEMS CAN WORK

Emma Gannon doesn't have a job. She used to— for a while, she worked in advertising, then moved to magazine writing. But for the past several years, Emma has earned money from many sources, including podcasting, online teaching, self-publishing, speaking gigs, affiliate links, and a subscription newsletter platform called Substack. She recently sold the rights to her podcast to the book-summary platform Blinkist. She spells out her career-development process in books like **The Success Myth** and **The Multi-Hyphen Method: Work Less, Create More, and Design a Career That Works for You.**

"I always have money coming in from multiple income streams," Emma said over lunch at a New York restaurant, "and even if each stream isn't lots of money, together it makes me feel very secure."

Like living things in an ecosystem, different elements of Emma's career wax and wane. This doesn't bother her, she said; she freely adapts to the constant change and shifts her focus depending on her own variable interests. For instance, Emma stopped recording her wildly successful podcast not because it wasn't performing well but because she felt her attention shifting. "The podcast was no longer my passion point," she said. "I felt my throat close over when I would go near the microphone. All I wanted to do was spend time on Substack."

Within a year, Emma's income from Substack went from bringing in "pocket money" to an earning level that could have financially supported Emma all by itself. But she continues to give her genius to the world in many ways, doing it for love, not money, and offering many services for free. "Sometimes, if you take the pressure off and there's no monetary exchange, it gives you a playground," she said. "If it goes wrong, who cares? If people didn't like it, who cares? So it's a good testing ground." She charges for services once she's sure they're valuable and interesting to others. The way she described her process revealed it to be a textbook example of "dedicated play":

My career is like sound waves coming in and me just changing the knobs. It's like, "This one is working better, so . . . turn it up, turn up the heat. This one's fading. Turn it down." I feel like I'm playing. All of it is play.

This doesn't mean that Emma doesn't work hard to master whatever craft she uses to make money. "I'm not comfortable with the whole 'Oh, I'll quit my job and be a TikTok influencer' thing," she said. "That's not what we're talking about." She believes in mastering skills that are genuinely valuable.

"A thriving business starts with just you thinking, **That looks fun,**" she said, "but then experimenting to see what works. We're told we can only earn money in a certain way, that we have to go to an office and do a job. But we're in an infinite universe of opportunities. . . . You can absolutely earn money from just things you love doing."

Your list of favorite pastimes and creative urges may be utterly different from Emma's. But because technology now puts you in touch with people who share almost any interest, **something** you love to make or do—maybe several things you love to make or do—is going to interest someone. If you let your creativity flourish, mastering a craft to the point where you can do-without-doing it, your efforts will have real value to others, who will either want what you create or want to learn how you created it.

David Sedaris's economic ecosystem is somewhat similar to Emma Gannon's. It consists of continuous creativity in the form of books, articles, stories, performances, and recordings that highlight his writing chops and quirky worldview.

We've seen a very different but no less relevant example in my friend Alex van den Heever, whom we met in chapter 9. Alex makes his living tracking animals, doing nature conservation, producing porridge, training safari guides, giving public speeches, and writing. All of his activities feel like part of his personal mission, and each one supports the others—for example, a child who benefited from Alex's nutritious porridge might grow up with an awareness of Alex's passion for wilderness rehabilitation, then join his tracker academy and provide new information and stories for Alex's books and speeches. Alex doesn't do this in a calculated way, but because all his activities flow from his creative center, they end up benefiting one another like the components of any ecosystem.

I've seen many people form economic ecosystems—what Emma Gannon calls "the multi-hyphen method"—by indulging all sorts of creative interests. Rob combines his love of outdoor sports, from skiing and surfing to rock climbing, with a passion for self-knowledge. His clients pay him to make them better athletes as they confront their physical fears, a skill they then translate into facing and quieting their inner demons. Cecily loves to bake and has created online viewings of her baking projects for hundreds of customers, who pay her a few dollars a month to watch live as she creates and demonstrates new recipes. Owen and Greg are brothers who write and perform their own music. Though they've never had a recording contract, their Patreon account brings in a tidy sum on a regular basis.

All of these people are continually looking for new platforms, adding interests and monetizing skills they've had for years. They haven't created new iron-cage jobs; they've constellated new ecosystems that they expect will change over time, and they intend to let their careers change with them.

"It's a living thing," Rob said of his own ecosystem. "It's going to change. Everything is always changing. That's a given. If you can stop focusing on having the kind of job our grandparents did, you can see the beauty of always being challenged to change and to let the changes in you transform your way of getting by."

HOW TO GET STARTED

I'd like to tell you that the day I quit academia, sitting in Delmer Fancyhat's office, I felt confident and secure. But I was actually close to a panic attack. My anxiety only grew in the days after I quit. I tried to think of other jobs I might pursue, but between my disabilities and my children, nothing occurred to me.

As a result, I ended up doing something I wish everyone would do: dealing with my anxiety as a problem in itself before I had a source of income. Paradoxically, this approach is what ultimately allowed me to make a living. As I began to pull my energy out of anxiety spirals and follow my creativity, I also encouraged other people to do this, and many were interested—so interested that they offered to hire me. What I now call my career gradually coalesced, almost without my knowing how it happened.

Now I know that this way of living really can and does work. But I also know how much courage it takes, how much faith. Every day I encounter more people who are ready—sometimes desperate—to leave their iron cages and begin living creatively. Often, the only thing stronger than their longing is their anxiety. They've been socialized to favor their left hemispheres, with the whole built-in anxiety spiral. And they want to break social-role rules, which attracts a lot of nay-saying and negative pressure from most of the people around them. If that sounds like you, here's my favorite assignment for folks in this predicament: feed the birds.

New Skill

CONSTELLATE A LITERAL ECOSYSTEM

---

1. If you can afford a bird feeder, get one. If not, just nail a metal dish to a branch

and fill it with sunflower seeds, or sprin-
kle birdseed on the outside sill of your
apartment window.

2. Keep your seed supply clean and fresh.

3. Watch as the birds **don't** show up to eat it.

4. Until they do.

I gave this assignment to Marielle, a school psychologist, who lived near me during the time I spent
in Phoenix. I often wondered if Arizona's capital got
its name because the summers were so hot that birds
would spontaneously burst into flames if they happened to fly anywhere near the city limits. Perhaps
the heat was one reason why Marielle felt burned out
and depressed. Though she wanted to run her own
learning center for at-risk kids, she felt that she'd be
financially safer by keeping her low-paying but steady
job in the public school system.

Marielle was so exhausted, and so used to following
orders, that when I told her to deal with her financial
fears by putting out birdseed, she barely asked why.
I told her anyway. I wanted her to see how offering
something truly nourishing attracts beings who need
that nourishment, the way I believed parents needed
Marielle's ability to help their children.

Marielle's initial bird-feeding attempt was a spectacular failure. She initially hung the feeder in a place where it couldn't be seen from the air. A week went by. No birds. Ten days. Nothing. Then one day it occurred to Marielle that she could move the feeder to a more visible location. The next day she saw a couple of English sparrows; a week later, mourning doves. When she saw her first bright little goldfinch, Marielle was hooked. Long story short: she ended up learning a lot about local birds and putting out all kinds of food. She attracted hundreds of gorgeous little creatures, including rare indigenous parrots and a flock of green-and-pink lovebirds that had escaped from pet stores and set up house in the desert.

Things didn't stop there—with ecosystems, they never do. As Marielle learned, experimented, and included more interesting items in her bird-feeding station, little foxes, coyotes, and small piglike animals called javelinas began to visit her feeder. If she'd kept expanding the ecosystem that formed in her modest backyard, she probably would have seen some jaguars. Maybe a dragon.

As she watched a literal ecosystem coalesce around her bird feeder, Marielle came to believe that parents might really pay her to help their kids. She began designing what she called a "play process" to help rebuild happiness and self-esteem in children who hated school. She offered this online to local parents. At first, no one signed up . . . until someone did.

Marielle's first clients were just friends, she told

me; they didn't really count. But her work proved so powerful that those delighted customers talked about it to other parents, who talked to others still, until Marielle was doing such good business she was able to quit her job and spend her time not only working with children in ways that really helped them but also dreaming up new ideas for services. A burned-out counselor offered sustenance to a bunch of burned-out children and their burned-out parents and, in the process, created a thriving economic ecosystem.

As you feed the birds—literally and then figuratively—you'll spark the creativity that helps you find the places where your deep gladness and the world's deep hunger meet. But first, you'll need to pull your mind away from the iron-cage job titles you've always called "work." In fact, stop thinking in terms of job titles altogether; the career you ultimately create may not even have a name. Instead, focus on whatever activities put your nervous system into a "deep green" peace, and allow yourself to slip into your right hemisphere's wordless creativity.

ENERGY, WATER, AND SPACE: HELPING YOUR ECOSYSTEM FLOURISH

As Michael Crichton famously wrote in **Jurassic Park,** "Life finds a way." Ecosystems emerge in places even more inhospitable than Phoenix, such as the deep, dark seas around thermal vents. If you refrain from cleaning your fridge for a few weeks, you'll find all sorts of exciting new species and interactions going on in there, without any additional input from you.

The word for this is **autopoiesis** (ah-toe-po-EE-sis), which means "the property of a living system that allows it to maintain and renew itself." You can't **do** autopoiesis. Only the intelligence of nature can. But it does so constantly, relentlessly, unstoppably.

Biological ecosystems constellate wherever three things come together: energy, water, and space. You have a metaphorical set of these same components. The **energy** is your desire, the longing for what you truly, deeply want. The **water** is your creativity. It flows from the deep wells of your personal genius in forms you yourself can't predict or completely understand. Finally, the **space** in which your economic ecosystem can form is your lifespan, this precious stretch of time during which you occupy the planet.

This book isn't about just managing your anxiety while functioning in a system that is (1) hostile to human life, and (2) falling apart. It's meant to help you go far beyond anxiety by creating the conditions that will lead to the autopoiesis of your best possible life.

If you follow all the suggestions I've made so far, I believe you'll continuously generate the conditions needed to keep your economic ecosystem flourishing. Calming your anxiety creature removes inner toxins, the frightening, inaccurate stories that anxiety dreams up. Then you can begin to reawaken your childlike curiosity and playfulness—but with the resources and knowledge of an adult. When you begin spending more time on whatever lights you up (possibly breaking role rules), some people will disapprove, but others will get curious. These people will become customers, clients, partners, helpers.

If you stay out beyond anxiety long enough, you won't be able to stop systems of energy and value, including money, from constellating around you. You'll spot ideas and feel drawn to people who truly interest you. You'll get comfortable with the fluidity of an ecosystem, the way different parts of it wax and wane. You'll see your true career displaying its own astonishing autopoiesis: forming, growing, and developing new features almost by itself, like mold in the back of your fridge. Life finds a way. Your life will find a way.

THE BLANK STARE OF GENIUS: OFFERING THE "BIRDSEED" THAT ATTRACTS INCOME

It's 2020, and for a full year, I've been recovering from a tricky foot surgery. My body is a mess: one leg atrophied, the other cramped from overuse, my back and hips a tangled clot of muscle spasms. I've taken to doing Pilates because it lets me exercise without having to stand up.

One day, my Pilates teacher, Ray, says, "You need to go to my physical therapist."

"I've had physical therapy before," I say doubtfully. "Usually, I ended up feeling worse. I have this wonky body. It doesn't work like a normal one."

"Hmm," Ray says, gazing into the middle distance. "Well, Bridget isn't a normal physical therapist. She's more like . . . magic."

Ray himself is like magic. I've tried doing Pilates with other teachers and **hated** it. But Ray seems to instinctively know exactly how to help me stress my body enough to strengthen it without causing damage.

It takes weeks, but I finally manage to get into Bridget Sanphy's packed schedule. She turns out to be a soft-spoken woman in her thirties, with the tawny hair, eyes, and taut physique of a puma. She asks me about my recent surgery and my general decrepitude, then watches me hobble around so she can "see me move." There's something almost unnerving about the blankness of her expression, the quality of her silence. I feel the hairs on my arms prickle.

"Okay," she says after a few minutes, "try this." Bridget then demonstrates a series of exercises, all of which look ridiculously easy when she does them but turn me into a sweating, panting, quivering hobbit. A man icing his knee nearby thoughtfully tells Bridget, "You're going to have to send that woman to the hospital." But Bridget will not do this. I strongly suspect she's trying to kill me.

The next day, my whole body feels better than it has in years.

I can't afford **not** to hire Bridget. Committed to good health and blessed with a streak of masochism, I go back to her studio week after week, grunting my way through many exercises so torturous that I'm pretty sure they're illegal. Also, miraculous. A thousand little aches and pains I'd long ago accepted start disappearing.

Clearly, Bridget is very well trained. But her ability to help me so much, so quickly, far exceeds that of the many doctors and physical therapists I've consulted in the past. One day, I ask her how she always knows exactly what will heal my various twinges and injuries.

Bridget pauses. Her eyes drift down and to the left, which often indicates activation of the right hemisphere. After a minute, Bridget looks up and says slowly, "I watch a person's body move, and then I get a hunch in my own body. I test it to see if I'm right, and we go from there."

"When was the last time your hunch was wrong?"

Bridget thinks again, then smiles shyly. "To be honest, I don't remember."

Throughout my adult life, I've been quizzing "outliers" like Ray and Bridget, people who are so good at what they do that customers and clients flock to them like finches to a bird feeder. I've interviewed artists, chefs, physicists, musicians, tax accountants, literary agents, home organizers, movie producers, journalists, comedians, event planners—any skill is fair game, so long as the person I'm quizzing has become successful just by offering their favorite pastime to the world.

Over and over, I've seen the same behaviors in these people that I noticed in Bridget: an almost unnerving inner stillness; that wide-eyed, expressionless gaze; the eyes that drift, usually to the left, when contemplating a question.

When I imitate that expression, the mirror neurons in my own brain fire up and remind me of times when I do the same thing. It often happens when I'm just walking outside, but also when I'm drawing, writing, coaching, or meditating. In fact, when I really have to solve a pressing problem, I deliberately adopt the "right-hemisphere gaze." I mentioned this in chapter 2 when I asked you to soften the focus of your eyes, to lose the sharp stare of the yellow-light alert state and go into the broad, contemplative state of a resting animal.

When someone generates "work" from this state, people notice. Reputations grow by word of mouth: "You really have to see this person. They're like magic." This is why patients wait weeks to see Bridget, though there are plenty of other physical therapists around. It's why Marielle has a yearlong waiting list for her workshops with parents and students. It's why people happily sign up for Emma Gannon's Substack, though the internet is swarming with competitors. It's how David Sedaris fills up Carnegie Hall in an era when no one goes to book readings.

THE SOFT MAGIC OF CONSTELLATION

Autopoiesis is a core attribute of nature, but when it happens, it can look a lot like magic. It's been thirty years since the day Delmer Fancyhat condemned me to life as a lowly faculty wife. During that time, as I learned to trust nature, inexplicable things happened to me more and more often. And they still blow my mind.

For example, when I began researching this book, I was especially obsessed with the work of the frequently mentioned Jill Bolte Taylor, Richard Schwartz (founder of IFS therapy), and Gavin de Becker, whose classic book, **The Gift of Fear,** published in 1997, still stands as the best guide to eliminating anxiety while honoring healthy fear. I'd never met any of these people. But as I researched away, ensconced in my house during the global lockdown, all three of them contacted me out of the clear blue sky.

No one knew what I was researching. No one knew whose work I found especially interesting. Yet without **any** effort on my part, I ended up having long conversations with them and got the incredible gift of drafting on their genius. Jill and I spent many hours talking about the brain and about how to form economic ecosystems. Gavin emailed me at the very moment I was telling a friend that I wanted to reread his books. I can't remember why Richard reached out to me; he just did. Obviously, there are logical reasons why they connected with me. But it looks a lot like magic from here.

So the last bit of advice I'd like to give you as you set out to create a career beyond anxiety is this: let yourself relax into the magic. In most children's books or fantasy novels, making magic is a grueling effort, one that makes the veins pop out on the wizard's head and leaves the hero exhausted. Only one writer I know, Philip Pullman, author of the book trilogy **His Dark Materials,** describes it differently. In the first novel of this series, **Northern Lights** (or **The Golden Compass,** as it's titled in North America), Lyra, the heroine, learns to read a magic compass by adopting the soft right-hemisphere attention I've seen in so many geniuses.

> [Lyra] found that if she . . . gazed at it in a particular lazy way . . . the long needle would begin to move more purposefully. . . . [I]t swung smoothly from one picture to another. . . . [S]he gained a deep calm enjoyment from it, unlike anything she'd known.

This, I believe, is how "magic" actually works. It turns us into satellite towers, sensing and transmitting good ideas like Bridget the physical therapist. It draws in people and conditions we need, and **the process feels like "deep calm enjoyment," not gruesome effort.** If you are committed to living without anxiety, you'll eventually end up going so deeply into your right hemisphere that you run into enchantment. I'm not a fan of religion, but I believe in the metaphysical. After all, love is metaphysical, as are our hopes and dreams. Metaphysical realities not only exist but are primordial aspects of nature, essential for life outside the iron cage. To end this chapter, here's an exercise to help you tap into them as you constellate your economic ecosystem.

New Skill

USE DEEP GREEN MAGIC TO CONSTELLATE YOUR ECOSYSTEM

1. **Go into a "deep green" state.**
   Use every anxiety-soothing technique that works for you to calm your nervous system. Throw in every breathing technique, every sort of KIST, every glimmer. Remember the most relaxing moments of

your life, and focus all your attention on them. Go into green-light energy, as discussed in chapter 3, and then into **deep** green energy.

2. **Staying very relaxed, imagine a natural ecosystem that appeals to you.**

   It might be in the ocean, the mountains, a forest, a savanna, or a river delta. Imagine this ecosystem as it might have been ten thousand years ago. Notice how everything in the ecosystem is balanced and responsive, everything caring for everything else year after year, century after century.

3. **Sense the overall feeling of this peaceful, self-sustaining system.**

   Imagine your body filling with the energy of that ecosystem, as if it were inside your body. Feel it humming and thriving. Imagine that energy as your own internal state. You **are** the meadow, the savanna, the coral reef.

4. **Picture your ideal life three or four years in the future.**

   In this fantasy, you don't have a huge sum of money in the bank, but **everything you need to fulfill any true desire is automatically funded**, the same way sunshine gives energy to flowers or water falls from the sky in a rainforest.

5. **Calm your creature again.**

   If the desire for this life spikes any worries or anxious questions (**How can I build this?** or **Where will I get the money?**) or even excitement (**Oh, I wish that would happen!** or **I hope I can have this!**), calm your creature. Go back into deep green peace and quiet.

6. **Use this little meditation every morning and/or evening for at least a week.**

   Then, as you go through each day, notice how things related to your imaginary game will begin to "pop" as you train your attention. Write them down in a journal or notebook.

7. **Expect and allow the elements of your ideal life to constellate around you.**

   If you begin having anxious thoughts (**Why isn't it happening yet?** or **Where will I get the money?**) just calm your creature, calm your creature, calm your creature.

As you live this way, your brain may keep sliding toward anxiety—mine certainly does. If we let the anxiety take over, the whole process of autopoiesis can be short-circuited. We won't see our desires trying to constellate, because they'll be hidden behind the fear stories generated by our left hemispheres. No worries. If you notice this happening, use the processes outlined in this book to return to your deep green state of calm. If you're anxious about money, deal with the anxiety first. When you return to peace, you'll be able to attract and deal with money far more effectively.

In fact, living beyond anxiety will ultimately reverse the way you've been taught to think about money. Even though you may still participate in iron-cage jobs to pay your rent or put the kids through school, your mind will remain open to your natural passions, and ideas for indulging them may very well turn into new ways of making a living.

You'll be amazed at how much less frightening financial issues feel when your first focus is on living a purposeful life and earning money is subordinate to that. And once you do begin making money through creativity, purpose, and a liberated imagination, the ups and downs of financial life will be far less upsetting. You'll feel that seasons change, that tides come in and go out. It's all part of the balance nature uses to keep ecosystems running indefinitely.

Spending more time in creativity, you'll also see opportunities to build up multiple ways of supplying your needs—all of which can serve your deepest sense of purpose. You'll have ideas that you didn't think of before and begin reaching out to explore them. And then you'll start to experience that incredible, beneficent magic: a sense of the world reaching back toward you from all around, as if the vast intelligence of nature is exploring **you.**

By the time this happens, you'll realize that making a living is less about hoarding money and more about funding a creative lifestyle. It's not about punching the clock, gutting your way through miserable hours in an iron-cage job. It's about getting lost in the deep green magic as you walk along whatever road you choose, picking up trash, cleaning your little bit of the world, enjoying the fresh air, and musing over what you might create next.

11

Don't-Know Mind

Here's something to ponder: your body is, at most, seven years old. In a process known as cell regeneration, every human body releases and then replaces every single atom of itself every seven years. All the physical forms you called "me" more than seven years ago—the "you" who went through puberty, who learned to drive, who acquired that unfortunate tattoo—were made of other atoms. Even the tattoo, though it sadly still looks the same, consists of different molecules than the ones originally punched into your skin. An entirely different skin from the one you're wearing now.

So if not an atom of your current body was present during all those past experiences, what remembers them? What lived through those events? Your consciousness. Whatever that is. It's exceedingly difficult to pin down a verbal definition of consciousness because we can't grasp, count, or clearly describe it. We just use it. We just **are** it.

Most scientists will confidently state that consciousness is created by the brain. The conventional wisdom is that life emerged from the primordial soup, evolved animals that were **kind of** conscious, and finally produced the amazing machine of the human brain, which generates all the wonders of consciousness as we experience it. Other scientists, following the intricacies of quantum physics, believe the opposite: matter doesn't make consciousness, they claim; consciousness makes matter. I happen to agree with this version, but whether you believe that consciousness makes matter or the other way around, the relationship between them is deeply mysterious.

More mysterious yet, how did your **particular** consciousness come to be, and how does it keep regenerating your body year after year? Beats me. Beats everybody. As philosopher Jerry Fodor said, "Nobody has the slightest idea how anything material could be conscious. Nobody even knows what it would be like to have the slightest idea about how anything material could be conscious."

All of this is just to say that your very existence is a mystery. And as you go further and further beyond anxiety, you may encounter Mystery in a life-changing way. In this chapter, I'll discuss the shift of perspective that is sometimes called "awakening." If you decide to ride your creativity a long, **long** way, I believe this ineffable experience may very well happen to you.

WHAT IS AWAKENING?

"Awakening" is one of many terms for a dramatic transformation in an individual's way of experiencing reality. Though very rare, this phenomenon has been reported consistently by people from all over the world, at every point in history. It's also known by other labels: "enlightenment," "insight," "realization," "liberation," and probably thousands of other terms in languages living and dead. All awakened people agree that language can't fully describe their experience, but their attempts are remarkably consistent, whatever culture they belong to.

At the moment a person awakens, so these sages tell us, everything suddenly looks different. The universe no longer appears to be a collection of solid, separate objects; instead, it's an indivisible field of living energy: one interconnected Being. Everything in it shares an infinitely compassionate consciousness. The awakened person **becomes** this consciousness, no longer identifying as a vulnerable body but as the awareness looking out through the physical form.

It's easy to see the similarity between reported stories of awakening and, for example, Jill Bolte Taylor's description of right-hemisphere perception. But most people who've reported these experiences didn't have strokes. Some quieted their thinking minds through meditation until they seemed to dissolve into full perception of the present moment. Others suffered so much from painful internal stories that in moments of grace, surrender, or sheer exhaustion, the story-telling parts of their minds finally let go, and they experienced a profound sense of being both liberated from their individual woes and interconnected with every aspect of a benevolent universe.

After decades of studying awakening from every angle I can find, I've come to suspect that it involves shifting identity out of a heavily left hemisphere–dominated mindset and into a worldview that grounds one's sense of self (or "no self," as many awakened people put it) in the right hemisphere's perceptions. It's a bit like changing the dial on a radio: by shifting our focus of attention, we pick up different "music," different perceptions. Both versions of reality have been broadcasting all along on parallel frequencies. **This doesn't mean that the brain itself is the ultimate source of the conscious mind, any more than a radio is the ultimate source of Bach or Beyoncé.** In this analogy, the brain is simply the transmitter of different ways to perceive reality.

Though the unawakened mind can't see the reality of the awakened perception, the opposite isn't true: people who are awake can access all the information coming in through their senses and logical thought. After recovering from her stroke, Jill Bolte Taylor was careful not to ever fully leave the part of her mind that had landed her in bliss during her stroke. In **Whole Brain Living,** she talks about connecting with her right hemisphere by identifying its wise, calm perspective as her primary viewpoint, and by lovingly caring for the left hemisphere's anxieties. She dubs this "calling a brain huddle," or bringing together all the perspectives from various parts of her brain to calm and comfort them, appreciating that each part has a role but designating her calm right hemisphere as the one who gathers and leads the rest.

I believe that, like Jill, awakened people throughout history have learned to use their whole brains. But once they've done so, they identify with nonphysical awareness rather than with their physical bodies. And this view of the world feels much more real and reasonable than their previous way of perceiving it. They feel calm, safe, and loved by the entire universe. Everything simply makes more sense, the way our everyday lives appear after we've woken from scary dreams.

STRANGE BUT NOT INSANE

One person who seems to have "woken up" is the philosopher Plato. In the **Republic,** he asks his readers to imagine a world where everyone lives chained up in a cave, facing away from the light. These people think that reality consists solely of the shadows they can see on the cave wall.

If someone got out of the cave and wandered around, Plato writes, that person would experience a much more vivid, interesting, and convincing world than the shadow wall. They would probably adopt a totally different set of priorities based on what they had discovered about the reality of the world outside the cave. And the cave people who were still chained up, Plato says, would very likely think that the traveler was insane.

I've mentioned several times in this book that going beyond anxiety will make you feel good and look weird. If you pull away from left hemisphere–dominated social norms, if you begin creating a life out of whatever brings you the most joy, and **definitely** if you have an awakening experience, other people may be confused. They may mock you, proclaim you've lost your mind, or attack you for failing to follow their beliefs.

So let me assure you again that awakening doesn't involve far-out psychedelic psychosis. In fact, many awakened people have said that it's the most normal thing they've ever experienced. I've met several people who I believe have "awakened." All of them told me that the awakened state is always present in everyone, and that staying in it is simply a continuous choice to direct our attention toward whatever connects us with the perception of a benevolent universe.

You've probably touched this state in many ordinary moments. If you've ever watched a person or an animal sleeping and suddenly seen them as deeply beautiful, even completely perfect, you've seen them through awakened eyes. Maybe you can recall having an argument with a loved one and suddenly seeing the whole conflict as silly—even to the point where you dissolved into laughter. That's a switch to an awakened perspective. Whenever you feel swept up by a wave of peace, or deep love, or awe, I believe you are touching the awakened state. Of course, to the fear-and-control parts of your mind, these kinds of experiences seem to contain nothing interesting— no drama, no stories, no events. So the part of you that's reading these words may not have even noticed your own flashes of awakened perception. Remember, the left hemisphere may fail to acknowledge the reality of your own left leg, so we really can't expect it to track a state of being that's absolutely still and silent.

At the end of this chapter, I'll offer you an exercise that might help you deliberately dip your toe into the fringes of "awakened" perception. But first let's talk about the fact that everything I'm saying may sound ridiculously woo-woo or far too simplistic. If you're like most citizens of the WEIRD world, you've been trained not to credit awakening as anything important, or as anything at all. That socialization may have created inner obstacles I'd love to address now.

WHY YOU MIGHT BE FEELING QUEASY RIGHT ABOUT NOW

If all this talk of "waking up" and falling in love with the universe is making you roll your eyes until you develop motion sickness, you are probably an educated person in a WEIRD culture who equates truth with empirical evidence. Or you may be a religious person who's deeply offended that I've boiled the ineffable experience of awakening down to a mere neurological shift. In any case, your hackles might be thoroughly raised.

We've all been conditioned to react this way to discussions of awakened consciousness. The Western world doesn't contain much of a cultural legacy that invites or accepts awakening. The dominant religions that helped shape this civilization may ascribe awakening to famous figures, but as they lay down the laws about what to do and believe, these religions rarely include any instructions for inducing transformations of consciousness. In fact, awakening might make someone question, or even wander away from, the teachings of religious leaders.

The scientific method appeared in more recent centuries partly to fight back against this kind of religious oppression. Science and religion have been at each other's throats ever since. These days, at least in WEIRD cultures, many religious people see science as a threat to basic goodness, while many scientists view religious devotees as dangerously delusional.

I've experienced both sides of this cultural bias from right down inside the trenches—an experience that ultimately made me sort of squirt out sideways. As a child, I once asked a Mormon teacher about factual claims in the Book of Mormon that don't square with scientific evidence (such as the belief that all Native Americans are descended from a Middle Eastern family that immigrated six hundred years ago). I was told, "You can tell that science is wrong because it changes all the time. One day scientists say this, the next day they say that. You can know the Church is true because it never changes."

When I left Utah for Harvard, still a malleable teenager, I was happy to discard "Intellectuals are evil! Mormons know all the things!" and replace it with "Religious people are stupid! Intellectuals know all the things!" But I hit a snag as a graduate student when my son was diagnosed with Down syndrome. All my academic advisers, and the doctors at Harvard's medical center, told me Adam's life would not be worth living and advised me to institutionalize him. Neither my heart nor my logical brain could feel this as Truth.

That's when I noticed that my advisers and doctors seemed to worship analytical intelligence in very much the same way my childhood community worshipped the Book of Mormon. For all their differences, the antiscience religious believers and the antireligious scientific thinkers all shared the same basic credo:

"WE KNOW ALL THE THINGS!"

You may recognize this as the characteristic viewpoint of the left hemisphere. When we're fully immersed in left-hemisphere thinking, we **absolutely believe** whatever story we're telling. We also want to manipulate other people into believing it with us. Religious or atheist, a mind locked on the idea that WE KNOW ALL THE THINGS is thinking dogmatically. When we're entrenched in this mindset, we go mind blind to much of what we're experiencing. We live in mental projection—the terrifying, anxiety-riddled existence awakened people call the dreamworld. So what's the alternative that can help us regain our mindsight? It's not rocket science. It's just acknowledging this:

Maybe we don't know all the things.

THE JOY OF DON'T-KNOW MIND

Socrates famously said, "I know nothing except the fact of my ignorance." The French philosopher Réne Descartes agreed. People often quote Descartes as saying, "Cogito, ergo sum" (I think, therefore I am). What he actually wrote was: "We cannot doubt of our existence while we doubt." He then concluded:

"Dubito, ergo sum, vel, quod idem est, cogito, ergo sum" (I doubt, therefore I am—or, what is the same—I think, therefore I am). It was doubt, not thought, that formed the foundation of Descartes's reality. But no one ever mentions that. Doubt is anathema to religious and scientific dogmatists alike.

When I was twenty, having absorbed both religious and intellectual versions of the WE KNOW ALL THE THINGS mindset, I went to live and study in Asia. I expected to find new, Far Eastern versions of WE KNOW ALL THE THINGS, and I did. Sometimes. Confucianism, for example, is rigid enough to please the Spanish Inquisition. But many branches of Asian philosophy take an approach I'd never encountered. They rest on the belief that **we will never know all the things.**

It takes about half a second of logical thinking to realize that a human mind can't grasp the totality of the universe. But when I first met people who were comfortable with that idea, I felt quite dizzy. It was like reaching out to touch a solid wall and finding . . . nothing.

Instead of stuffing themselves full of knowledge the way I'd always been taught to do, the most revered Asian philosophers aspired to a state they called "don't-know mind," which sounded to me like the definition of stupidity. I knew that the European Enlightenment happened when a lot of intellectuals learned enormous amounts of facts and logical processes. But these Asian sages used the term "enlightenment" to describe the **release** of all fixed ideas.

At first, I saw all of this as a kind of strange, abstract word puzzle. I thought it had nothing to do with me. I'd probably still think so if it weren't for my old nemesis, anxiety.

As the years went by and I got more and more unbearably anxious, adding chronic pain to my list of worries, I finally resorted to the one thing I could still actively **do:** learn to meditate. So I embarked on endless hours of excruciating boredom and mounting unease. And then, when I'd stopped even hoping for it, I felt the first faint hints of what all those Asian mystics had been talking about. For fleeting instants, I would sometimes slip into a gentler, sweeter, more vivid world and get a brief but intense feeling that I'd come home.

The skills you've been reading about in this book are some of the practices that brought me these moments of grace. If you practice these skills, or any others you might find lying around the house, you may occasionally feel a pause in your own anxiety, like the silence in the eye of a hurricane.

In these moments, you may lose track of time, along with guilt, regret, and fear. Again, your verbal mind—the part that's reading this—may not record these experiences at all, since nothing it values happens within them. But if you start paying attention to the silent spaces in the streams of thought rather than to the thoughts themselves, you won't just move away from anxiety. You'll wake up. And these days, even science is finding that every step we take toward this mindset is very, very good for us.

THE SCIENCE OF AWAKENING

Dr. Lisa Miller has a lot of nerve. I mean that in the best way. A professor at Columbia, Miller has compiled a small mountain of research suggesting that our brains have what she calls "a docking station for spiritual awareness."

Miller and her colleagues have found that individuals who are open to the idea of a spiritual reality in the universe are, statistically speaking, far happier than others. When we open our minds to the possibility of a metaphysical element in the universe, she says, "we access unsurpassed psychological benefits: less depression, anxiety, and substance abuse and more positive psychological traits, such as grit, resilience, optimism, tenacity, and creativity."

The reason I say Miller has so much nerve is that though her research is impeccable, it's also, in her stomping grounds, downright embarrassing. Championing spirituality at an Ivy League institution is like standing up during Sunday Mass at a monastery and shouting to the monks, "Hey, friends, we've all got sexual feelings, and it's time we explored them!"

When Miller first presented her data, disapproving

colleagues said there had to be "hidden factors" that would explain away the whole spiritual thing. But so far, no one has found such factors. And other scientists are observing phenomena that back up Miller's findings.

For example, neurologist Andrew Newberg and his coauthor Mark Robert Waldman, who call the spiritually tuned brain "enlightened," reported the same link between spiritual openness and mental health benefits that showed up in Miller's data set. When Harvard's Daniel Goleman and Richard Davidson used MRI machines to peer into the heads of those Tibetan monks, they saw brains that looked much younger, and much more wired for happiness, than the brains of most other people. The effect was stronger in monks who'd spent more time meditating, which means the men weren't just born with happy brains; they had transformed their own neurology through spiritual practice. These practices were not about learning dogmatic beliefs but about **letting go of the need for certainty.**

Mental health practitioners also report that the compassionate core of the self is open to the mystery of the universe. Therapists who use IFS report that people's "Selves," the loving, wise, fearless cores of identity, often seem to be overtly spiritual. In fact, Richard Schwartz told me that it can be hard for people to describe their Selves without using spiritual concepts and vocabulary. When they "go inside" to talk to various parts, many patients say that they en-counter spiritual aspects of themselves, one of which is the Self. Other parts may identify themselves as guides, aspects of a person's consciousness that help them find their way through life.

In short, many different approaches to neurological research and clinical psychology are leading very well educated, scrupulously scientific scholars to a place where "accepting the data" includes acknowledging that the human brain has the "docking station" for spiritual connection that Miller describes.

If we follow the creativity spiral very far, we may begin "docking" with experiences that feel intensely mysterious and metaphysical. In these moments of awakening, we sense that we're being drawn out of our small, frightened selves to mingle with the whole vast span of Creation. Our anxiety drops out of sight. Our health, happiness, and ability to realize our senses of purpose all take a dramatic upward turn.

I'd love to help you experience this. But I'm not going to suggest that you need some massive person-ality shift or to go dancing with angels. I believe that accepting the limits of our own perceptions is all we have to do to begin waking up. The road to wak-ing up is paved not with new knowledge but with **unknowing**—really knowing how deeply we don't know things, like what reality actually is. We start down this road by accepting not-knowing as a fun-damental quality of being human.

THE WAY INTO AWAKENING: ACCEPTING DOUBT

I've just mentioned research done by Dr. Andrew Newberg, the director of research at the Marcus Institute of Integrative Health and a physician at Thomas Jefferson University Hospital. As a young man, Newberg embarked on a compulsive search for absolute truth. He was anxious and depressed, in deep psychological pain. "But then," he writes, "it happened."

> Suddenly . . . I found myself floating in what I can only describe as a sea of Infinite Doubt. . . . Instead of fighting the doubt, I became united **with** it. . . . It was incredibly intense, profoundly clear, entirely uplifting, deeply emotional, and extraordinarily pleasurable. In fact, it became the most important turning point in my life and philosophy. [Italics in the original.]

It wasn't **thinking about** doubt that helped Newberg begin to wake up; it was **becoming the consciousness in which doubt occurs.** I've met other people who also dropped out of certainty into the wondering, open, curious, intensely present aspect of themselves and felt as if the whole world became "incredibly intense, profoundly clear, entirely uplifting, deeply emotional, and extraordinarily pleasurable."

Very few of these people are famous or revered. They live completely ordinary lives. For example, my client Dinah, a mother and freelance writer, visited Taiwan when she was a teenager, before the internet or even cell phones existed. She wandered away from her student group and got lost—for three days. Speaking no Chinese, unable to even read street signs, she became intensely aware of the energy around her. She felt drawn to certain people and somehow made herself understood by them, despite the fact that they spoke no English. They fed her, gave her a place to sleep, and eventually helped her contact her group through the American embassy.

Dinah was transformed by this experience. Years later, she told me, "I realized that **not knowing** anything about my surroundings forced me to tune into a more open kind of awareness. In not-knowing, I found a way to connect with everything and everyone. I felt beauty and love like a matrix that holds all of us, everything."

Since then, Dinah has lived according to a phrase she heard in a yoga class: "I exist in continuous creative response to whatever is present." This is the way of life that arises when we accept that we don't really know much, and what we do think we know may be false.

Asher is another ordinary person who I think may be awake. Asher's granddaughter, like my son, has Down syndrome. We met at a conference and ended up talking for hours with two or three other attendees. Late in the evening, Asher told us about an experience that, in his words, "blew my mind and saved my soul."

Asher reached middle age feeling that life was pointless and depressing. He suffered from terrible anxiety and was haunted by the suffering, death, and horrors he saw in human history. "Then one day," he said, "I stopped backing away from all that pain and kind of mentally stepped **into** it. I don't know how. But as I did, I joined all the people and beings who had ever suffered—only I wasn't them; I was the thing that made them exist. And I thought, **Oh, it's like a movie! All these stories are real, but they're only real projections from something much** more **real.** And that something is Love. Love beyond Love. I can't express it. I just try to live in it."

These people aren't superhuman, just human. Newberg is just a scientist. Dinah is just a writer. Asher is just a retired landscaper. They're ordinary people, but they're a lot less anxious and a lot more creative than most of us. Instead of generating internal suffering, they are constantly creating. Newberg creates experiments. Dinah creates poems, essays, and books. Asher creates activities and adventures for athletes in the Special Olympics. They choose, moment by moment, to stay awake. And they all believe, as Newberg writes, that "in every child, and perhaps every adult, there is an artist that is capable of reaching out beyond the confines of a limited human mind to touch some deeper essence of life."

The way to discover this inner artist is to walk into doubt with wonder and curiosity instead of anxiety. Here's an exercise that helps me do that.

New Skill

ACCESS YOUR DON'T-KNOW MIND

Below are a few descriptions of documented events. Respond to each description by noting whether you know, or don't know, exactly what is going on in that situation. Use your self-calming skills to relax if you begin to feel anxious.

- Eşref Armağan is a Turkish artist. He was born with one eye, which is the size of a lentil and totally nonfunctional. His other eye is completely absent. Armağan has literally never seen anything. Yet he paints recognizable portraits and realistic landscapes that feature birds in the air and linear perspective. Armağan has been

studied by researchers from multiple uni-
versities, including Harvard. They verified
that no one is assisting him in any way as
he paints these realistic images.

☐ **I know exactly what's going on
here.**

☐ **I don't know exactly what's going
on here.**

- Studies have found that twins reared apart
often share many characteristics and even
life experiences. In one heavily studied
case, twin boys were separated and adopted by different families at the age of
four weeks. They were reunited at age
thirty-nine. Shortly after learning of each
other's existence, they realized that they
also had these things in common:

  - Both of their adoptive families named
  them Jim.

  - As youngsters, each Jim had a dog
  named Toy.

  - Each Jim had been married two times.
  Their first wives were both called Linda,
  and their second wives were both called
  Betty.

  - One Jim named his son James Allan.
  The other named his son James Alan.

- Each twin had repeatedly driven his light-blue Chevrolet from Ohio to the same small beach in Florida for family vacations—though they never saw each other there.

- Both Jims smoked Salem cigarettes and drank Miller Lite beer.

- Both Jims at one time held part-time posts as sheriffs.

  ☐ **I know exactly what's going on here.**

  ☐ **I don't know exactly what's going on here.**

- A researcher named Monica Gagliano from the University of Sydney has published numerous peer-reviewed scientific papers about the way plants can learn, remember, and communicate. Her inventive, highly successful, and highly replicable experiments have shown, among other things, that plants rest, play, learn, emit sounds, and respond to the sounds in their environments.

  Gagliano claims that the ideas for these experiments came from the plants themselves. She uses practices learned from rainforest shamans to "listen" to plant communication. And the experiments she runs to test the information turn out to be scientifically valid.

- ☐ **I know exactly what's going on here.**

- ☐ **I don't know exactly what's going on here.**

- In 1898, a writer named Morgan Robertson published a novella about the wreck of a ship called the **Titan**. Though this was years before the real ship **Titanic** was even conceptualized, Robertson's story paralleled the sinking of the **Titanic** to a remarkable degree. For example:

  - Both ships (fictional and nonfictional) were the largest ever built at the time.

  - Both ships were called "unsinkable."

  - Both were British.

  - The **Titan** was 800 feet long, the **Titanic** 882.5.

  - Both were made of steel and had three propellers and two masts.

  - Each ship had a passenger capacity of three thousand.

  - Both ships had twenty-four lifeboats.

  - Both struck an iceberg at around midnight.

- Both had a hull breach at the same location on the ship.
- Both sank in April.

  ☐ **I know exactly what's going on here.**

  ☐ **I don't know exactly what's going on here.**

- For the past century, physicists have known that the universe isn't a set of physical objects bumping into each other. Subatomic particles, the building blocks of all matter, are just fields of energy—until we measure them. Somehow, whenever we set out to do that, the wave probabilities "collapse" into physical points of matter.

  Some think this means that being observed by consciousness literally creates matter from energy. Others say that the way we perceive things is nothing like reality; we see the universe as matter, but in reality, every electron, every researcher, every bit of equipment, and the entire universe are really just energy fields.

  ☐ **I know exactly what's going on here.**

  ☐ **I don't know exactly what's going on here.**

How did you do? Is there anything here you can explain with certainty, or are you content to doubt that you know anything for certain? You might be thinking, **There's no way all that could be true. And even if it is, I'm certainly not going to go all mushy headed based on a few anomalies. I'm sticking with a** proven **version of reality.**

Hello, left hemisphere. Hello, anxiety spiral.

All these strange facts, and a great many more, will be waiting for you if you ever decide to release your grip on certainty and wander into the mystery. And if they occur, your moments of awakening will feel not alien but completely familiar, like coming home. You won't think, **I have never known this until now!** Instead, you'll realize, **Oh, yes! This loving reality is what I've always known in my heart. It was just masked by the way I was thinking.** You'll have far less "magical thinking" in an awakened moment, simply soaking in the present situation, than you would on an anxious day buying extra lottery tickets and hoping to cash in on The Secret.

That said, the more often we allow ourselves to access our awakeness, the more life really does start to feel purposeful, loving, and capable of giving us adventures that—at least to the left hemisphere—look a lot like magic.

A FEW MAGICAL ADVENTURES

I seem to have a lot of "magical" adventures—not because I'm anything special or one of the awakened but because I actively, repeatedly use all the advice I've given you in this book. I mentioned in the last chapter that "magic" happens when we extricate ourselves from anxiety. I think this may be because a brain working normally has the "docking station for spirituality" that Lisa Miller describes. She claims we need access to the Mystery to "make full use of how we're built." Free from anxiety, happily knowing we don't know, we enter a reality where improbable, wonderful things seem to happen all the time.

I've told you a few "magic" stories from my own life already. I use them because I know for sure they aren't exaggerated, since they happened to me personally. Here are a couple more, just to show you how odd reality can be.

One evening, I bought dinner for an anthropologist, a woman who had spent her career studying Siberian shamanism. I wanted to grill her about the metaphysical aspects of that ancient culture. As we chatted and ate, she matter-of-factly mentioned that there are practical applications to acknowledging that physical reality is fundamentally interwoven with consciousness. When I asked her for an example, she said that a spoon may allow you to bend it if you connect to your own core consciousness, which is intermingled with the spoon's consciousness, and ask the spoon to play with you. If it agrees, you can bend it like clay.

I know this sounds crazy. It certainly sounded crazy to me. It sounded crazy as I picked up a fork, asked it to play with me, and suddenly felt it bend double under light pressure from my hands. Try this yourself if you want to—but remember that to make it work, you need to be in an anxiety-free state, the "particular lazy way" and "deep calm enjoyment" Philip Pullman wrote about in **Northern Lights** (a.k.a. **The Golden Compass**). If you stay in calm don't-know mind and do some deep play, you'll easily master this skill. (Just please use your own spoons. People at hotels where I go to speak are always asking me to demonstrate and then practicing spoon bending in their rooms. They get anxious when they can't bend them back to exactly the original shape, which leaves a lot of mangled spoons, and I feel responsible.)

This little party trick is far from the weirdest way I've felt the consciousness of physical things that seem to be playing with me. It often happens in nature, especially when I get the chance to interact with wild animals. For instance, one freezing winter day in Pennsylvania, where I live, my family rescued a broken-winged blue jay from our backyard. We wrapped the bird in a towel and put him into a box so that I could drive him to the wildlife rescue center.

It was a fairly long way. Every time I turned, braked, or accelerated, an unnerving scrabbling sound would come from the box. "It's fine," I told myself. "He can't get out."

We got to a stretch of freeway where I sped up to about sixty miles per hour to merge with heavy traffic. The scrabbling from the box got louder. It began to sound frantic. I kept my eyes on the road and silently repeated, "He can't get out. He can't get out. He can't get—oh my God, he got out."

I don't know how he did it. I just glanced over and there he was, standing on top of his box in the passenger seat right at my eye level, looking much larger and more vivid than I remembered.

As I forced myself to carefully navigate out of the high-speed traffic to a place where I could pull over and stop, my mind played out a million terrifying scenarios: the bird trying to fly through the windows, flapping in my face, fighting me as I grappled with him, possibly hurting his broken wing, getting my eyes pecked out, causing a massive accident with multiple fatalities. The poor blue jay was in a profoundly new environment, one that I imagined would terrify any wild animal.

Since I didn't know what to do, I did what I knew. I put the car in park, then used all my anxiety-calming techniques. I realized that, as always, my anxiety was dread of what might happen in the future, even if that future was in the following second. I slowed my breathing, relaxed my muscles, and began repeating little KIST phrases: "You're okay. It's all right. You're good. This is fine. Everything's okay."

It took a minute or two, but I finally felt my anxiety slow down, then slow down more, then stop. I went deep into that open, present state that is always waiting beyond anxiety. I let out a long, slow exhale and turned to face the bird.

Who, at that very moment, hopped off his box, walked over the gear shift, climbed into my lap, and settled down as if he'd arrived back home to his own nest.

My heart did a little hitch, then started up again. I stroked the blue jay's silky feathers and talked softly to him until he closed his eyes, apparently enjoying himself. Then I wrapped him in his towel and placed him back in the box, a procedure to which he submitted very calmly. I carefully set my purse on top of the box and headed to the wildlife rescue center, feeling a little dazed. A woman took the box into an office, from which there immediately emerged much whooping and yelling.

"Damn!" the woman said, bringing my towel back to me. "He's a feisty one, isn't he?"

Well, not always.

I'll never know why the blue jay acted as he did. Maybe as I calmed down, the mirror neurons in his brain reflected my quick drop into peace. Maybe he felt some sort of energetic emanation. Maybe he developed Stockholm syndrome. Or maybe he just thought it through and decided he'd try to melt my squishy human heart. If that was his intention, it worked.

Now, I couldn't have deliberately forced that blue jay to calm down, any more than I can heal the fears of everyone in this anxious world. What I can do is kindly extricate myself from anxiety, turn to curiosity and connection, and become an intentional, focused point of consciousness in the sea of creation.

My favorite practice for doing this is the following meditative exercise. It begins by using a technique discovered by psychologist Les Fehmi at the Princeton Biofeedback Centre. He found that saying or thinking certain sentences caused the brain to go into what he called "open focus." This is the same calm, relaxed state that can help you commune with a spoon, a bird, or your own best Self. It is one of the infinite paths to waking up.

New Skill

DISSOLVE INTO SPACE, SILENCE, AND STILLNESS

---

1. Begin by taking a few minutes by yourself in a calm space. Sit or lie down and relax. Breathe easily and regularly.

2. Repeat this question silently several times: **Can I imagine the distance between my eyes?** Don't try to figure out an answer. Just repeat the question.

3. Now mentally repeat: **Can I imagine the distance between the crown of my head and the bottom of my chin?**

4. Next, mentally repeat: **Can I imagine the distance between the top of my head and the center of my chest?**

5. Now remember that the atoms in your body are almost entirely made up of empty space. Silently, several times, ask yourself: **Can I imagine the space inside the atoms of my body?**

6. Next, think: **Can I imagine the space inside my body as continuous with the space all around me?** Silently repeat the question several times.

7. Next: **Can I imagine the silence that underlies all the sounds I hear?** Silently repeat the question several times.

8. Now: **Can I imagine the stillness in which all activity occurs?** Repeat.

9. Allow whatever physical and emotional reactions surface as you ask yourself these
   odd questions. Be very kind, gentle, and
   undemanding. Feel the field of space that
   fills your body and extends to the ends of
   the universe. Listen for the silence under
   any sounds you hear. Rest into the vibrant
   stillness that holds all activity.

You may have noticed, as Fehmi reported, that
asking these questions puts your nervous system into
"deep green" faster than almost any other prompts.
This is strange to the "I know!" mind, because the
whole meditation consists of asking questions without worrying about the answers. If we can let ourselves ride the not-knowing out beyond our bodies
and into space, silence, and stillness—all of which
are endless—our little brains seem to open up to a
state of almost surreal calm. Once that happens, be
on the lookout for magic.

THE BOTH/AND MINDSET

I think this deep green calm is what sacred texts call
"the peace that passeth understanding." We don't get
to that peace by knowing anything. We get there by

diligently striving to know all we can and then being willing to not know. We spend many hours in dedicated play, then acknowledge the obvious fact that we still aren't omniscient.

An experiment that has been called "the most elegant in the history of physics" (the double-slit experiment) showed that every object is **both** boundaryless, unified energy and a collection of separate physical things. Einstein proved that time, which appears relentless and irrefutable from our usual perspective, is "only a stubbornly persistent illusion."

In other words, what science shows us—even working through the "I know!" mind—is the don't-know mind. Reality is unfathomably paradoxical. The mind that excludes can't handle what we actually are. Only the mind that includes can hold the paradoxes of being. When we embrace don't-know mind, we can find ourselves as drops of consciousness existing beyond space and time, and as small physical creatures who are inching closer to death even as you read this.

Did the death thing just give you a jolt of anxiety? Yeah, that happens. Even after a thousand moments of looking at the universe and noticing that you're as connected to it as you are to your own left leg, you can slip out of the peace that passeth understanding and into the anxiety that is completely understandable.

But as I believe we've established, anxiety feels like hammered crap. You can use that suffering as motivation to relax, breathe, and ask yourself, **Can I**

imagine the space, silence, and stillness I share with everything? In other words, you can use that suffering to return to peace. To awaken, moment by moment.

I've done this to relax into excruciating physical pain and have found paradoxical relief. I've used it to cope with failure, the deaths of loved ones, and rejection by the people I cared about most. It's always there—not a wispy phantasm I have to imagine but the rock-solid fact of my own not-knowing. It's like discovering the same priceless gift, then forgetting it, then finding it again, over and over and over. The Self holds the paradoxes of space and being, time and eternity, in an unalterably comforting embrace.

I think this may be why Buddhist nun Pema Chödrön, after years of spiritual practice, wrote, "I am awake. I will spend my life taking off this armor." There is nothing new we must learn, no ritual or ceremony needed to connect us to our natural gift of spiritual awakening. In order to be fully awake, all we have to do is take our armor off, over and over again until one day we forget to put it back on.

12

Deep Green Self,
Deep Green Earth

The first time I flew on an airplane at night, the view took my breath away. The cities below me blazed like galaxies, the roads between them sparkling like strings of stars in jet-black space. I remembered this sight a few years later, when I read a famous description of the brain written by neurophysiologist Charles Sherrington. This is what Sherrington said happens inside our heads every morning:

The brain is waking and with it the mind is returning. It is as if the Milky Way entered upon some cosmic dance. Swiftly the head-mass becomes an enchanted loom where millions of flashing shuttles weave a dissolving pattern, always a

meaningful pattern though never an abiding one;
a shifting harmony of subpatterns.

This shimmering fabric of energy allows us to do
uniquely human things: think about the new day,
chat with loved ones, check our calendars for appointments and our email accounts for messages.
All of this relies on the human neocortex—a surprisingly meager structure, only about the thickness
of four credit cards stacked up. From this little skiff
of cells wrapped around our brains has come every
uniquely human invention: agriculture, science, literature, mathematics, the Great Wall of China, the
space shuttle, the mocha Frappuccino.

In many ways, we humans are like the earth's neocortex: a thin layer of highly active entities, interacting and communicating constantly across the outer
surface of a sphere. Like brain cells influencing the
entire body, we have disproportionate power over the
globe we live on. We can (and, on a daily basis, do)
eradicate species, demolish whole biomes, shift the
planet's weather. And, like the brain, we have the collective capacity to awaken—not just out of our nightly
nap but out of our illusions. And virtually all of our
most damaging illusions, from the dread of our own
mortality to the rejection of people who seem different from us, have anxiety at their core.

Healthy psyches, like healthy brain cells, are self-
generating, self-healing, and self-driven to creative
action. If we let ourselves gravitate to the places we

love, doing things we love, with people we love, we generate results much greater than the sum of their parts. These days, when thoughts can flash from one mind to billions in an eyeblink, we may spark ideas that light up the whole human population—a planetary Eureka effect.

This chapter will discuss the impact you may have on the world if you choose to live beyond anxiety. Since people are drawn to calm, joy, and creativity, existing in this way tends to automatically draw like-minded folks together into groups called "social cells."

This social structure is not held together by a set of rules that assemble groups in order to make objects, wealth, or war. Instead, the people who form a social cell are loosely bound by idealism and affection. As we'll see, social cells may generate collective wisdom that is greater than the sum of its parts. Historically, such groups have often been the source of monumental changes in human ideas and activities. In other words, if you can calm your anxiety and live from your creativity—strictly for your own well-being— you just may end up helping to save the world.

CARE OF THE CELL, CARE OF THE SELF, CARE OF THE SOUL

Most cells are squishy, delicate little things. Yet they can repair themselves, good as new, after being punctured, torn, or even ripped in half. The same goes for our selves and our souls. All of us face a world full of sharp edges. The slings and arrows of outrageous fortune pierce, cut, and rip us all. But even after sustaining terrible damage, a cell—or a self, or a soul—can not only survive but also heal and thrive. We can recover from almost anything as long as we do the two things our cells are designed to do: keep out toxins and take in nourishment.

The toxins of the mind, the things that can get right inside us and tear us apart like viruses collapsing a cell, are lies. As we've learned again and again throughout this book, our brains and bodies hate to lie. Believing anything that doesn't align with the truth of our **entire** experience—thoughts like **There's not enough stuff for me!** or **I'm a worthless waste of space** or **I can't do anything right** or **No one cares about me!**—erodes our mental and physical health. Lies, even the lies we believe innocently because they're part of our socialization, can send us down dangerous paths, make us self-destructive, or simply distance us from reality so that nothing we do seems to work anymore.

This is why I wrote a book called **The Way of Integrity** in which I argue that integrity is the one thing necessary for psychological well-being. I don't mean performative "integrity" (a pious politician holding up a Bible to impress believers). I mean **structural** integrity: being united and aligned, like a living body with all its parts in working order. This kind of integrity requires that we let ourselves know what we really know, feel what we really feel, and act in accordance with what we genuinely believe.

After **The Way of Integrity** came out, many readers told me, "I live in integrity, but I still feel awful. I'm so, so anxious!" That reaction led me to write **this** book. Because these good, honest people were lying to themselves without knowing it. They couldn't see a fact that may be clear to you now, though you might not have accepted it if I'd just blurted it out at the start of this book:

Anxiety always lies.

Always.

Remember, healthy **fear** is the truth: a clear impulse to act when, for example, there's a leopard in your bedroom. Anxiety is only a thought: the fear of leopards when no leopards are present. You'll always have your healthy fear. It can save your life; anxiety can only ruin it. Psychologists Dan Grupe and Jack Nitschke called anxiety "aberrant and excessive anticipatory responding under conditions of threat uncertainty." In other words, it's the terror of imaginary monsters in an imaginary future that may never happen.

KEEPING OUT THE TOXINS

Given the structures of our neurology and our society, it's obvious why we terrify ourselves with such fictions. It's not easy to stay grounded in truth when anxiety's terrible stories are not only wired into our brains but also threaded through our entire culture.

Individually and collectively, we suffer from the left hemisphere's solipsism, its utter conviction that its beliefs are factually correct, no matter how bizarre they may be. We truly believe that one political party (the one we don't like) will bring total destruction on us all. We may feel certain that a specific diet—no meat, no carbs, no preservatives, no whatever—will prevent all the diseases we fear. Some of us order children around, while others permit them to do whatever they want, everyone believing that their own preferred method of child-rearing will protect their progeny from life's hardships.

The reality is that all these well-meaning anxiety-based beliefs (and many, many more) are impossible to prove. We simply can't know what will happen if a given politician wins. Some people get sick despite eating "clean" their whole lives. Children encounter suffering no matter how they're raised. Insisting otherwise, trying to prove unprovable points, is stressful and draining. But if you use anxiety-calming skills, including the ones in this book, you'll begin to see through anxiety's deceptions. You'll notice, question, and dismiss stories that only serve to frighten you, choosing instead to focus on what makes your life enjoyable and meaningful. You'll be like a healthy cell, one that recognizes and automatically repels the virus of a frightening lie.

At this point, you may be thinking, **Hold on a minute! Have you checked the news? Bad things really** do **happen; they really** are **happening, and someday they** will **happen to me. My anxiety stories are true!** Again, this is an understandable reaction, but it's still not the truth about your own present moment. Take a long, slow breath. Exhale completely. Look around you for "leopards"—that is, for any **imminent danger that is physically here and now,** as opposed to frightening thoughts. If you see danger, take action. But if you're physically safe in this moment, you may want to say right out loud:

"Oh, how interesting! I am having aberrant and excessive anticipatory responses under conditions of threat uncertainty!"

Or, much better:

"You're okay. We've got this. You can relax. I'm right here with you."

Keep up the KIST until you can access Self-energy—enough of it to begin breathing more easily and feeling your muscles loosen a bit. This will put you back in touch with what you innately **are:** a consciousness that is calm, clear, confident, curious, courageous, compassionate, connected, and creative.

Remember, there's nothing to **do** here. You don't have to direct your psyche's healing process, any more than you have to heal your own cells after they've been damaged. You couldn't if you tried. But the intelligence of nature can, and will, if you simply surrender to what's really here and now.

LETTING NOURISHMENT IN

Avoiding the toxicity of false beliefs is half of what we need to thrive. The other half is taking in nourishment. This starts with watching our anxiety rather than believing it, like a calm mother watching her scared child. The moment we begin to **observe** and **wonder** about what's happening to us, we trigger curiosity, which leads to courage and connection. We regain that critical mass of Self. Then we can use our imaginations, not to tell horrifying stories but to transform challenging situations into catalysts for creativity.

For example, in 2021, journalist Maria Ressa won the Nobel Peace Prize for reporting on corruption in the Philippines under President Rodrigo Duterte. In response, Duterte launched a massive, highly organized smear campaign to destroy Ressa's reputation and threaten her life. Hundreds of thousands of attack emails and social media posts poured onto the internet. At one point, Ressa was receiving more than ninety hate messages and death threats an **hour.**

And what did Ressa do? She and her team refused to succumb to what could have been truly massive anxiety. Instead, they accessed curiosity. They decided to study the attack campaign itself. They found something fascinating: on the internet, lies spread faster than facts—six times faster. The simple truth about what actually happened just can't compete. But Ressa's team also found the one thing that **does** spread as fast and powerfully as lies: inspiration.

Just as anxiety is the end product of a **paranoid** imagination, inspiration is the end product of a **creative** imagination. When we allow ourselves to be inspired, our minds relax out of anxiety, choosing to focus on possibilities that nourish our souls.

You can do that right now, wherever you are. Ground yourself into the present moment by breathing deeply and slowly, noticing what's around you. Knowing that you're safe for this moment, remember one of the occasions you listed in chapter 4: a time when you were **calm**, **clear**, **courageous**, **creative**, and so on. Remember this occasion in as much detail as you can. Dwell on it. Drop false humility and be inspired by your own capacity to step up and embody your best Self. You are an extraordinarily brave human doing your best to navigate a difficult world. That's inspiring.

One paranoid person caught in fight, flight, or flop mode can spread a lot of anxiety. But one person living with courageous creativity can spread a lot of inspiration. One of my life's heroes, Ruth Killpack, was a homemaker and mother of five teenagers when her husband died from a brain tumor. "I didn't know what to do, but I knew I could figure it out," she told me. Ruth went back to school in her midforties, earning a BA and then a PhD in psychology. I met her some twenty years later, when I was struggling with anxiety, depression, and physical illness. Ruth became my therapist.

To be honest, she wasn't as gentle as most counselors. In the group therapy I shared with seven other women, Ruth functioned more like a coach. "I don't care what's going on in your life," she would tell us. "There is a way to make it work. There is **always** a path to some kind of solution. Figure it out, figure it out, figure it out."

With Ruth's encouragement, my fellow patients and I attacked all sorts of nontherapeutic issues: how I could care for my children on days when I was in too much pain to walk or use my hands; how another woman could fix her own bathroom pipes (she couldn't afford a plumber); how several others could start careers after leaving abusive situations; how we could all become activists who resolutely defied unfair social systems.

Mostly, Ruth "counseled" by walking her talk and choosing calm, creative, courageous, compassionate responses to any and every life dilemma. She was never rich or famous, but inspiration rippled out from her to everyone she knew, changing countless lives, mine among them.

GLOBAL CONSTELLATIONS

Like Ruth and Ressa, inspiring people tend to attract clusters of others who want to learn from them or serve the same causes. It's interesting that, as I've mentioned, such groups of individuals may also be called "cells." All humans tend to self-constellate into cells, finding people who share their tastes, interests, or values. You may belong to several social cells: a circle of friends from school or work, fellow fans of your favorite music group, other potbellied pig fanciers, committed rock climbers, gamers, pastry chefs, or gardeners.

The cells inside our bodies group up as well, and no one is quite sure how. When you were knee-high to a grasshopper (I mean that literally—you were two millimeters long), some of your cells clumped up and began pulsing in synchrony. All these years later, your heart—now three billion cells strong—is still beating. The brain is even more astonishing. Its 171 billion cells not only run your body and think your thoughts but also constantly resculpt themselves, aggregating to achieve different ends. Confronted by a problem you really want to solve, some groups of your cells complete "far transfers," illuminating your inner world.

Both the groups of cells in our bodies and the social cells formed by shared ideals are incredibly resilient. This isn't as true of our usual social organizations (governments, bureaucracies, factories), which don't run on the desire to connect. In these machinelike organizations, people who might not know or like each other are arranged according to abstract rules. They assume particular titles and ranks: some issue commands, others follow orders.

You can destroy a structure like this by eliminating the top leaders, or by fomenting rebellion among the people at the bottom of the pyramid, or by placing it in a larger environment where rapid changes are happening.

Social cells, on the other hand, are almost impossible to destroy. That's why resistance fighters in occupied territories use this structure, as do those with darker intentions, like terrorists. For good or ill, people whose ideals are countercultural naturally tend toward this structure. If someone from a cell is "outed," they can't betray everyone in the group, because they don't know everyone in the group. And they can't hand over the group's leaders, because there are no leaders. The cells are self-forming and self-repairing, their connections always gently shifting in loose, voluntary ways, like a brain with Sherrington's "shifting harmony of subpatterns."

If you've lived your whole life in structured hierarchies, you may not be able to see how social cells can form around you. Maybe you were born into a family hierarchy where men were more powerful than women, or raised in a society where white people were favored over people of color, or employed by a system whose "golden rule" was that "whoever has the gold makes the rules." You might have spent your adult life in organizations where everyone wakes up terrified and works very hard at grabbing stuff all day, every day.

Anytime you stop following this culture of anxiety and begin tuning into your creativity, you'll soon experience the constellating magic of creation. And the word **magic** will not sound like an exaggeration. As an example, let me describe a constellation that seems to have drifted toward me my whole life, though I truly have no idea why.

Even as a very small child, I felt an intense sense of mission. Maddeningly, I had no idea what my mission was. But growing up, I'd see other people—strangers, mostly—who seemed almost lit up, as if a spotlight were shining on them. Looking at such a person, I'd think, **Oh! We're on the same team!**

What team? I had no idea.

For decades, I told no one about this. It seemed very odd to me, and I was pretty sure I'd sound crazy if I talked about it. But as I reached my adult years, things just kept getting weirder. Long before I became any kind of public figure, people I barely knew would sometimes approach me and ask, "We're here on the same mission, right? Do you know what we're doing?" This seemed to happen at random. I had nothing to say to these people except: "I don't know, but for what it's worth, I feel the same way."

As I studied toward my PhD and began thinking

like a sociologist, I started making a list of patterns I saw in this self-aggregating "team." Along with having that powerful sense of mission, the people who connected with me tended to share common traits. For example:

- They all felt an intense desire to heal broken things—individual hearts, human cultures, certain biomes like oceans or forests, even the whole natural world.

- Many had felt compelled to learn certain subjects—biology, ecology, social science, medicine, specific languages.

- They had little interest in wielding power, yet these folks had often attained positions of authority in business, science, or politics.

- They often had significant neurodivergence and/or a loved one who was neurodivergent to the point of not being able to function "normally" in society.

- They were often genderqueer or resistant to society's gender definitions.

- They were highly imaginative, creative, original thinkers.

- They loved nature and disliked living in highly structured hierarchical communities or environments.

- They were emotionally sensitive to a fault; they couldn't ignore the suffering of other beings.

- Their sensitivity made them vulnerable to anxiety, depression, and various addictive behaviors that helped dull their emotional pain.

- They all had the sense, usually present from early childhood, that they were here to help with a massive shift in the way human beings think.

A lot of people have a few of these characteristics, but as I encountered more and more of these "team" folks, the consistency and specificity with which they described **most** or **all** of these qualities came to seem much more than coincidental. Looking feverishly for a common link, I realized that my "team" matched the personality profile common to the medicine people, shamans, and other mystical folks in many traditional cultures. In fact, some of them **were** medicine people or shamans in traditional cultures.

When I reached middle age, I finally decided to "come out" as a believer in my loose, self-generating community of "team" members. I wrote about it in a book called **Finding Your Way in a Wild New World.** I expected to get my ass kicked, and I did. Many people in academia, publishing, and the general reading public told me I'd slid way out of my genre, out of my depth, out of my mind. I truly thought my writing career was over. But then there were other people who wrote to tell me they'd read my description of the "team" and burst into tears, realizing for the first time that there might be others like them.

Nowadays, of course, I make no secret about my sense of team and mission. Some comedians yell things like "Anyone out there from Cleveland?" That's how I yell to audiences: "So, how many people out there have always suspected you're here to help with a transformation in human consciousness?" Depending on the crowd, 5 percent of the people may raise a hand, or 25 percent, or virtually everyone.

Upon further investigation, it turns out that some of these people believe the Holy Cheeseball is coming in a spacecraft to shower them with gold right after lunch on Thursday. But the overwhelming majority seem completely sane. Many are highly accomplished: doctors, therapists, professors, CEOs, scientists, educators.

For decades, I've wondered deeply about this constellation, this group of compassionate "sleeper cells" that seems to keep forming itself, guided by something I can't pretend to understand. **What's happening here? What are these people doing, and why?**

The only answer I get, tossed out by my right hemisphere (which, you may recall, uses language mainly for jokes, songs, and poetry), comes from T. S. Eliot's poem "East Coker." He writes, "I said to my soul, be still," specifying that his soul must wait without hope, love, faith, or even thinking. "Wait without thought," Eliot says, "for you are not ready for thought."

From a WEIRD culture perspective, these are very strange instructions. They're a recipe for don't-know mind. And they are excellent guidelines for anyone who hopes to experience a transformation of consciousness. Because if the change will be to one's way of thinking, no present way of thinking can adequately anticipate it, let alone understand it.

So I watch and wonder, constellating my way through baffling situations as a Dimly Understood Global Mission Toad. I stay firmly in don't-know mind (which isn't difficult, since it's the only mind I have) and wonder if my feeling of being drawn to my "team" is what a brain cell feels when it aligns with other cells. What guides such things? The Tao? The Force? The Sea of Infinite Doubt? I don't know. So I wait, and the faith and the love and the hope are all in the waiting. And whenever the opportunity and inspiration arrive, I'm available to play.

YOUR CONSTELLATIONS

Imagine that fulfilling your mission—stitching away at your sanity quilt, living the life that no one but you can create, shifting from an anxious brain to an awakened one—is the best way for you to constellate with other members of your own "team." Imagine that playing with these like-minded companions, learning and creating with as much deep practice as you can, will allow you to contribute to ideas and solutions so vast, subtle, and complex that your little left hemisphere could never fully grasp them.

Let that image be your inspiration.

You can't **think** such an adventure into being, any more than a single brain cell can think through its juxtaposition with the cells around it. But you can move away from anxiety's lies. You can get off anxiety spirals and follow your curiosity into creativity and creation, over and over and over again. With each recovery, you'll come closer to the truth, the magic, the mission. As David Foster Wallace wrote, "The truth will set you free. But not until it is finished with you." As your truth sets you free, you'll find yourself being used in the most remarkable ways.

WHAT WE MIGHT DO

Every time I visit Londolozi, I feel my whole body relax into a natural environment much like the one we humans first experienced when we evolved in southern Africa. But Londolozi's story is one of paradise interrupted. The land was once used to farm cattle, who overgrazed it until the native plants died and the soil went barren. Then two teenage boys, David and John Varty, who inherited the land after their father's sudden death, decided to try something they called "restoring Eden." They started by cutting alien thorn scrub and packing it into eroded furrows in the soil, which repaired the area's natural water cycle. Native plants returned, and animals followed. Today that ecosystem is almost wild again—**almost,** because the humans who live there deliberately tend their environment, serving all its inhabitants, from plants to animals to people.

All over the world, similar restoration efforts are taking place. In 2011, an organization called Rewilding Europe began working to restore the ecosystems of ten different landscapes in twelve European countries, including Germany, Italy, Romania, and Bulgaria. In China, regreening projects have reforested 31.74 million hectares of land, with plans to add an additional 2.7 million hectares by 2025. These efforts transformed an area that was farmed into desert thousands of years ago. After only a decade of restoration, it became a "Green Great Wall" that prevents sandstorms, conserves water and soil, and safeguards agriculture.

In 2001, I met environmentalist Paul Hawken, whose goal is "ending the climate crisis in one generation." When we met, he was about to publish a book called **Drawdown: The Most Comprehensive Plan Ever Proposed to Reverse Global Warming.** The word **drawdown** refers to pulling carbon emissions out of the atmosphere and reversing climate change. In Hawken's book, dozens of scientists and ecologists offer descriptive blueprints that show different ways we can do this.

And, yes, we really can.

The opening words of Hawken's book describe the first step each of us must take when confronted with anything that makes us anxious: "The genesis of Project Drawdown," he writes, "was curiosity, not fear." Obviously, he cares very much about preventing apocalyptic destruction of our planet's atmosphere. But by deliberately choosing curiosity over fear, Hawken sent his own research in a profoundly positive direction. He ended up interviewing scores of ecologists and climate specialists and found multiple solutions that could heal the biological systems we need to survive.

This group formed like any other social cell. "To be clear," Hawken notes in the book's introduction, "our organization did not create or devise a plan. . . . [W]e found a plan, a blueprint that already exists in the world in the form of humanity's collective wisdom." Over and over, that wisdom chooses creativity over anxiety.

Small groups of people following their individual creativity, compassion, and genius can make big changes happen, fast. Think of the firefighter Wag Dodge, staring at what appeared to be inevitable doom, then suddenly knowing exactly how he could survive. His own men were fighting and fleeing too hard to understand, but after Dodge survived, firefighters all over the world began using his epiphany.

If our whole species is a global neocortex, an idea from one person's creative right hemisphere can travel almost instantly to the whole population. One awakened brain can create a flashover of comprehension and motivation, inspiring all of us to live our most fulfilling, purposeful lives while mending the hoop of the earth.

Hawken and I met not at an ecology summit or scientific conference but at the home of a mutual friend, a spiritual teacher named Byron Katie. Her specialty is healing individuals by helping them question the thoughts that make them miserable. As I mentioned earlier, her method (which I strongly urge you to investigate) helped me see that my anxiety is always lying and that, in fact, the **direct opposite** of a frightening thought is often my next step toward awakening.

An example of this is Hawken's reversal of the thought that "global warming is something that is happening **to** us" to arrive at another possibility: "Global warming is happening **for** us."

If we change the preposition, and consider that global warming is happening **for** us—an atmospheric transformation that inspires us to change and reimagine everything we make and do—we begin to live in a different world. . . . We see global warming . . . as an invitation to build, innovate, and effect change, a pathway that awakens creativity, compassion, and genius.

As odd as it sounds to go against the left hemi-sphere's frightened convictions, thinking this way—creatively rather than anxiously—opens us to possibility. Both Hawken and I needed this under-standing to move forward in our lives' missions, so we constellated in a loose, self-organized cell around Katie's work. We shared instructions and ideas, then moved on to our respective teams and tasks.

A culture that forms this way is like an organism, not a machine. It's the opposite of the iron cage. Where our left-hemisphere culture is rigid, social cells are fluid. Where WEIRD societies require climbing pyramids of wealth, power, and status, social cells form because of enthusiasm, sharing, and inter-weaving creative insights. Like five-year-olds who can build a spaghetti tower faster and better than a group of trained engineers, people serving their own creative genius come to solutions that a hierarchical structure could never find.

History abounds with examples of this process. The framers of American democracy, whatever their flaws, got together with a plan for government that broke with the monarchical systems of Europe. The French impressionists pushed past the limits of lit-eralism and began painting light and emotion. The Bloomsbury Group, which included thinkers and writers like Virginia Woolf and E. M. Forster, changed the way people think about literature, aesthetics, eco-nomics, feminism, pacifism, and sexuality.

If you want to access the power of a social cell to solve problems in your own life, join an online group that shares your interest in decorating a house without spending much money, or breeding friendlier hamsters, or planning delightful family vacations, or living comfortably in a van, or making chairs out of driftwood. Don't be too intense about this, and don't latch on to everyone you meet. Allow yourself and your attention to drift and wander; notice which people or comments spark your creativity or help you feel connected.

Whatever you want to address, whether it's fanciful topics like those I just mentioned or life-changing skills like coping with serious illness, there are others out there who are wondering about the same issues and working the same problems. Joining forces with some of these folks—which can be as simple as posting your own question in an online forum—will link you into an exchange of insight and information, a living social cell, that could change your whole world.

THE PYRAMID AND THE POOL

One day, as I wandered around my neurodivergent brain, hopping Toad-like from one interest-based thought to another, I asked myself what human culture might look like if a critical mass of individuals experienced their own awakening. The answer came not through left-hemisphere concepts but through a right-hemisphere picture. In my mind's eye, I saw a pool of water, a metaphor for the aggregation of human thought, feeling, and experience. Each individual's contribution was like a raindrop landing on the surface of the pool, and every raindrop created waves that interacted, the personal energy of each human being affecting every other.

But how, I thought, **does our culture—a rigid pyramid of wealth and privilege—become a pool, where there is no such thing as hierarchy?** In the next instant, my brain tossed up another picture, this one so clear and intense that I set about making it real. I found a flat glass pie dish. Inside it, I built a pyramid of sugar cubes. The structure was solid, angular, crystallized. **That,** I thought, **is the consciousness that has dominated human society for the last few centuries.** Then I got a glass of water and thought, **This is awakened consciousness.**

I poured the water into the dish and waited.

At first, nothing happened. But then the sugar cubes at the bottom of the pyramid began to crumble and fall apart. Capillary action pulled water up to the next row of cubes, which also began to dissolve. The pyramid started gently collapsing from the bottom upward. The top remained dry and solid until almost all the sugar cubes had melted. Then, even the very highest cube began drawing in water, and disappeared.

Not a single bit of that sugar was destroyed. Everything that had started in that pan was still there. Only the rigidity and opacity were gone. And given time, water can also wear away soil, or cement, or granite. To us, with our left-hemisphere focus on grabbable **stuff,** fluid things appear less powerful than rigid ones. But "water falling, day by day, wears the hardest rock away." That which adapts and includes will win over that which rejects and excludes. Or, as the Tao Te Ching puts it, "When two great forces oppose each other, the victory will go to the one that knows how to yield."

Since the day of my "pyramid and pool" experiment, I've looked at our moment in history through the lens of that metaphor. Because suffering causes people to seek awakening, individuals who are near the bottom of our social pyramid—or who have been entirely excluded from it—are more likely to awaken early. They simply have less to lose than people born into privilege. As these people "wake up" and their ego structures dissolve, each of their minds becomes fluid and open, able to embrace rather than polarize.

We don't need more "revolutions," those brutal massacres in which one powerful group deposes another, grabbing the top of the pyramid. What we need is the **dissolution** of ego that happens in awakening. The right hemisphere's consciousness—the water in this equation—doesn't reject the sugar; it includes its essence while making it clear and fluid. In the same way, our right hemispheres acknowledge every point of view, holding paradox and polarity, both "I know!" mind and don't-know mind without destroying anything.

HOW THE SELF MELTS EGO

Lawyer and activist Valarie Kaur was devastated when a beloved friend was killed by a racist who announced at a bar that he was going out to shoot anyone in a turban and then did it. But Kaur refused to let the murderer make her close her mind and heart. She and her family healed by following a process that Kaur described to **Parenting** magazine. It has three steps:

1. HOLD THE HURT. "Ask where it shows up in our bodies," Kaur said. "It's important to notice the hurt, because if we push it down, it will show up later."

2. LET IN LOVE. "Imagine a place or person who loves us and notice how it feels in our bodies," Kaur advised. "When we let in love, it's like the warm water that slowly melts the ice in our bodies—and allows us to feel empowered again."

3. CHOOSE ART AND ACTION. "Write a poem, paint a picture, create a story, or start a campaign that makes meaning out of what happened," Kaur

said. When we access and share our creativity, we find that "we are not alone and have the power to create something loving that sets others free."

To the left hemisphere, this sounds pathetic—sheer idiocy at best or an invitation to more destruction at worst. But it also sounds a lot like the advice of Chris Voss, the FBI hostage negotiator, for calming the emotional part of the brain and defusing dangerous situations. And here's the thing about water, love, and awakened consciousness: you can't stab, shoot, or bludgeon them to death. They'll remain unharmed, ultimately wearing away your violent energy and your weapons. Nothing can hurt space, stillness, and silence.

This is why Gandhi said, "When I despair, I remember that all through history, the ways of truth and love have always won. There have been tyrants and murderers, and for a time, they can seem invincible, but in the end, they always fall. Think of it—always."

If you follow your joy away from anxiety and into creativity, you'll find yourself interacting fluidly in social cells fueled by creation itself. Each person, each gathering, will create ripples that affect the whole pool of humanity. Structures held in place by anxiety, within your psyche and all around you, will begin to melt. Right now, Earth's entire human population is already interacting with a fluidity that's unprecedented in all of history. And the more we connect, the more we increase our access to wisdom.

THE WISDOM OF CROWDS

In 1907, a scientist named Francis Galton reported an odd phenomenon: A crowd at a county fair had been invited to guess the weight of an ox. When all their guesses were added up and divided by the number of guesses to calculate the **average** guess, that average turned out to be closer to the ox's true weight than the estimate of any single individual in the crowd. Economists believe that this phenomenon, dubbed the "wisdom of crowds," holds true in many situations; crowds can be more accurate than any of the individuals who comprise them.

You and your social cells, the people who interact with you, can be this kind of "crowd." Together we can create outcomes that include but transcend us all, just as a molecule includes but transcends its atoms, cells include but transcend their molecules, and your body includes but transcends its cells. If awakened hearts and minds are allowed to freely interact, we may include but transcend our individual wisdom, creating something wiser than even the wisest among us.

One of the most counterintuitive things about the wisdom of crowds is that **the more diverse the crowd, the wiser it is.** Some crowds are possessed by propaganda or illusion. This is less true when a crowd is characterized by a diversity of opinions and experiences. Just as an ecosystem or a social cell is more resilient if it is more diverse—with more streams of input, more living things, more ways of living—human crowds need difference to be wise. And each person's opinion should be "independent and free from the influence of others."

THE MESSAGE

If a wise crowd is a diverse one, then a crowd that includes my son, Adam, who has Down syndrome, may be wiser than a crowd made up entirely of intellectuals. Adam happily admits that he knows very little ("I don't have a clue" is one of his favorite responses to any question). But he also dwells in the Mystery, in a reality far more wondrous than anything our culture teaches us to value. Many times, in brief flashes, he has shown a deep and ineffable relationship with the intelligence of creation.

Adam can go years without doing anything unusual. But every now and then, he calmly shatters what's left of my "I know!" mind. That's what happened one day when some friends and I had gathered around my laptop to listen to a YouTube video called "All Planet Sounds from Space (in our Solar System)."

You should google this phrase—you won't be

disappointed. Your computer or phone will play for you the radio emissions gathered by spacecraft as they zoom past different astral bodies in our solar system. Translated into sound, these recordings show that everything out there has its own eerie or beautiful signature tune. Planet Earth makes a wild churning sound, like wind howling through dense trees. Venus thrums like a huge Tibetan bowl. Jupiter is apparently playing a pipe organ. Uranus sounds like the chirping of a million small birds (and I challenge you to say this to someone at a party while keeping a straight face).

As my friends and I listened to all of this, fascinated, Adam walked past us, then did a double take and came into the room.

"What are those sounds?" he asked. "I have those sounds in my body."

In his **body**? Filing the strangeness of that claim in the back of my mind, I explained to Adam that we were listening to the planets.

"Oh, right," he said, nodding casually, as if I'd just reminded him it was Wednesday. Then, before he turned to leave, he added, "That's the mfflve." (He has trouble enunciating, and even after decades of practice, I often can't understand him.)

"Wait," I said. "What did you say? The . . . mfflve?"

"Yes," he said. "Always send same mfflve. All times."

One of my friends joined in. "Adam, could you say it one more time so we can understand? We're not too good at this."

Adam smiled patiently and held his hand up to his ear like a phone, thumb and little finger extended. "The MFFLVE!" he repeated. "The call!"

"Oh, a **message**!" we all said in unison.

Adam beamed and nodded. "Right!"

We were so pleased by this breakthrough that I almost forgot to ask: "Wait, Adam! Are you telling us the planets are sending us a message?"

"Yes," he said, seeming surprised that I didn't know. "Always."

"Well, what is it?" one of my friends asked. "What's the message?"

Adam shook his head in apparent pity for our ignorance and said, "That we're safe."

YOU BELONG

When I'm lost in anxiety's hall of mirrors, this sounds impossible. How can we be safe with catastrophes small and large happening everywhere in our lives, everywhere on our planet? How can we be safe when we are all "born astride the grave"? How can this one frail specimen I call myself possibly ever be **safe** in a universe ruled by entropy?

Because we can wake up.

Because we are not just these bodies, not just our anxiety. Because we can allow the intelligence of nature to work our missions, our unique creative genius, as part of its overall strategy. Your mission is an essential part of the quilt being stitched together all over the world by an intelligence that may be our collective subconscious, the Tao, the Force, the wisdom of nature. No label can define it, but we can experience it. It is, in fact, the end state of moving beyond anxiety.

Once we've left anxiety behind us, what will occupy our minds and our time? Full immersion in the present moment and the equanimity that comes naturally to our core Selves. In this state, we know that we're indispensable elements of creation. We belong. Everything about us belongs, including the part that fears not belonging. Instead of living as a tight, clenched ball of anxiety, we can choose to open into our own creativity until we find ourselves inextricably blended with creation itself. We can let go and dissolve. That is how we all become one emergent force of love.

Do I know this can save the world? Of course not. I may be imagining this entire book in a very long, focused sort of dream. Dubito, ergo sum. I doubt, therefore I am. Knowing that I can't know, my mind is open. I am right here, taking off my armor. And I truly believe that's all this perilous moment in history calls us to do: stay calm, curious, creative, and ready. Here's a visualization that may help.

New Skill

STAY CALM IN SPITE OF IT ALL

---

1. Get into a state of calm by using the techniques you've learned in this book. Spend a little extra time connecting with your core Self, your compassionate center. Offer KIST to any parts that might feel anxious.

2. Think of something you want very much to control, something that has proved, in fact, to be either difficult or impossible for you to control: illness, aging, war, injustice, the behavior of someone you love.

3. Picture yourself rising out of your body, through the ceiling of the room, and up into the atmosphere. Look down from a distance at the problem that troubles you. Be still.

4. Kindly tell all your internal parts, "We can't control this situation."

5. Notice whether anxiety arises. If it does, offer more KIST ("May you be well. May you be happy . . .").

6. Breathing deeply and regularly, staying in Self, say to all the parts of your psyche, "It is **absolutely okay** that we can't control this. We don't **need** to control it." Allow this thought to sink in.

7. Notice any resistance. If one of your parts protests (e.g., **No! I must control that thing!**), gently remind the part, "But, sweetheart, we **can't** control it."

8. Once you can get calm about your lack of ability to control the situation, make an offer to the universe's Magical Chicken, the Force, the Tao, or whatever you want to call creation. You don't need to believe this offer; you just need to feel calm while saying it. The offer is:

   "I'm available for action in this situation if needed. I'd like it to be different, and I'm willing to show up and do my best to make it that way. Please let me know when and how I can help."

9. Take one more deep breath and shake out your hands and feet. Then go do something you enjoy. See if you can let go

of the whole issue. If so, you're FINISHED! If not, go on to step 10.

10. If you can't let go of your worries, say, "I can't control the fact that I can't stop wanting to control this thing." Repeat this whole exercise, using your inability to let go as the thing you can't control.

11. Pay attention: An opportunity to take positive action may occur. It may be an idea or a situation that appears around you. If and when it does, do what feels most peaceful.

Once you've begun to awaken, you can maintain "a critical mass of Self" at all times. This means you always have a place to go when you need to feel calm. It means you can calm down other brains, both human and animal. It means the world cooperates with you in unexpected ways. It means you can help. Follow the flow of your truth as it plays out, your creative mind embracing all your anxieties, calmly waiting until their frenzy resolves into stillness.

Feel what's working in you, through you, for you.

This is lila, the play of consciousness as it takes on matter, forms itself into beings, and then leaves them again. It is consciousness playing in the field of matter, dancing with human bodies more beautifully than they know how to dance. It is consciousness as a generation of human beings going much, much further toward their ultimate capacities than members of any previous generation. It is consciousness using incredible technologies and then leaping forward with the Eureka effect, solving problems in ways that will only seem obvious once someone thinks of them. It is all of nature, all of the earth, as one intelligent organism working its incredibly complex algorithms, playing with form.

Here is the true miracle of life: when it is awake, it heals. I don't just want you to believe that. I want you to live it. Not all at once, and not without wobbles, but consistently and then continuously, you can release your illusions. There will come a time when you feel the message "I am safe" in every cell. Living beyond anxiety will heal your torn and punctured heart, filling you with peace, joy, and the urge to share your freedom with every other being.

So now imagine the earth at night, all those points of light moving, clustering, spreading, and connecting. Around the people who are using those lights, other forms of energy are flowing: radio waves, digital communication, electromagnetism. We are all overlapping fields of energy and matter, flashing shuttles in the enchanted loom of the world, where we weave a dissolving pattern.

When we go beyond anxiety—when we reject the

lies that cause so much heartbreak—we don't just discover the magic of life; we **are** that magic. It is magical that as long as consciousness inhabits a physical form, it can move, act, think, and automatically repair its broken parts. It is magical that you and I can heal from the sorrows and torments of our lives. Using that "magic," we can heal as a species, connecting with the courage and curiosity that lead to harmonious cooperation without needing rigid structure. And together we can heal our home, this planet where we move around like a busy little neocortex, tired of its fears, poised to go beyond anxiety.

If we are the brain of the earth, the brain is waking.

ACKNOWLEDGMENTS

I'm gobsmacked with gratitude when I think about how many people contributed to the conception and completion of this book. First and foremost, I'd like to thank the thousands of clients, readers, and participants in my online courses who shared their experiences and helped me test various methods of solving life problems. If you are one of these people, know that I deeply appreciate your openness and your insights.

My agent, Linda Loewenthal, was an invaluable presence in my mind (and on the phone!) as I roughed out the general ideas for **Beyond Anxiety.** She patiently listened to my excited ranting about various scientists, then gently reminded me that she wanted to hear **my** ideas. Oh, yes, that. Linda is a friend, a champion, and a wonderful editor. I am so lucky to know and work with her.

My first readers and constant supporters as I hacked

my way through the various drafts include some of my best beloveds: Kitt Forster, Sam Farren Beck, and Paula Keogh. Thank you all for your literary brilliance, your immense generosity, and your kindness. I love you.

As I was writing **Beyond Anxiety,** I shared phone calls and visits with my dear friend Elizabeth Gilbert, during which we each read aloud new material from our respective books. I loved seeing the beautiful, spontaneous illustrations Liz would draw as she listened. I've never met anyone so gifted at turning all forms of energy into artistic creation. What a gift she is, and how grateful I am for her.

I also had amazing opportunities to speak in person with a few of the experts and scientists whose work formed the armature of this book. Huge thanks to Jill Bolte Taylor, who generously shared her knowledge and experience in conversation and in her powerful books, which I hope everyone reads. Jill's heart is as huge as her expertise, and I feel blessed to know her. Richard Schwartz, founder of Internal Family Systems therapy, was also incredibly generous with his time and ideas. Alexandra Barbo, a highly trained expert in IFS, not only gave me excellent therapy but explained the process brilliantly. I am so very grateful to these amazing people, whose work helps so many people every day.

Of course, none of this would ever see the light of day without a dedicated team working to publish what I've written. Great thanks to everyone at The Open Field, Penguin Life, and Penguin Books.

Pam Dorman was the first to believe in this book

ACKNOWLEDGMENTS

and read the proposal. She is a legend, and I am so grateful for her help and support, with this book and my previous one. Brian Tart, Kate Stark, and Meg Leder were there to launch me into the writing process and support my efforts. I can't thank them enough.

The Open Field operates under the guidance of my inimitable, longtime dear friend Maria Shriver. Her commitment to serving the world, her kindness, and her energy are almost unfathomable. Did I mention feeling overwhelmed by gratitude?

My editor, Nina Rodriguez-Marty, is a truly lovely human being, with a sharp eye for detail and story, a gentle way of correcting course where I went astray, and a constant willingness to offer encouragement. Working with her has been wonderful. Randee Marullo, my production editor, and my copy editor, Lauren Morgan Whitticom, also went the extra mile, combing through the manuscript for errors and putting things right. Huge thanks to both of them.

Most of all, I thank my family. Lila Mangan and Adam Beck bring grace and joy to every day. I would never have finished any book without the endless patience and constant support of my beloved Karen Gerdes, who tirelessly takes on tasks that would stop my writing in its tracks. My gratitude to her is beyond expression.

Rowan Mangan, my other beloved, is my constant, loving sounding board. She's there to discuss every faltering new idea, to read first and second and third and tenth drafts, to challenge my errors and bring her own brilliant perspective to every page. She came up with the phrase "feeling good by looking weird," which describes our family—and my life—about as well as anything ever could.

Finally, thanks to every reader who looks at or listens to **Beyond Anxiety.** Once it reaches your hands, eyes, ears, and mind, you become a factor in constructing a new interpretation, unique to you. We are all a part of every thought we share. I'm so happy to be sharing and creating with you.

ABOUT THE AUTHOR

MARTHA BECK, PhD, is a Harvard-trained sociologist, **New York Times** bestselling author, world-renowned life coach, and speaker. She is the author of nine nonfiction books and one novel, and contributed to **O, The Oprah Magazine** since its inception, as well as **Oprah Daily.**

Visit marthabeck.com
Instagram and X TheMarthaBeck
Facebook MarthaBeck